LOVE & JUSTICE

MAYA MOORE IRONS and JONATHAN IRONS

WITH TRAVIS THRASHER

LOVE &
JUSTICE

A STORY OF TRIUMPH ON
TWO DIFFERENT COURTS

FOREWORD BY
BRYAN STEVENSON

ANDSCAPE
LOS ANGELES   NEW YORK

First Edition, January 2023
10 9 8 7 6 5 4 3 2 1
FAC-004510-22336
Printed in the United States of America

This book is set in Acta, Hoefler Text, and Adobe Caslon
Designed by Amy C. King

Library of Congress Cataloging-in-Publication Number: 2022938154
ISBN 978-1-368-08117-7
Reinforced binding

SUSTAINABLE FORESTRY INITIATIVE   Certified Sourcing
www.sfiprogram.org
SFI-01681

www.AndscapeBooks.com

Logo Applies to Text Stock Only

To Granny, Papa, Cheri, and Reggie.

Your faithfulness made a way for this miracle.

CONTENTS

FOREWORD

by Bryan Stevenson

IN AUGUST 2003, the United States Bureau of Justice Statistics (BJS) issued a startling announcement. Based on radical changes in crime policies and sentencing laws and an unprecedented commitment to incarceration that shaped the end of the twentieth century, the bureau projected that one in three Black male babies born in the United States in the twenty-first century would spend time in jail or prison during their lifetime. One in three. The projection for Latino boys was one in six. Despite the devastating scale of this forecast, based on data and trends, very few things changed in response to this dire prediction. Government policies and practices were not reconsidered. State and federal entities did not engage in serious strategies to prevent the predicted painful futures for Black and Brown families. Most Americans, if they took notice at all, shrugged their shoulders while the United States continued to imprison its people at a higher rate than any other nation in the world.

The incarceration epidemic grew in the years that followed. The number of women in jails and prisons—most of them mothers with minor children—increased 750 percent from 1980 to 2017. By the end of 2018, some 113 million American adults had immediate family members who were formerly or currently incarcerated. And by 2014, the United States, despite having less than 5 percent of the global population, held 22 percent of the people imprisoned on Earth.

At the time of the BJS forecast, fourteen-year-old Maya Moore's extraordinary talent for basketball was emerging, setting her on a journey to international fame, acclaim, and achievement as one of the most dominant and successful players of her era. Two Olympic gold medals, multiple national titles at the collegiate level, multiple world championships, and MVP honors as a professional basketball player would cement her status as a sports icon and legendary superstar.

In a much less glorious space, Jonathan Irons already knew about the horrors of mass incarceration for young Black men. In 1997, six years before the BJS report, sixteen-year-old Jonathan was falsely accused of breaking into the home of a white man in Missouri who was shot by an intruder. After the shooting victim misidentified him, Jonathan was arrested, convicted by an all-white jury, and sentenced to fifty years in prison.

The case of Jonathan Irons exemplifies the many flaws in our criminal legal system. He was prosecuted as an adult in the late 1990s—after elected officials in almost every state lowered the minimum age for prosecuting children as adults. Entranced by the politics of fear and anger, elected officials authorized an era of excessive punishment of children, placing kids as young as twelve in adult prisons and condemning thousands of children to decades of traumatizing confinement.

Criminologists in the 1990s falsely predicted the nation would be overrun by a juvenile crime wave, spreading fear that children—mostly children of color—were not really children but "superpredators." New policies vilified and demonized children as policymakers built frighteningly efficient pipelines from schools to jails and prisons. The prevailing "zero tolerance" rhetoric was devastating for poor kids and kids of color, who were at much greater risk of arrest and excessive punishment. Jonathan Irons was one of thousands who were swept up by a harsh system that treated young people as nothing more than the crimes they were accused of committing. Today, thirteen states still have no minimum age for trying children as adults.

Jonathan Irons was not only a child wrongly prosecuted and incarcerated as an adult—he was also innocent. As Maya and Jonathan's powerful story makes clear, criminal justice in America is shockingly unreliable. Over the last forty years we have invested billions of dollars to build scores of prisons around the country. State and federal governments have funded exponential spending increases for policing, prosecution, and punishment but made no corresponding investments to ensure that people living in poverty are fairly prosecuted and represented by capable lawyers. Most states do not fund indigent defense systems that can mitigate the challenges imposed on poor defendants. This imbalance has resulted in a criminal legal system that treats you better if you are rich and guilty than if you are poor and innocent.

Even in capital cases, where prosecutors and courts are supposed to be more careful and outcomes more reliable, scores of innocent people have been identified on death rows across the country. For every nine people who have been executed in the United States since 1973, one innocent person has been exonerated and released—a shocking rate of error.

Jonathan's case also reveals our nation's continuing failure to deal honestly with our history of racial injustice. Even after the end of slavery in 1865, the American legal system allowed white mobs to violently and lawlessly lynch thousands of Black men, women, and children with impunity for nearly one hundred years. Maya Moore and Jonathan Irons grew up in communities where Black people had been terrorized by racial violence, segregated by Jim Crow laws, and constrained by narratives of racial hierarchy for decades.

Even without a particular animus directed at him personally, Jonathan Irons was caught in a system where fairness was elusive and unjust outcomes likely. It is a grim narrative surrounded by many tragic and painful accounts of injustice and inequality.

But this book presents another side of this story.

It tells the story of how some individuals have responded to unfairness, harsh and extreme punishment, and unreliable convictions by insisting that we do better. Some Americans have refused to accept that people can only be defined by their crimes—they emphatically believe that millions of incarcerated people are not beyond hope, redemption, and rehabilitation. Like Maya Moore and Jonathan Irons, they work to embody the words of the great theologian Reinhold Niebuhr, who said, "Love is the motive, but justice is the instrument."

A decade after Jonathan was wrongly convicted, as Maya was leading the University of Connecticut to back-to-back undefeated, national-championship seasons, I was preparing to argue a case before the United States Supreme Court. I represented Joe Sullivan, who had been sentenced to life imprisonment without parole for a nonhomicide offense in Florida when he was just thirteen. We had argued that Joe was innocent, but the Supreme Court case was about the constitutionality of life-without-parole sentences for children convicted of nonhomicide offenses. In the companion case of *Graham v. Florida*, the Court ruled in our favor, holding that children cannot be condemned to die in prison for nonhomicide convictions. I represented many people who sought their freedom after being unfairly convicted and harshly sentenced as teenagers, and many people, like Joe Sullivan, were eventually released.

I found my work gratifying and uplifting, but I worried a lot about the people I represented. Many had been abandoned by their families. Some had spent years in solitary confinement; others had been targeted for assault and violence in prison because of their young ages. Some had become severely compromised by years of trauma, isolation, and dehumanizing treatment.

Working with the imprisoned, the condemned, and those forgotten for decades behind bars can be dispiriting. Which is perhaps why I find myself so deeply moved by Maya and Jonathan's story. Some will see this book as the tale of a legendary basketball player who stepped away from her career in its prime to crusade for a man who was wrongly imprisoned, leading to an inspiring romance and freedom. I see *Love & Justice* as even more than that. To me, it's a compelling and powerful narrative exhorting all of us to care more about one another, to bear one another's burdens. Maya Moore could not have become the extraordinary player she is without a community of people caring for her, loving her, and believing in her before anyone knew what she could do with a basketball.

Maya's connection to Jonathan came about because ordinary people made the extraordinary decision to go inside a Missouri state prison to offer hope, redemption, and compassion to people who had been discarded by our system. The teachers, choir directors, ministers, and caregivers who wrapped their arms around Jonathan resisted condemnation and chose instead to reflect a deeply held commitment to the forgotten that merits our attention and recognition.

Maya suspended an unbelievable career as a basketball superstar to advocate for more justice in America. The story she and Jonathan tell, in its essence, inspires all of us to do justice, love mercy, and walk humbly with God. Their fight for justice, for freedom, and for love is something we all must embrace if we want to disrupt the terrifying Bureau of Justice Statistics forecast about the future of incarceration in America that ushered in this century.

This is an important book filled with love, grace, humility, and compassion. It takes us on an unflinching journey through degrading confinement, dehumanizing violence, bigotry, and shameful indifference to the suffering of others. It is a triumphant story of ordinary people doing extraordinary things in the name of love. And in the end, it shows us something beautiful, something redemptive, something we should all celebrate.

PROLOGUE

(2019)

MAYA (M)

"GOD IS A CHAIN-BREAKER."

I think of Jonathan's words as he's taken out of the courtroom in his orange jumpsuit and handcuffs. After seven long hours, his evidentiary hearing is finally over, yet I don't know whether we've won or lost. We've been hoping for this hearing for years, for a chance to give Jonathan his day in court and to have the truth be seen and shown. A chance for his conviction to be overturned and for justice to finally be obtained. But as I escape to the bathroom in the courthouse just to get away from everybody and take a moment to gather myself, I feel super heavy and angry. A cyclone of emotions tears through me.

What just happened?

I am confused by how the hearing ended. I don't have a full understanding of what was happening as Judge Green told the prosecutors to "amend your pleadings to conform to the evidence." What did this mean? And Mr. Logan has seven days to respond? *Seven days?* Then they will set another hearing? All I know is that I heard the date of December 9 set and felt my soul begin to fall into a tailspin.

Why the whole extra month when everything's going to be in by October 31?

My spirit feels weighed down, having witnessed firsthand the discouraging actions of the state prosecutor. The darkness of their one-track mind to maintain the "win" and blatant disregard for truth was excruciating to watch. As I sat and witnessed the State trying to poke holes into everything we presented, it was so hard to not jump over the railing and drag them into the prison Jonathan was trapped in. It felt so evil to see that up close. How could they look at the evidence that was being presented and then intentionally try to confuse it or muddy it or attack it? But unfortunately, it's just the reality of some or maybe even the majority of the prosecutors wanting to uphold and defend the original conviction despite the facts presented before them. I am more convinced than ever that reform must happen in our prosecutorial realm. I couldn't believe they were even claiming to have new "evidence." You could tell the document was a forgery. They literally planted a page in the box in an attempt to get rid of the fingerprint Brady violation. I'm so angry about how these people who went to law school and took an oath to uphold the law were clearly planting evidence. Right in front of everybody!

Despite all this, I feel gratitude and have a new level of respect for Judge Green in how he handled his courtroom. He acted extremely fair and our prayers that he would have a heart for justice and a heart for Jonathan were literally being answered. It was encouraging to see the judge humanize Jonathan in how he let him tell his story and to see how he was courteous in both warning him about testifying for a possible appeal and telling him "Be careful" when J left the stand.

As the bailiff takes Jonathan to the van that will carry him back to a maximum-security prison, I fight back tears and head outside to address the media.

"Unfortunately, it's another step to another step—but it's a big step to finally have the truth be told in this context. To leave here knowing it could possibly be another two months before another step is made is just—it just doesn't feel good."

Eric Schmitt's people are playing games with someone's life.

I know that not all prosecutors are heartless, but the evidentiary hearing was disorienting as I watched a team of people literally ignore facts and fight to muddle the truthful path of justice. And not even think twice about it. It was nuts.

As we work to improve our criminal justice system, I think this hearing will be a powerful illustration of how bad it can be if we don't reform. I know in my head a lot of good things will come out of this fight to free Jonathan. But right now my heart just hurts.

PART ONE

Chapter One

THE BOY WHO SMELLED LIKE SMOKE

(1980–1996)

JONATHAN (J)

GRANNY. That's what everybody called her.

Florence Bell Spears was technically my great-aunt, but in reality, she was the only parent I had. She was like a grandmother to everybody in the neighborhood—my friends, white people, Black people . . . it didn't make a difference. She treated everybody like they were her own; everyone was important to her. Granny was a guardian angel; she wouldn't turn anybody away. I can remember my great-aunt taking in so many family members who had nowhere else to go that we even had little kids sleeping on floors. At one point, there were close to twenty-five people staying at my grandmother's house. At nighttime, there were so many bodies lying down everywhere that you had to be careful where you walked. Our house wasn't always that crowded; there were also times when it was just the two of us living together. But whenever bad luck or misfortune happened in the family, it would happen in waves, so people brought their kids to stay with Granny until they could get into a better situation. Somehow, she managed to feed everybody with her retirement checks.

I grew up below the poverty line in Wentzville, Missouri. I sometimes joked that we were so poor we had to climb up just to get to the poverty line. I lived in an old one-story A-frame house with a basement that wasn't finished because my grandmother couldn't afford it. There was no functional bathroom installed in our house. Instead of a toilet, we used a five-gallon bucket and threw a stack of folded newspapers over it, then dumped it outside about a quarter of a mile back in the woods behind our home. We bathed in a five-gallon tin tub, the kind you see people bathing their dogs in. I wore second- and third-generation hand-me-downs, clothes that had been bought at the local thrift store, then given to older relatives in the family before getting to me. They often smelled like smoke as well. Since my grandmother heated the house with a wood-burning stove, I would chop wood, carry it into the house, and stack it for use all year round. The kids teased me at school. "You live in a furnace, you stink . . ." they would tell me.

Yeah, we were poor in resources, but we were rich in love. My grandmother made sure we were raised that way.

Our house was rickety and unfinished because the first two houses my grandmother had lived in burned down. The first fire came courtesy of a Molotov cocktail somebody threw in our house trying to kill one of my uncles while yelling racial slurs. After the house burned down, my grandmother bought property behind it and then had another house built. This one was torched after some of my older cousins were playing with fire. She didn't have insurance, of course, so from the little money she had left, she had the A-frame home built.

Florence Spears was born in 1915. In her youth, she worked as a maid for wealthy white people in St. Louis, scrubbing the floors on her hands and knees and cleaning counters from sunup until late in the evening. Years later, she was also a postal worker until she retired. Being on her knees all day as a maid caused severe damage to her knees, so by the time she was hired by the post office, she was quietly enduring great knee pain. Not only did she walk long postal routes with a heavy postal bag, but she also had to walk to and from work every day. She always came home exhausted, yet this didn't stop my grandmother from taking care of everybody in her household and neighbors in need, too. She was an amazing woman who made miracles from the small pension she received from the post office. Granny could feed ten of us off five dollars, going to the grocery store and finding all the ingredients for a delicious meal. I can still hear her humming and singing along to Al Green, Marvin Gaye, and old gospel hymns from a little radio while she cooked. She had a big garden that I helped her with, growing everything from tomatoes and corn and watermelon to her own homegrown greens. My favorite meal she made was breakfast, with biscuits made from scratch. To this day, I still haven't had a biscuit as good as the ones my grandmother made.

Our house had a living room and a family room. The former was the most pristine room in the house, one nobody was allowed to go in unless you were guests. You had to be a special person to be able to go in the living room. "Better not go in there and dirty something," Granny warned us. "That's lookin' for a whuppin'." The living room was where Granny spent most of her time, either resting on the couch or in a chair watching TV. We watched *Wheel of Fortune* together, *The Golden Girls*, local news, and even some of her soap operas. After viewing her shows, she would let me watch cartoons.

Granny pretended like she didn't like dogs even though we always had them around, whether from somebody giving them to us or having them show up on our property. Like the stray puppy that showed up at our back door one day, barking and whining. My grandmother didn't hear him, so I went outside to discover this little pit-bull mix desperate to come in. I picked him up and then hid him in a box, feeding him and playing with him in secret for about a week. Since my grandmother never went down in the basement because it was dark and dank and not finished, I brought the little dog down there. We didn't have a septic tank, so water backed up down there, but there were still some dry spots. I named the pit-bull mix Cujo, and every morning I went down there to feed him.

Hiding Cujo from Granny only lasted so long. One day, she heard a noise coming from the basement. "What's making that sound?" she asked me. I tried to hide the dog, but she figured out what it was. Once she saw how much I loved him, she let me keep him. Even though she always complained about the mutts roaming around her house, I knew she enjoyed them. One afternoon when I came home, I found Granny sleeping on the front porch with Cujo curled up on her lap. As she woke up, she gently petted the dog.

"Granny!" I said in surprise. "What are you doing?"

I'd caught her, and she knew it.

"Go on—get away from me," she told Cujo.

"Okay, Granny. It's all right."

As Cujo took off running, she called out after the dog, "Filthy mangy thing."

Even as a kid I knew this was a term of endearment.

◆ ◆ ◆

We grew up around woods and fields and ponds. I loved to be outside, climbing trees and running around on trails, riding my bike over gravel roads on rolling hills, having fun exploring. I loved a good adventure. My neighborhood friends and I would go fishing in small lakes that surrounded us. I also called myself a mechanic in training since I always helped the mechanics who showed up at our house to work on our cars.

The area we lived in was rural and not very populated. Several miles away from our house was an older farmer named Mr. Crooms. He was friends with my grandmother, and he was the reason we were able to have extra food in the house like meat and eggs. He was an older white guy with a good heart, and I learned a lot about farms from him. He let me work on the farm, and I also learned how to drive from him. Mr. Crooms taught me how to drive this old, rusted-out truck in the field and get used to it. I was ten years old, sitting behind the wheel, stopping the truck, then accelerating, turning it as it rolled downhill. He let me drive him around town doing errands for him. On the farm, he let me drive big tractors along with a four-wheeler.

I'd chase down chicken and hogs. For several years, I probably spent more time over at the farm with him just listening and talking to him than I did with my grandmother.

Early on, I knew there was something different about my life, but I never truly understood that until the bring-your-parent-to-school day at my elementary school. I knew my other friends had mothers and fathers, but I had never really thought about what the term "parent" meant. When I heard our teacher talk about this upcoming day, I asked a buddy of mine about it.

"What's a 'parent'?" I said.

"My mom and dad," he told me.

I was simply thinking, *Well, my granny's my momma*. But it dawned on me that I didn't really know who my actual mother and father were, so when I went home, I asked my grandmother if she was my parent. She sat me down beside her before she answered.

"Johnny, I knew this day would come," she said. "I'm not your mother or your father. And actually, I'm not your grandmother. I'm your great-aunt. I've taken you in, and I've raised you as my own child."

"They're having a bring-your-parent day at school. Could you come?"

She told me yes. "I'll go, but just realize I'm not your mother or your father. And don't forget about my knees. They're not the way they used to be, so I can't sit there for long 'cause they'll end up aching."

I knew she struggled to sit or stand anywhere for too long, and my grandmother ultimately decided against coming to school. It wasn't that she didn't want to come; it was just too much strain for her to take. I understood and wasn't hurt or angry at her. When I got to school, there were maybe only three kids out of thirty who didn't have a parent there. What I had been missing my entire life suddenly became very visible. I felt left out. More than that, I found myself curious about my biological mother and father. Who were they?

A door opened that day, letting in the seeds of doubt and confusion. I began to notice all the things that were wrong with my family and started to hear more about them from others. My cousins who lived with us teased me and told me that my mother put me in a dumpster and left me there because she didn't want me, and I believed that and latched on to it. For my entire childhood, I would believe this lie. It fueled the anger and hurt inside me.

My only thoughts about my mother were *Oh, you didn't want me? Well, I hate you, then.* But they were not telling the truth about my mother. I didn't know this was just kids being mean. That's sometimes just what they do. This cruel lie became the story I bought into about my mother. Only years later, while I was in prison, would I finally discover the truth.

Like many things, Cheri and Reggie were the ones who helped uncover this deception I was living under.

◆ ◆ ◆

It's easy to connect the dots looking back, to see how one thing in my life influenced another, to spot how one situation turned into a different circumstance, how events continued to build. Yet at the time, I felt like I was stuck in a maze I couldn't get out of. Every path seemed to arrive at a dead end, and the only way out was the wrong way.

As I became older and kids became more cruel, I dealt with being made fun of the same way I did in our household. The way we were raised, if you teased somebody, those were fighting words. So, when I heard someone saying to me, "Oh, look at you with your dusty pants on," I'd bop them in the eye and then dare them to say it again. When I got in trouble, Granny would ask what I did.

"They were making fun of me," I said.

"You can't keep fighting," she told me, adding, "But don't let nobody pick on you."

Of course, it wasn't just other students mocking me. Teachers used to pick on me, too. One day a teacher put a Stick Ups air freshener underneath my desk, something that amused the entire class and gave them fodder for months afterward. I'd always been a very active kid with a lot of energy, so it was hard for me to sit down in class. I'd always be tapping my foot or bouncing my knee, and teachers didn't like that. Many got angry at me, and

I didn't respond very well to that. They didn't want to understand me or reach me, so I grew to resent them telling me what to do.

When I first started to go to my friends' houses when I was young, I began to realize that something was different about my home. Like the time I was at a buddy's house and I asked him if I could use the bathroom. He pointed to a room down the hall, so I went expecting to find a bucket just like the kind we used, but when I walked into the small room, I couldn't find it.

"Where's the bathroom?" I asked.

"It's right there," my friend said.

"What's that?" I asked, pointing at the round white thing by the sink.

He looked at me to see if I was joking, then said, "That's a toilet."

The disparity in my life only grew as I entered middle school. Things like clothing mattered more, so the jokes about my flooding pants and my no-name-brand shoes only hurt worse. They jolted me from the joy I felt as a child. I began to believe the ridicule. I was beginning to feel like I was unworthy of friendship and that I was less than human. The poverty that consumed me and my family only served to slowly give confirmation that nothing was going to change for the better in my life; things were only getting worse.

Something's really off in my life.

The pain of the teasing and the proof of how different I was than others made me question my circumstances.

Why do I have to live like this?

Living in Wentzville, Missouri, only made things worse. Even though it was a suburb of St. Louis, Wentzville was totally segregated from the metropolitan city and didn't want to have anything to do with it. It felt like the majority of people living there—maybe 90 percent—were white, so there were pockets in Wentzville where the Black folks lived. One area was the area I grew up around on the south side of town. Right next to us was Lake St. Louis, where rich kids lived. There was overt racism that we saw when you got called the n-word or fights happened, but for the most part, being Black was just another clique like the preppy kids or the jocks. We got along with most of our classmates, since we'd grown up with them. The problem was with the police. The older we got, the bigger the problem became.

One of the biggest streams of revenue in Wentzville came from the General Motors plant that opened in 1983. As lots of people moved into the town from all different places, including St. Louis, they began to build Section 8 houses, and with that came the baggage these residences brought, such as more drugs and violence. The added workers in Wentzville meant there were also more drug dealers, and since we were so close to downtown St. Louis, more people would come to our town to buy drugs. Other dealers would learn about this and try to get into the market, meaning there was a battle for clientele and resources. This was what brought in more violence. It's also what brought in my older cousin.

KJ had moved away from Wentzville when I was younger, and when he came back around while I was in middle school, he made a big impression. I noticed his shiny new car and his clothes and the jewelry around his neck. When I first asked him where he was working and how he was getting all the money to pay for everything, he told me not to worry about it, to stay in school. But I wasn't gonna listen. When he took me for a ride in his car one day, I saw how everybody liked him. *Man, this guy is cool*, I couldn't help thinking. Older ladies used to say, "Oh, he's so handsome." I even began getting noticed, being called "KJ's nephew." As I began to hang out with my cousin more, I knew exactly where that money came from, and I wanted in on the action. I was tired of being poor. He assured me that this was a way out of living in poverty.

One day I was looking for KJ and asked my grandmother where he might be. She had seen me running after him and laughing at his jokes and always wanting to hang out with him.

"Let me tell you something," Granny said. "Something that happened when you were younger. Just to show you what you're messin' around with. To show you what could happen if you keep hanging around with KJ. Do you remember when your mama came around when you were seven years old?"

"Not really. I kinda remember something about it."

"She had been living in Minnesota after getting out of a mental hospital and ended up with this guy who claimed to be a preacher. She saw how we were living, so one day she came and told me that she had a way where we didn't have to struggle anymore. I looked your mother up and down and asked if she had a job, and then she told me the truth, how this preacher she was with was selling drugs. She wanted you to go with them because a kid could help move the drugs. The preacher would've paid a lot of money for you to work for him."

The preacher reasoned that if a kid got in trouble, he was only going to go to juvenile detention and they could try to get him out.

"Your mama said they'd send you back, but they needed a kid for a while."

My grandmother didn't tell me at the time that she told my mother to go ahead and ask if I wanted to go with them. When they did, I ended up telling them no. I wanted to stay where I was. I loved being around Granny, and I loved going out with my little toolkits and pretending to work on these old cars with older guys. I didn't know this woman who had come around hugging me and kissing me. All I could remember was asking Granny, "Who is this lady?" She wasn't my momma. Granny was my momma.

Learning about my mother's attempt to use me to sell drugs for a fake preacher only fueled my hate for my mother, but it also planted a seed in my heart that I was about to go in the wrong direction. This seed did not grow, however, because it was choked out by the hunger pains of poverty. A dark cloud of hopelessness was also clouding my judgment; I was starting to feel trapped.

"You don't want to get involved with people like that," Granny said about my cousin.

I wish I would have listened to her. At that point in my life as a thirteen-year-old, I'd been doing stupid stuff like finding cars being worked on and stealing them so we could go joyriding. I was beginning to fully embrace being a delinquent. I realized that school wasn't for me, and I also knew I needed to make money for me and my grandmother. So I told KJ I wanted to sell marijuana. I didn't want to mess with crack and cocaine—I knew that it was bad, and I'd never liked how it made people behave.

"No, man, it's just weed," KJ assured me.

"Well, how do I do it?" I asked.

That's when he showed me. He was a gang leader, so he basically groomed me to be a gang leader myself, to lead my homeboys in my area. I began selling weed, traveling around making money off little joints. Since they didn't have GPS back then, I used a map, stopping and spotting the mile markers and the street signs. Sometimes I even traveled out of the state.

We called our gang the Bloods, but we weren't like the notorious gang founded in Los Angeles. Our gang just consisted of our friends, but cops gave us the gang moniker since we were young Black guys selling weed and doing stupid things. This was the '90s, so a lot of people really hated the young Black gang member stereotype. My gang consisted of the guys I'd grown up with. We were simply tight and didn't have many other options. We weren't innocent, yet I found a sense of safety and security and empowerment with my gang. I discovered my identity. These weren't just my friends; they were my brothers. Most of the time, we were scared to death, just trying to be tough and protect our neighborhood. We got shot at and robbed, but we weren't really trying to hurt anybody. We fought with our fists, but when people brought guns out, we'd get out of there and run for our lives to safety.

As I began to sell pot for my cousin, he told me he was going to keep some of the money, saving it for me in case I wanted to invest it one day or if I ever needed a lawyer. I was too young and naive to realize he was keeping that money for himself so he could buy things or support a crack cocaine habit I didn't know he had.

The first thing I did when I made some money was to give it to my grandmother. At least I tried to give it to her. Yet she refused to accept the cash in my hand and looked at me with distrusting eyes.

"Where'd you get that money?" she asked, knowing I didn't have a job. I couldn't open my lips or even give an answer.

"I don't want that—that's bad money," she said with the sound of heartbreak in her voice as tears started streaming down her face.

When I couldn't convince her to take the money, I started taking it and hiding the money around the house, like under a cushion in the sofa or on the kitchen counter. Granny might find a twenty-dollar bill on the floor and pick it up. "I can't believe I dropped this money," she would tell me. "Yeah, you're always dropping money," I responded with a laugh. This was how I managed to get her to take some of the money I'd made. I knew how hard she worked, so she deserved it. This little game continued until the day Granny found my supply of weed.

"You're not going to be selling drugs in this house," she said in a powerful voice. "Not under this roof. If that's what you want, then you're going out on the street."

"No! This is not what I want, Granny. I'm just trying to make some money. I want something better for my life. For our lives. Why do we got to live so poor?"

So I became homeless for a while, spending up all my money trying to get food and stay in hotel rooms. I couldn't stay with my friends because they were young and their parents would ask questions like "Why are you staying here?" At one point, things got so bad that I was eating food off my friend's plate like old scraps for a dog because I was so hungry and didn't want to steal from a store. I didn't want to stoop that low. I just tried to make ends meet. So that drove me to figure out how to be more effective selling weed.

Eventually I ended up getting a car and my own trailer. Since I was only fifteen years old, I couldn't pay for it in my name. I decided to try to have a crack addict I knew buy a vehicle for me.

"I'll give you this money if you buy this car for me," I told him. "All you gotta do is sign your name on it." I gave him $2,000 for the car and paid him $500 for his help.

This guy helped me out, signing for the car and later doing the same thing with a single-wide trailer. I told him I'd take care of everything, just to say that the trailer belonged to him. For a few months, I lived in that rhythm. Turning sixteen and living alone. Dropping out of school and selling weed. Joining a gang and feeling like I was part of something. Sensing I was protected. But this environment didn't protect me. It only pushed me further out into that pitch-black world where enemies always lurked, trying to get at me.

I started noticing strange stuff with my cousin. I noticed KJ coming around not dressing as clean and cool as he used to. He wasn't just selling weed—he was selling other stuff, and I could tell he was getting high on his own stash. The car he showed up in was a rusted-out bucket. I asked him what was going on with him.

"Man, I'm good. Just putting the money aside, saving it up for an emergency."

This was the ugly side of this universe, and it kept getting more unseemly. I got robbed several times, and one of those times I got pistol-whipped. After this, I decided this world wasn't for me.

I'm done. No more. I'm gonna get a legitimate job.

So that's what I did. I ended up getting a job at a McDonald's not far from my house. It was my first official job. I was trying to turn the page, trying to find another purpose.

No kid should want to hang out in the streets living an aimless life. This was a hard truth I would come to realize years later. The sense of belonging and being a part of something bigger was a false narrative I'd bought into. Even though I believed I was succeeding, I was in fact setting myself up to fail. The street life will accept anyone, but that way of life will chew them up, spit them out, and then ask for more, just like an all-consuming beast that cannot be satisfied. The street life will always be hungry for more souls to consume, taking everything and leaving nothing.

It waited for me, but it wouldn't have to wait very long.

Jonathan
Irons

Granny, Jonathan, and his aunt

Chapter Two

THE GIRL WITH THE BRAIDS

(1989–2000)

(M)

ONE THING MY mom taught me at an early age is to put yourself in a place where you have opportunity. If you pursue a goal and want something to happen, you have to work at it and think ahead. You need to put yourself out there. You must be thoughtful about how you pursue your goals in life. When I was ten years old, I took her advice and set out to achieve the biggest dream my fifth-grade self held: owning my very own drum set.

Coming from a musical family, I grew up watching people around me playing instruments and singing. A song could always be heard somewhere in the air. Before I ever shot a basketball, I learned how to sing. I was memorizing songs by the time I was three. When I was ten years old, we were visiting some of our extended family in Atlanta, and that's when I first discovered my love for drums. My cousin at the time was a music producer and very talented at playing several instruments, and he had his drum set out. It had so many parts that I didn't know by name just yet, but I knew I wanted to play them.

"You wanna try them out?" my cousin asked me.

I took the drumsticks and sat on the padded stool. The first thing I did was press down on the bass pedal with my foot, feeling the boom of the bass drum bounce off me. I began to beat on the floor tom with the stick in my right hand, then alternated with my other stick on the snare drum. For the first time, I found a rhythm behind a set of drums. These instruments fascinated me.

"Let me show you how to play," my cousin said.

He taught me a few things on the drums before we left to go back home to Missouri. By the time we were on the road, I was determined to get some of my own.

"Mom, I want a drum set," I said in the passenger seat of our car while she drove.

"Well, do you have the money for a drum set?"

"No." I didn't know exactly how much they cost, but I knew I didn't have enough money saved to buy anything as big as that.

"So what do you think you should do?" my mom asked.

Little did I know my mom was using this as an opportunity to teach me a valuable lesson about life. If you have a goal, make a plan and work it out. Seeing how motivated I was about this drum set, Mom helped me come up with an idea. That was how "Maya's Mobile Car Wash" was born.

Right around this time, Windows 95 was all the rage, making clip art and graphic design more accessible to the everyday person. Mom and I used this program to create a flyer. It had a cheesy little car standing right next to a bucket and a sponge with goofy eyes on them with the following words in big, bold type:

Maya's Mobile Car Wash.

We'll come to you and wash your car!

We bought sponges and buckets and windshield squeegees and super-absorbent towels. We even purchased some car wax. This was a serious enterprise. And I promise you, there were quite a few people who let me wash their car. People like my mom's coworkers and our neighbors. It was hard work, but I didn't know anybody else on the block who was washing cars like that. And I'm still proud to say that Maya's Mobile Car Wash was kind of successful. By the end of the initiative, I had raised a whopping $200. Back in 1999, that was a lot of money.

The drum set I wanted cost around $400, but Mom had told me that if I could raise half the cost, she would pay for the remaining amount. This is such a vivid memory that sticks with me, such a great life lesson I discovered at a young age. If you want something, you go out and work for it.

I was ecstatic on following through with my goal of owning a drum set. God bless my mother, because this meant I would be making a lot of noise for several years to come. I don't know if she knew what she was getting into, but I do know she's a very gracious momma, because most parents do not want drums banging around in their house! After I learned the basics from an instructional video, I was self-taught the rest of the way. Just listening to music and trying to imitate it, maybe picking something up from an artist here and there. It was a hobby, but even to this day, I enjoy the drums and play them every now and then. I still have that same set.

Whenever I can learn a song, I feel like I am part of the music and I can connect with something bigger and beautiful. It's almost like the feeling in basketball when everyone's on the same page, flowing right, moving the ball steadily with purpose and precision. The drums taught me the joy of finding a good rhythm and moving to the right tempo. I would come to learn how this not only applied to playing basketball but also how it applied to living a fruitful life.

◆ ◆ ◆

Music wasn't the only constant in my family. Growing up, I became very aware that almost everyone in our family was a teacher. Both my mother and my godmom have taught at some point in their lives. My great-aunt and -uncle are teachers, and so are my grandparents and several of my cousins. My grandmother taught kindergarten in the inner city of Chicago for forty-nine years, a feat that is amazing to think about. My grandparents would bring me books anytime they came from Chicago to see me. Teaching is a gift, and it was impactful to have teachers in my childhood to look up to. They taught me the value of having role models and the true effect a person can have on another individual.

The combination of a passion for music and teaching brought my great-uncle and -aunt to Missouri. Hugh and Janett Flowers were known as Papa and Hamaw to my younger cousins and me, and in 1972, they left Chicago to move to Jefferson City. Papa had taught music and directed several choirs at Parker High School in Chicago, and this led to him accepting a position at Lincoln University to continue his musical teaching career. Papa was more than a teacher to his students; he was a mentor and an encourager. For more than fifty years, he nurtured and established loving relationships with the students he taught.

My mom's parents grew up in Detroit and early in their marriage settled in Chicago, where they would raise my mom and her siblings. My great-aunt and -uncle also settled in Chicago alongside my grandparents and began raising kids of their own, the oldest being my godmom, Cherilyn. Missouri entered the picture after Papa got the job at Lincoln University. Cheri was ten years old when they moved.

My mother, Kathryn Moore, was the baby girl in her family with two older brothers. After she turned eighteen, she decided to go to Los Angeles to make it on her own, to go to college and prove that she could be independent and build a life for herself. When I became old enough, my mom admitted to me that this was not the wisest decision.

"It was silly, being out there all by myself," Mom once said. "I didn't have guidance. I didn't make great decisions."

"Well, I'm glad you did, because I'm here," I told her.

Even this was a lesson for her to share. As I grew up, my mom told me things like this in order for me to learn. "You need to be mindful of when you go places," she said. Knowing what we know now of the importance of family and support and having safety in a community, my mother moving to California was very risky. A woman only eighteen years old going out there on her own was quite bold, but that's what Kathryn Moore did.

While in LA, my mother worked part-time and attended classes while also getting long-distance financial support from my grandparents. She persisted through the challenges of navigating her new college life and eventually earned a bachelor's degree in history. Her passion has always been fashion and retail, however; she's been sewing since she was a kid. While in California, she dabbled in retail and also worked in sales. After being there for thirteen years, my mom found herself pregnant with me at the age of thirty. A single expectant mother living in Los Angeles far away from a family support system.

Through some sound advice from a faithful friend and after talking with my grandparents, Mom decided it would be best to move to Missouri to raise me around a very stable and very familiar group of family members. As a teenager, Mom would go down to Missouri every summer to visit her aunt and uncle and the cousins who she was very close with. She missed them after they moved away from Chicago, but they would at least be able to see each other during summer break. So she decided to raise me around the people she was raised with. I was born in Jefferson City on June 11, 1989. After the delivery in the hospital, a nurse came to take me to the nursery, but my mom refused. She wanted to hold me in her arms. It was just the two of us now. We were a team.

With Papa and Hamaw's four kids growing up and starting their own families in Jefferson City, I became the first "grandkid" in that group and the first cousin born in my generation there. Papa and Hamaw became my second set of grandparents while my own grandparents came down from Chicago to visit all the time. As the eldest cousin, I grew up feeling like my younger cousins were siblings, so naturally I developed a lot of big-sister tendencies. This meant if something went wrong or if we all got in trouble, I was the one getting blamed for it. Of course, that was mainly because it was probably my fault.

◆ ◆ ◆

My mother didn't have grandiose aspirations when she hung the toy basketball hoop on the door of our apartment when I was only three years old.

She simply needed something that could occupy my time and keep me busy while she was making dinner or doing chores. To say I was an active child is an understatement. I never stopped running or moving, whether I was inside or outside. At first, it really didn't matter what I played with—it could have been a basketball or a soccer ball or a rock—but I needed something to keep me occupied. I was a kid who loved to play.

When I entered elementary school, I was still a very energetic and active kid. Very social. Even then I had a personality that liked to perform. I loved giving tours and explaining things and teaching my younger cousins how to do stuff. Some might say I was a natural leader, but maybe I simply liked to talk a lot. Those sorts of things—always moving and always talking—got me into trouble, whether I was in school or out in our neighborhood.

Jefferson City was a fairly safe suburban town with probably no more than thirty thousand people living there at the time. It wasn't the most diverse area of the country, but there was a little bit of diversity on my block. I spent as much time as I could outside, climbing trees and making up games and trying to build tree houses or construct go-karts. The only rule I had was when the streetlights came on, it was time to come inside. Every so often, our neighborhood would have "Junk Day," when you put big items on the curb that the garbage companies would haul away; I always marked the dates on my calendar.

"We're going to go find some good stuff," I told my friends.

We would go and pick through people's junk and see what we could drag home in order to build something. My mom was often horrified when she came home to see the trash people had left on the curb now sitting in our backyard.

I wasn't only active; I was adventurous. Somehow, I made it out of my childhood with only a couple of fractured bones. The house we lived in sat on a partial cul-de-sac at the bottom of a hill, so I loved to take whatever I could find—a bike, a skateboard, a pair of Rollerblades—and figure out a way to ride it down the incline. If it had wheels, I was going to attempt to take it on a ride. I liked to stand up on my bike seat or ride down backward on my Rollerblades. I loved making ramps on the street to jump off despite them barely holding together. Every now and again, I talked some innocent neighbor or cousin into doing something with me. This didn't always work out so well. Those poor children.

One day, I thought it was a good idea to ride a wagon down the hill. This wasn't any ordinary wagon; this was an old red wagon I'd bought at a garage sale for seventy-five cents. I loved garage sales because you could actually pay for your neighbor's junk. After bringing the wagon home, I began to take it down the hill, and I got pretty good at steering it. Somehow, I persuaded a couple of my neighborhood friends to ride in it with me. They were siblings, and they trusted that I knew what I was doing, but I wasn't really prepared for having other passengers in the old wagon. As we took off and began racing down the hill in a wagon without brakes, I couldn't control the front wheels despite how hard I tried to steer. We ended up crashing, falling out of the wagon, and getting pretty scraped up. Needless to say, my friends' mother made sure they didn't play with me for a few days.

My high energy and how it expressed itself was not easily handled by my teachers, and around second grade, the school was telling my mom that I needed to be on Ritalin. Looking back now, I feel like Ritalin was being handed out left and right for kids growing up in the '90s. Thankfully, my mom got some advice from a friend:

"Do not let them put her on Ritalin. There's nothing wrong with her."

My mom agreed and didn't let them. I didn't have ADHD; I was just very active. I'm grateful that she made sure that I was well supported and she advocated for me. I thrived in group activities and creative ways of learning. When they tested me for the gifted program in third grade and I got in, I discovered other options for learning and getting my energy out. Once a week, I attended the gifted classes, and I loved them.

Entering fourth grade at Moreau Heights changed everything. That's when I met Joni Henderson, one of those life-changing teachers who is anointed to impact children. She looked at each student and saw what they needed, and she gave us a sense of responsibility and ownership in the class. She truly is a diamond. I'd never had a teacher like her before. She was instrumental in helping me learn how to channel my energy and my focus. If

I needed to stand up to do my work, Mrs. Henderson would let me stand up and work. She had a classroom environment that was very family-oriented and gave kids tasks and responsibilities so you felt like you were a part of helping the class. Her encouragement really helped change me and allow me to grow.

I was a good student, someone who always made good grades. The older I got, the harder I worked on achieving those strong marks. Knowing myself now, I realize I'm an achiever. That's one of my strongest traits. I'm not necessarily as motivated by the competition as I am by the achievement. It's never been so much about beating someone else but rather about accomplishing the goal. My class projects and assignments excited me. And I always enjoyed learning, so if there were positive learning environments for me, I thrived.

Of course, one of the biggest outlets to focus my energy on and the best way I found myself thriving was in active games. My mom realized early on the value of putting me in structured activities like sports. She knew I loved being around other kids, and she saw that letting my energy out in constructive ways was good for me. I played every sport you can think of, from gymnastics to T-ball, softball to basketball and dance (the latter only lasted a couple of days because there wasn't enough action in it for me). I didn't miss anything. I loved to swim, and I even played two-hand touch football with the boys at recess and kickball and four square. I loved playing anything outside, so I'd always try to rally up the neighborhood kids to do something.

Around this time, the X Games were starting to get popular, and for a while, I wanted to be in the X Games. Watching those athletes compete in extreme sports with skateboards and Rollerblades and bikes excited me. That changed the day my mom took me to a skate park where I could see firsthand what it looked and sounded like to be jumping and flying high in the air and then landing hard on the ground. I realized that the ground *was* in fact really hard and that this was a little too scary for me, so I decided I was only going to Rollerblade down my street.

My mom, seeing that I needed some structured activities, signed me up for my first basketball team at the YMCA in second grade. We wore green and white, and I was the only one who could really score. At seven years old, you're just trying to make sure the ball stays in bounds. In third grade, I started playing AAU (Amateur Athletic Union). There was one AAU team in Jefferson City. When I was seven, they wouldn't let me play because they said I was too young, but after turning eight, they let me play on the ten-and-under team. I played on the team for two years. I'm sure we were very entertaining to the parents who were watching these little eight-, nine-, and ten-year-olds running around shooting air balls and traveling. In the '90s, we liked to wear big clothes, so everything was baggy and didn't fit. Since my mom knew how to braid, I was always rocking braids. Mom always kept my hair in twists or braids, something low-maintenance because I was super active. That's how you knew it was me out there. There's the girl with the braids. I was very skinny, all muscle and bone, very wiry and long. And of course, I was pretty much taller than everybody in my class for almost my whole school experience.

I always had a knack for sports, but around the time I was eight years old, I started to realize I liked basketball better than anything else. Basketball was perfect for me because there is never a down moment: You're either on offense or defense. Soon the other sports started to drop off, especially when I told my mom I wanted to stay home to shoot hoops instead of having her drive me to some other activity I didn't enjoy as much. My mom told me that was fine but that I needed to decide which activities I wanted to commit to because I couldn't do everything, and I chose to stick with basketball.

Another reason for my love of basketball around this time was because the WNBA had just started. The league was founded in 1996, and the first games began a year later. I was really drawn to the WNBA as I watched the athletes on television. My favorite team was the Houston Comets. Since there was no team really close to Missouri, and since the Comets won the first four WNBA championships in a row, I naturally latched on to them. There were so many players that I looked up to and who ignited my excitement for the game, players like Cynthia Cooper, Sheryl Swoopes, Tina Thompson, Janeth Arcain, Lisa Leslie, Teresa Weatherspoon, Rebecca Lobo, Andrea Stinson, Dawn Staley . . . I could keep going. As I watched them on the screen as the years went by, I began to realize something about basketball.

There are other women who do this. This is something that could be out there for me.

Looking back, I see how so many family members and coaches helped to inspire and influence my basketball journey. One of them was my uncle, Preston Moore. He was always so supportive behind the scenes. One Christmas, he gifted me with my first WNBA indoor and outdoor balls. I almost lost my mind. From age eight to sixteen, I took that indoor WNBA ball with me to every single AAU event and practice. It was always with me until I graduated high school. I always had a ball. There was no way I was going to be in a gym and not have access to a ball. No way. I had my WNBA ball thanks to Uncle Preston. I carried that ball around with me everywhere. I remember when I was fifteen, I dunked for the first time on a full ten-foot hoop. I shared so many memories with that ball.

Playing on that ten-and-under team when I was eight allowed me to push myself. I remember Coach Steve teaching me the fundamentals and basic plays. Sure, it was really just about having fun and the games weren't extremely competitive, but we were still working. It was fun being able to go to basketball practice. Every year I got a little a better. I ended up playing nine seasons of AAU basketball before I went to UConn.

◆ ◆ ◆

The most consistent thing in the first eleven years of my life was the love from the extended family I grew up with. Papa and Hamaw lived on a small farm about fifteen minutes away in the next town over, and every weekend we went out there for a family meal. It was a close-knit, very supportive, and positive environment to grow up in. My extended family were all solid people of faith, not perfect but full of a lot of love. I grew up feeling loved and sensing the stability in my extended family. They had stable marriages, they were faithful in the church community, and when we gathered, alcohol was never abused. There never was a lot of drama that I witnessed. It was just a really healthy, safe environment to grow up in.

My mom describes me as a very compassionate kid, someone who loved people no matter what they looked like. One of my best friends was a kid with a disability, and we had tons of adventures in our neighborhood. I also really gravitated toward babies and older people. As all the cousins were popping out one year after the other, I was ecstatic to love on and play with each new baby. I was all about every newborn that came along. So much so that parents would have to get my attention every now and then.

"Maya, you have to play with the other kids, too. You can't just play with the baby all day."

Loving and enjoying people was role-modeled for me through my extended family. But my biggest role model was my mom.

As I grew up, my mom and I were close. When I was little, I didn't understand what it meant to be raised by a single parent, but kids are very perceptive and know when something's off even when they can't verbalize it. I knew that there was something different about our home and family, and as I grew older, I came to realize the truth.

I don't have a mom and a dad. I have a mom.

Yes, I had this loving extended family. I had Reggie, my godfather, and I had my grandfather, uncle, and other males in my family, but there wasn't the presence of my biological father. I feel this made things challenging for me in ways I didn't yet understand as a kid, and my mom was determined to make it work and carry the whole load as best as she could. We had so much support from our loved ones around us, but I still saw my mom get up every day and go to work. In living her life, my mom taught me the value of a strong work ethic. You show up every day, and you work hard. I saw that lived out through my mom. She was always present for me, whether it was for my games or the other activities I had going on. My mom was always there. That consistency of going to work every day and showing up and being present was ingrained in me and shaped the woman I would become.

When I look back and think of what it would have been like raising a high-energy kid like myself, all I can say is "God bless you, Mom." I know it was not easy. I definitely had my ups and downs as a kid, but this created a deep, deep bond between my mom and me. We've always been a team for my whole life, and it's been a blessing to have been raised by her. To watch her grow over the years. To witness the heart that she has for me and for others. And to see her determination to seek out opportunities for the two of us.

When I was in sixth grade, my mom saw another opportunity and she acted on it.

She was working for a phone company at the time, and she received a promotion in her job that would relocate us to Charlotte, North Carolina. She knew that we both could benefit from moving somewhere that offered more potential for growth. And she did a great job of painting that picture for me, so I focused on that. I had to tell my friends that we were moving, and the reality of leaving began to hit me. I would miss everyone, but there was an exciting new adventure ahead.

At the time, my extended family was all pretty shocked by the decision and it was extremely hard for them to see us go. We didn't have any family in Charlotte. From the outside looking in, it didn't look like the smartest move. It didn't look like the safest move.

But moving ended up being a game changer.

At the Women's Basketball
Hall of Fame in Tennessee

Mom Kathryn

Chapter Three

A LION ON THE STREETS

(1993–1997)

(J)

IN MY EARLY teens, I already understood the lyrics of "Trapped" off 2Pac's first album. Back in the early '90s, we didn't have social media and cameras and national commentary, but we did have hip-hop music. With songs like LL Cool J's "Illegal Search" and Ice-T's "Cop Killer" and Geto Boys' "Crooked Officer," the gangsta rap we listened to accurately reflected the reality of our lives. We weren't living in Compton in southern Los Angeles County, but we still experienced the same sort of police misconduct and brutality living in Wentzville in western St. Charles County. It became commonplace in our lives.

A clear portrait of this occurred when I was thirteen and hanging around with Bob, another kid I'd grown up with. One night we were walking in the city limits of Wentzville, not doing anything, when a police officer slowed down in his car, put his cherries on, and pulled in front of us.

"Get in the back," he ordered after rolling down the window.

Bob and I did as we were told. This wasn't the first time a cop had slowed down and even told us to get in the squad car without any explanation for why. We knew the real reason was the color of our skin. He didn't say much as he got on State Highway Z and began driving into the pitch-black night. After ten minutes, I began to get nervous. Then when he pulled off and entered the small town of New Melle, I grew afraid.

This was an extremely racist town, a place that actually had a sign that read "If you're not from here, don't let the sun fall down on you."

Meaning "If you're Black, you better not be caught here after sunset."

With a population of just over two hundred people, New Melle was a rural town that was settled by immigrants from Melle, Germany. They were an all-white and conservative community that wanted to be rural and remain removed from cities like St. Louis. Bob and I knew being seen out there at nighttime was an invitation to trouble, and the cop knew this as well. That's why he dropped us deep in the heart of New Melle and drove off.

The police officer deliberately drove way out of his jurisdiction just to try to taunt us and force us to walk nine or ten miles back home in the darkness of night. The only way a passing driver was going to be a good Samaritan was to not stop but to keep driving. If anybody did stop, we knew they'd not be offering us a drive. I was frightened, but more than that, I was angry. Thankfully no drama ensued on this night.

◆ ◆ ◆

When I was little, I used to dream about being a police officer. This began when D.A.R.E. cops visited our elementary school and spoke. The acronym stood for Drug Abuse Resistance Education, with the officers coming to speak to children from kindergarten all the way up to high schoolers. I also loved McGruff the Crime Dog, an animated dog in commercials who always said, "Help take a bite out of crime." I thought, *This is what I want to do one day.* Even the Police Academy movie series in the '80s inspired this dream. The Black guy who always made the sound effects cracked me up. More than any of this, however, I think I wanted to be a police officer because, at my core, I've always wanted to help people. That's always been my nature. It wasn't until I was in fifth grade that I began to see the darker side of law enforcement. I realized there were a lot of cops who were nothing like those friendly D.A.R.E. cops or McGruff the Crime Dog.

Being driven out to New Melle wasn't an isolated incident. These sorts of things happened repeatedly. We had white friends in Lake St. Louis that we played football with, so we'd go hang out with them and swim in the lake. The rules stated that you couldn't fish or swim in the two private lakes unless you were a resident of Lake St. Louis, so local cops would show up while we were swimming and ask to see our IDs. As young teenagers, we didn't even have IDs, so then they'd ask us where we lived and we'd tell them Wentzville.

"You're not allowed to be here," they would tell me and Charles and any other Black kids there.

The white kids who didn't live in Lake St. Louis were allowed to stay. This happened all the time. Sometimes we'd simply be playing basketball in the park, and the cops would swoop down there just to harass us. "Here come the police!" someone would call out, and everybody would disperse in every direction, hopping fences and running through yards. After experiencing this repeatedly and learning this was simply what the cops around us did, I decided I didn't want to be a police officer. I didn't want to have anything to do with them. This would only be magnified after I lost my job at McDonald's.

When I got hired to work at the fast-food restaurant, I was proud to finally have a legitimate job, but it didn't take long before I became resentful of where I was put. The manager put me behind a grill to flip burgers even though I was certainly able and qualified to be standing behind the counter taking orders. There were some young girls and another guy working there, and they were struggling. So I decided I was going to show my manager that I deserved to be up there behind a register. Someone would place an order, and I'd be able to figure out the exact cost with the tax in my head before one of the other workers could ring it up.

"That's seven dollars and fifty-six cents," I'd spit out above the sound of the sizzling patties below me.

After working there for a couple of weeks and continuing to do this, my manager had had enough.

"You need to stop doing that," he barked out. "I'm training them. This is your job."

"Why you got me flippin' burgers? I'm way better than those guys at the register."

"You need to be happy that you got a job. This is what you're going to be doing."

Once again, I was battling something bigger than simply a manager not liking me. I knew he was racist, not just because he forced me to work behind the grill and didn't give me a chance, but it was the way he talked down to me and the tone he took when he told me to do something. He treated me different than any of the other white employees, whether they were male or female.

When I got off work that evening, I grabbed some food and then started walking to my buddy's house down the road. My feet hurt and I was exhausted from standing all day behind a hot grill. My uniform smelled like grease and french fries. About a mile away from McDonald's, a police car approached on the other side of the road and the officer spotted me, then whipped his car around in a *Smokey and the Bandit* sort of way, with his tires screeching and his lights flashing. He sounded a few short blasts of siren just for dramatic effect, and he popped out of his car and positioned himself on the hood with his gun facing me.

"Freeze!" he called out. "Get down on the ground!"

Terror filled me as I did what I was told. I had no idea what was happening and why he was so angry. He looked like he wanted to kill me. I think if I had run, the cop would have shot me.

"Keep your hands up in the air where I can see them!"

Sprawled out on the hard concrete at the side of the road, sweat covering my back and face, I saw the figure walk toward me, still aiming the gun at my head. As he jerked one of my wrists while he put the handcuffs on me, I was so freaked out that I peed on myself.

This guy's gonna kill me, and I didn't do anything wrong.

The cop put me in the back of his car and brought me to the station, never saying a word to me. Nobody said anything. I wasn't questioned or spoken to. I just sat there in this room with no window and no clock, staring at blank walls and waiting. I had to go to work the next day and knew my manager already hated me, so I couldn't afford to be late.

What is happening? Did I do something I didn't remember? I don't have a gun. Nothing was on me.

The questions and the fear filled me all night long. After being locked up for hours, the window on the door slid open and a police officer I hadn't seen looked at me.

"Who are you?" he asked.

"I'm Jonathan Irons."

"How long you been here?"

"I don't know. Hey, man—why am I here? Nobody's come to talk to me."

"You don't know?"

"No," I said.

"I don't know what you're doing here," he said.

He disappeared, and then fifteen minutes later, they let me out. There was no explanation, no apology, nothing but "Go ahead, you can leave." I never saw the officer who arrested me. When I finally left the station, I realized that I had been there for twenty hours. I also knew I was late for work. My manager promptly fired me. On paper, he was justified. Because I was still on work probation as a new hire.

Like losing the desire to become a police officer, my dreams of having a legitimate job and getting out of selling drugs were over. Any hope I had felt crumpled up and tossed out.

Why am I tryin' to find something that's not gonna happen?

So I went back to selling weed and hanging out in all these areas around Wentzville, St. Charles County, and St. Louis County. It would be easy to reason that this decision prompted everything that came next, but that's not the case. What eventually happened could have easily taken place if I had become the manager of that McDonald's. I had a choice whether or not to sell marijuana, but I couldn't choose the color of my skin.

◆ ◆ ◆

The guy pointing the gun at my head was scared. Maybe more scared than I was. His arm shook as the barrel hovered only inches away from my face. The white, long-haired, and scraggly-bearded hippie yelled at me while I stood still. The bag of weed he wanted lay on the ground by my feet.

We were behind the gas station late at night near my grandmother's house, and I was going to sell this guy some pot, when he upped a gun on me. As he started hollering at me, I dropped the weed and put my hands in the air, watching him carefully. Then I quickly moved and grabbed his arm and pulled him forward. One of my hands clasped onto the .380 he was holding, and we wrestled a bit until I somehow grabbed the gun from him. I closed my eyes and fired a shot into the ground, the sharp crack making the guy jump. I tried to pull the trigger again, but nothing happened. The gun had fatally jammed; it could no longer be fired, and I didn't know how to fix it. The hippie darted off in one direction, and I ran in the other. I didn't bother to get the bag of weed. I needed to get out of there.

Desperate to feel safe, I ran to Granny's house. Even though I wasn't living there, she opened the door and let me in. She also proceeded to give me a good tongue-lashing since it was so late at night.

For a while I'd keep the .380 as a trophy, showing it off to my friends. I felt really tough and smart, and I had survived an armed robbery attempt. Little did I know that simply being seen with this gun would be a fact used against me in a court of law.

◆ ◆ ◆

Life as I knew it ended the moment I stood at the large front window of my friend's house and saw two white men pull up in a regular car. As they climbed out of the vehicle, I noticed they had suits on, and when they both pulled out handguns and started walking toward the house, one thought ran through my head.

There's a hit about to happen!

I'd seen enough Mafia and mobster movies to imagine what was happening.

It was January 21, 1997, and I was a week away from turning seventeen. I was visiting a friend named Tee in Troy, a town that was a twenty-minute drive from Wentzville. I'd come up there to sell some weed to people. I was starting to branch out my business because I was hungry and wanted to make enough money to eventually get out of selling drugs and do something else.

When Tee saw the men outside, he bolted to the back door and took off running. I did the same thing, still clueless about what was happening. Maybe Tee had done something and they were after him, or maybe we were being robbed. Twenty feet from rushing out of the house, I was blindsided by a big guy tackling me like he was a linebacker. At first, I didn't even know what hit me—I've never been hit that hard in my life. As he wrapped me up, I heard him saying into a walkie-talkie, "I got him, I got him," and then I noticed a badge and my mind whirled around in disbelief.

These guys are cops?

"What's this about?" I asked.

The guy didn't say anything except to order me to stand up. They initially took me to the jail in Troy, but soon I was taken by those same officers in plain clothes to the O'Fallon Police Department, where I was brought down a hallway and then shoved into this cold holding area where I had to wait. I thought of the McDonald's incident and wondered if this was another case of the cops messing around with me.

Maybe this is about the weed.

A detective named Michael Hanlen came to the door. "I want to talk to you for a minute," he said in a gentle tone. He took me to a room with no windows or cameras or recording devices. After we sat at the table, another guy came into the room, but the detective told him he couldn't be there.

"I got it," the detective told him.

Never once did the detective read me my Miranda rights, nor was there any notice of them on the wall in the room. Nobody gave my grandmother a call, and there wasn't another adult in the room with us. I scarfed down the food he had brought to me. He seemed to be a kind man as he patiently watched me eat while he opened a notebook and began to write in it. When I finished the meal, the detective began to ask me questions.

"Do you know a subdivision named Osage Meadows?" he asked.

"Yeah," I said.

"Know anybody there?"

"Yeah. I got some friends livin' there."

He nodded and continued writing as he asked more questions.

"You been there recently?"

"Yeah, I was there not too long ago."

The detective began to tell me about how just a week ago somebody's house in Osage Meadows had been burglarized and the owner of the house had been shot.

"I think you know something about this," the detective said.

"No, man—I don't know anything about that," I said. "I don't."

His hand stopped writing for a moment as he stared at me. "Okay, how about this? Why don't you give me some names of who you think might have been involved with something like this?"

I didn't know anything about a burglary or shooting anywhere in Missouri, but I did know that you never told on anybody. That was how I was raised.

"I'm not a snitch," I said. "I don't know nothing, but even if I did, I wouldn't tell you a thing."

The man didn't like my response and the tone I was taking with him.

"Really? If you don't give me some names or some information, I'm gonna put you away for a long time. Do you understand?"

"What're you talkin' about, man?" I said, feeling a mixture of being frightened and frustrated.

The longer the detective interrogated me, the more angry he became.

Every single accusation or inquiry I denied made him more hostile. When he began to yell at me, I yelled back, repeating that I didn't know what he was talking about. He grew so irate that he stood up, approached me, and pushed me in my forehead; then he left me alone in the room to wait and wonder what was happening. When the detective came back into the room, he appeared to be calm once again and tried to play the good-cop role.

"Look, I'm sorry," he said. "Let's try this again. I'm just trying to help you, kid. Just give me some names or some info—anything that can help. You gotta know something."

"No, man."

"Okay, how about I write down some names and all you gotta do is sign it to confirm they were involved."

"I'm not signing anything," I told him. "I plead the Fifth."

The detective shook his head and gave me a disdainful laugh. "Kid, you watch too much TV."

The detective was agitated once again, and he kept writing down notes, looking up to glare at me, then looking back down to jot down something. After what felt like a hundred denials to being involved in this robbery and shooting in any sort of way, the detective brought me back down to my cell. The interrogations weren't over, however.

Another detective named Richard Morrell came and brought me to a room that had a video camera perched on a stand. I thought it was odd and began to study it. I noticed that the recording light was on as I walked by it to sit down. Once again I wasn't read my Miranda rights. Morrell seemed cool and was much more relaxed than the last detective. He asked, "You want to smoke a cigarette and drink a soda with me before I take you home?"

Shocked and willing to do anything to go home, I said, "Yes, but my grandmother would be very upset if she found out that I was arrested." I had never smoked a cigarette before in my life before that point. I immediately fought the urge to cough but was unsuccessful. He softly giggled as I tried to recover from inhaling the tobacco smoke.

"I believe you are a good kid and I can help you get out of this trouble, if you give me some names of people you think are involved. I don't think you are the one who did it."

At that moment, I realized what he was doing. He was a bad cop, playing a cool-cop role with the aim of getting me to open up to him. I folded my arms, trying to appear like a tough guy, and said, "I don't know anything, and even if I did, I wouldn't tell you anything." Little did I know, I was about to learn that this was a big mistake.

"Can I leave now?" I asked him.

"No," he said in an aggravated tone.

"That doesn't make sense. Why not? You said I could go home."

"We'll figure it out tomorrow. Anything you want to tell us now?"

"No, I don't have anything to say."

I thought I knew what was happening, that this was all routine for them.

They're just trying to figure out what happened, so they're giving me a hard time. That's all.

Question after question kept coming at me, even when I didn't respond. He would ask it again or ask another one. It was becoming clear that Detective Morell wouldn't or couldn't accept my answers. Instead, he only grew more agitated and finally stood up, grabbed me by my shirt with both of his hands, and threw me against the wall so hard that the clock fell down off the wall beside me with a loud, startling crack. "Listen, kid, if you don't tell me the truth, I will put you away for good!" he said as his frightening eyes glared into my soul for what seemed like an eternity.

As terror filled my heart and my body trembled with disbelief, I could no longer hold back my tears and anger. In an attempt to retaliate and get him off me, I spat in his face. I wasn't going down without a fight, but I knew it was a fight I couldn't win.

I felt powerless. Helpless. I'd always thought I was a strong, powerful kid until that man grabbed me and shoved me into the wall. As soon as he grabbed me, I knew I was helpless against him. *He's gonna hurt me bad*, I thought. *This is serious.* But instead of touching me again, the detective let me go while he walked over to the camera, took out the video cassette, and left the room.

That recording never saw the light of day.

Left alone once again, I felt the burn of anger and fear racing through me.

I'm supposed to be hanging out with Charles and my brothers. They're probably wondering where I am.

I thought through the scenarios of what was happening. Clearly, they didn't know who had done this crime. Were they gonna accuse me of doing something or not? But after replaying everything that had happened, I came to a terrifying conclusion.

They really think I did this.

This only frustrated me even more, just the very notion that I was involved in some kind of robbery. When the booking officer got me and started rolling my fingerprints, I still couldn't believe what was happening. *These people are crazy. I ain't had nothing to do with this.*

"Man, what y'all doing my fingerprints for?" I said with bitter sarcasm. "Come on—did y'all find my fingerprints in the house?"

"I don't know. I'm just doing my job," he told me.

The booking officer knew what I meant, how it was ridiculous that they were bothering to take my fingerprints when I had nothing to do with this. I wanted to go home. They had told me I could go home whenever I wanted to, but that was obviously a lie. I couldn't go home; they had me. I was under arrest whether I had handcuffs on or not. I couldn't leave this jail even though they had said I could leave anytime I wanted to but just not now.

Later in my police report, I would discover that they made it seem as if I had asked if they found my fingerprints in a worried sort of way, but my words were never meant that way and this man knew that. As I would one day tell a court of law as a grown man, "I was being a dumb, smart-mouth kid, and I didn't understand the gravity of the situation that I was in."

When they put me back in the cell, I felt the walls closing in around me. My mind kept spinning as I breathed in and out just to calm myself down.

The next day, I was transported to the St. Charles County Jail by the St. Charles County Sheriff's Department. Shortly after being booked and placed in a county jail cell, I was taken to another interrogation room and interviewed by Detective John Neske.

"I want to talk to you and get everything on record," he said. "You don't have to talk to me if you don't want to."

Why is he being so nice? I have seen this trick before.

He had a Miranda form that he passed over to me. I knew what the form was and initialed it on the line marked *I refuse to make a statement at this time.* I knew my rights and chose to not say anything. At that point, I was well beyond trusting any more police officers. I was done talking. I was overcome with fear and anger. I didn't understand why I couldn't go home, and I was angry that I was being held against my will. I felt so helpless. But this time, the interrogation was short, lasting about ten minutes. He didn't ask any more questions. It was over. After signing the form, he made a phone call and had me taken back to my cell. This was the last interrogation I had to endure.

They're gonna figure this out and somebody's gonna come in and say they made a mistake, to let the kid go home, I kept silently hoping to myself.

The moments kept passing and nobody came.

They're gonna figure this out—they're cops. Cops do the right thing. They're the highest moral authority. They have integrity. They don't lie.

But I knew better. I thought of the detective slamming me up against the wall, thinking that I had either done it or knew something more about it. He was playing the bad-cop role, and yeah, I didn't respond well to him. To any of them. But that's 'cause I should not have been there. And I'd never seen a police officer treat someone like this guy treated me.

I wouldn't discover until my arraignment the next day that I was being charged with first-degree assault, armed criminal action, and first-degree burglary.

◆ ◆ ◆

According to Stanley Stotler's testimony at trial, his home was burglarized and he was assaulted with a firearm on January 14, 1997. This was a week before my arrest. Mr. Stotler claimed it was a Black male who assaulted him. After being taken to the hospital, he had emergency brain surgery and ultimately survived. Mr. Stotler would be hospitalized until March 1997, when he returned home, then was hospitalized again in July of the same year for additional surgery as a result of complications from the bullet wound to his skull.

That evening I had brought the .380 handgun that I'd taken from the guy who tried to rob me at the gas station. It wasn't loaded, and I didn't know how to make it work again. I also didn't know where to get bullets for it. I was bragging about how I took it from this guy and shot into the ground to scare him away. My friends' father heard me talking and told me about the trouble a gun could cause.

"You need to get rid of that gun," he said. "You know what was done with that gun? Do you know if any other crimes were committed with it? What about the guy trying to mug you? You're cruising for some trouble."

He told me to let him buy it from me, but I refused. In my mind, this was a cool trophy and it symbolized me surviving this encounter. Days after this, I decided that my friends' father was right, so I eventually threw it in the river. I never would have imagined that simply being seen with the gun would be something of note.

A week after this date, I got arrested, and I would soon learn that they were looking for me because I was a Black man in this predominantly white neighborhood. I was an easy target. People knew who I was.

◆ ◆ ◆

Fear shook me the moment I followed the sheriff into the St. Charles County Jail. In a matter of twenty-four hours, I had been to the police departments in Troy and O'Fallon and now was transported to this county jail. My body shivered as they stripped me naked and sprayed me down with some chemical. *Ain't no tellin' what that is*, I thought with my eyes closed and breath held. They gave me a jumpsuit and a bed bundle; then a guard led me through a corridor. The cold concrete frightened me with a raging terror that I could conceal but never fully extinguish. I arrived at a desk with a correctional officer sitting there in his uniform and badge. COs were the ones who maintained order within the prison. They were the police within the prison who didn't have guns but instead carried Mace, Tasers, a walkie-talkie, handcuffs, all that sort of stuff.

The guard brought me over to a door, then looked back at the CO.

"Where do you want me to put him?" the guard asked. "He's just a kid."

"Put him in there with the rest," the CO said.

The guard looked alarmed. "But he's a kid," he repeated.

"That's not our job to figure out."

The CO pressed a button and a loud *ZZZZZ* sound echoed as the door opened. I looked inside to see a holding tank packed with men from wall to wall. Staring at me were grim faces with hardened eyes. The area was supposed to be for around ten men, but it appeared more like twenty or thirty were in there, standing and lying down and talking on the three phones on the wall. The windows were foggy with dirt, and the air reeked of body odor and excrement. This was the sort of wretched place people talked about when they told stories about jail.

I couldn't move for a moment, standing there paralyzed by fear. All these grown men glared at me and I knew I had to stare back at them and look defiant, but all I could think about was what they were going to do to me. I didn't know anybody and had no idea who might be friends and whether anybody knew me and wanted to hurt me. I didn't know anything. So I just stood still until the guard began to push me into the holding tank.

"You better keep that jab up," the guard said.

I almost dropped my bed bundle, but I caught it just as the steel door behind me slammed shut. The thunderous sound scared me, and so did the laughter coming from someone in the background. I moved to another part of the room. As I stood there, a sixteen-year-old kid facing down a den of strangers, I saw one face staring at me too long, so I looked away at somebody else. I realized I was standing in the bathroom area as someone bumped into me. It smelled bad and I knew I needed to move. I spotted a seat in the far corner of the room, so I made a beeline over there, weaving and stepping over guys to get to that spot. I sat down and tried not to show how terrified I felt. As I looked up, fewer people were staring at me, but I could still see eyes on me.

The COs turned the phones off. The quiet felt eerie. I shoved my stuff up against the wall and then sat back. As I scanned the room full of lost and forgotten souls, I still felt all those stares. I looked down at the floor, unable to look these men in the eyes. A mocking voice sounded in my head.

You were a lion on the streets because you could get away, but look at you now. A scared little kitten.

I knew how to fight and always held my own, but suddenly in a place like this, my strength and toughness were gone. In their places were suspicion and trepidation. I continued to replay the last twenty-four hours in my head. I no longer felt powerful and couldn't stop my mind from racing. The room was spinning, so I closed my eyes tightly in an attempt to focus on the danger at hand. Beneath the surface of all the chaos swirling within my heart and mind, I felt like I was slowly falling into a pit of despair and had nothing to grasp on to even to save myself. I sat with my head down and swallowed, my throat dry and parched. I wanted to use the phone to call my grandmother and tell her that I was in the county jail, to ask her to come get me since I didn't know what was happening, but I couldn't even talk to her. I'd been up for over twenty-four hours and felt dizzy and thirsty. I needed something to drink or I was going to pass out.

I found some bigger, older guy sitting on the water cooler. He reminded me of the wrestler called "Stone Cold" Steve Austin with his bald head and bulging muscles. Tattoos covered him. As I approached, he watched me without any expression.

"I want to get some water," I said when I got to him.

The guy didn't say anything but just sat there, so I started to get some water, until he began to scream at me.

"Get away from that! Don't you touch my water! Get your n***** a** back over there!"

Nobody said a word, and nobody moved. The room was full of Black men, but they allowed him to talk like that to me without reacting. That said a lot. I shot back over to my little corner and then balled up under this bench shelf, curling into a fetal position. I felt scared and worthless as the stranger's words replayed in my head. The events of the past day were catching up to me, strapping me down like the belts on an electric chair.

I'm gonna die tonight. I'm about to die. It's all over.

Fear and dread suffocated me as I drifted in and out of a half sleep. I hated these feelings and how they sucked me down. But somewhere in the middle of the night, something hit me. I woke up and couldn't go back to sleep. I thought of the deep and desperate despair filling me.

No, J. No more. Stop it.

I didn't know exactly why I was in there and how I was going to get out and whenever that day might be, but I did know that I couldn't let fear destroy me. Something underneath my skin and inside my soul tightened like fingers making a fist.

Never again. Never will I allow someone to make me feel this low, this horrible.

I went back to sleep, and when I woke up in the morning, I knew I was going to have to confront the big guy. He was probably going to beat me up, but that didn't matter because I just couldn't go on living in that sort of caged fear imprisoning me. Yet the guy was nowhere to be found.

There were plenty of others I'd be forced to fight. My war had just begun. My goal was to simply stay alive.

Jonathan's lineup photo, 1997

LOVE & JUSTICE

Chapter Four

WHO AM I?

(2001–2002)

(M)

"KOBE!"

Standing in front of our apartment in north Charlotte, with the hum of the Ford Explorer's engine ready and waiting, I looked up in the sky to see if I could find my cockatiel darting around and flapping its wings. We had taken my spirited pet bird with us when we moved from Missouri only a year ago, and now he was nowhere to be found on another similar day: It was February, and we were moving to Atlanta, Georgia.

"Honey, we need to go," my mom said, standing a few feet away from our packed car.

I wondered if Kobe disliked the idea of having to move to another state so soon after just arriving here. He had darted out of the apartment door while the movers were working. I called out his name a few more times and tried to spot his bright orange-and-white face or hear his serenading whistle.

We can't leave without him.

Even though it only felt like yesterday when we were first pulling up to our apartment complex in Charlotte, I knew I wasn't the same girl who arrived here a year ago. So much had happened in the last twelve months.

I still remembered the first day we arrived in Charlotte. . . .

◆ ◆ ◆

"Mom—they have a pool here."

My mom was pleased to hear my excitement as she unpacked a box in the kitchen. "They have tennis courts, too," she told me.

Our new home on the south side of Charlotte was in a nice apartment complex. When we arrived I thought, *Yeah, this is gonna be amazing.* I started at a new middle school in January 2001. It was a bit daunting being the new kid, but I discovered a bigger city that was much more diverse.

Charlotte was a culture shock to me. We had gone from being in the minority in the middle of Missouri to now living on the south side of Charlotte and being around a much more diverse group of Black folk. Our apartment was close to the Charlotte Coliseum, the home of the NBA Charlotte Hornets and the WNBA Charlotte Sting. My mom had gone through a big move like this before, so it wasn't as dramatic to her, but for me the contrast between our old home and our new one was drastic. Not in a startling way. This was exciting, like going on a vacation to this really cool place and getting to stay there. I found myself having more exposure to Black culture and experiencing it in a broader way than in Jeff City.

Our excitement didn't last long. Before we had even settled into our new home, the unthinkable happened.

"I got some bad news today," Mom told me one afternoon after getting home from work. "My company has to let go of a lot of people, so it looks like I have to get another job."

We had only been in Charlotte for two weeks.

"Are we moving back to Missouri?" I asked.

"No, Maya. I'll find something else. We're going to be okay."

In 2001, the economy was shaky, and a lot of people all over the country were losing their jobs. For an eleven-year-old, I was remarkably confident in my mom. I knew she was always going to find work, no matter what it would take. And I was right. She did what she needed to do, taking temporary jobs and working nights as she looked for a more permanent place of employment.

Basketball offered us a close-knit community. More than ever, the sport remained a prominent thing in our lives. I ended up joining an AAU team north of the city called the Concord Blazers, and they were a majority Black team. It was my first time on a mostly Black team, and we were really good. After a great season over the summer, we ended up getting sixth at AAU nationals. Back in Missouri, it was a big deal just going to nationals—we had made it to the Sweet 16 my last year there. So finishing sixth at nationals on the twelve-and-under team in North Carolina gave me a taste of what was possible.

Wow . . . we did really good. We can get better.

My desire to grow as a player really started to come alive during that time. My passion for the game continued to grow, and so did I.

My age and my shoe size were identical from ages eight to thirteen years old. I sprouted like a weed in middle school. By the time I was in eighth grade, I was five foot ten, so needless to say, I was always one of the tallest in my class. I loved being tall, but it was nearly impossible to find cute shoes. Back then, the only ones that fit me were old-lady shoes. *I'm thirteen*, I thought. *That's not gonna work for me.* So my only other option was to wear men's shoes. I didn't love it, but we didn't know where else to shop.

By the time I reached my new school, I started to become a little more conscious about what I wore and how I presented myself. I wanted to dress cuter, and I also started to find identity in being a basketball player. Truth be told, I think the movie *Love and Basketball* changed a lot of things for us Black, athletic girls. The 2000 romantic sports film wasn't the most appropriate movie for children, but there were a lot of middle schoolers who saw it. Sanaa Lathan starred in the love story, and her role as a basketball player continued to help popularize women's basketball and portray the players as attractive. I noticed these little Black boys around me talking about *Love and Basketball*.

This is a thing. They think this is cool.

I remember boys starting to flirt with me. But I never became super boy crazy. Very early after moving to Charlotte, I was finding a real love in someone else.

Who are you, Maya? Who do you really trust?

We discover our true identity in the desert seasons of our life. For me, this period of isolation was during my middle school years, and it began in those months when I found myself on my own. My mom and I had moved to Charlotte without knowing another soul there, and now that she was having to work all the time, including in the early mornings and late evenings, I became a latchkey kid in some ways. I had to grow up fast. I was responsible for getting myself up in the mornings and making it onto my bus to school.

I ended up going to two different middle schools in Charlotte, and that meant being the new kid, again, and trying to make friends, again. Being the new kid creates many moments where kids question their identity: "Who is this new girl?" There were a lot of lonely times for me. But I think it's good to have seasons where you are by yourself. These are the times when you really get to see what you believe and what's real. Some of the noise dies down, and you have to deal with yourself. You get to answer one of the big questions of life.

Who am I?

Church had been an important part of my upbringing back in Missouri. Our whole family went to church on Sunday, and the heart of Jesus was modeled for me through the character of my relatives. I know in my early years of growing up that I was learning God's voice and sensing His call to life versus things that aren't life, and just like any person, I didn't always follow His voice, but I had a desire to know God. Now that we were away from our family and going through some hard times, my desire to know God was even higher, and the stage was set for my mom and I to decide if we were going to pursue knowing God even without the momentum of our family back in Missouri.

My mom and I decided we were going to try to find a church, so we visited a few until we found one we began to attend. I can't remember the name of it, but I remember that first Sunday when the well-dressed Black pastor stood behind a pulpit and began his sermon.

"I want you to open your Bibles and get out your pen and paper," the pastor told the congregation. "We're going to get after it this morning."

The invitation to dig deeper in learning about God through His word was an exciting one, and I was ready to lean in. "Mom, do you have a pen and some paper?" I asked her.

I was fired up. And in that church, the Bible came alive to me. This church became an environment where I began to really seek God for myself and wanted to understand what He was saying about who He was and who I was. The loneliness caused me to reach out to my Creator for comfort and stability, and in this season of moving through the challenges of the unknown, my faith became my own and I saw God more clearly as I grew in looking to Him. As I discovered more about the reality of God as my Creator, Father, Savior, and Friend, His love became so real to me.

Middle school wasn't the easiest time of my life; kids can be cruel, and I was struggling to find comfort in this season of change and challenge. We've all experienced these periods of growing and searching for identity. But when your Creator speaks to you and you realize who you are, it just anchors you. It gives you clarity instead of confusion. You're no longer the new kid in sixth grade or the tall girl being teased for her height. You're not confused, and you're not stuck trying to figure out how define yourself. Because I realized my identity was already defined by my Creator as His beloved daughter created by Him and for Him to light up this world. I knew my identity was not in my awkwardness as a middle schooler, but my identity was in who my Heavenly Father said I was.

I'm so grateful for this uncomfortable period of my life because God's presence became more authentic to me, more certain. It created something in my mom and me that has been crucial to how the rest of our story has unfolded.

◆ ◆ ◆

Our story. That's the way it's always been. Mom and I have been a team my whole life. It was no different in this current season of challenges.

Mom always found work and always took care of me. She eventually found a good job working at a bank while we were living in Charlotte. We weren't rich, but we weren't poor. And as I got older, Mom would explain to me how we couldn't have made it through those times without the financial support from my uncle and grandparents. Right after my mom lost her job, my grandmother came down from Chicago for a few weeks and was there for me when my mom had to work nights. We had our family show up and support us in many ways. More than anything, they showed us compassion.

Racism at its heart, as I understand it now, is an inhumane use of power and control. It attempts to put a group of people down by perpetuating lies about their humanity instead of acknowledging the fullness of our common humanity.

I had grown up living a pretty empowered life despite being raised by a single mother. We had family members who were very present, and education was such an integral part of why our Black family was as stable as it was. All the women on my mom's side were educated and found opportunities to work inside and outside of the home. I now know that it can be a very discouraging experience to be Black in Missouri, but my childhood did not end up being defined by that. Thankfully I never experienced racism in a way where I was afraid. I also didn't understand how it felt to be stuck like a lot of people do, shackled to a place where you felt like you had no opportunity. I am grateful to God I was born into a situation where I had a family legacy of education and a mom who had vision beyond Missouri's limitations because she wasn't from there.

Even though I did have a more protected experience than many others, I knew enough of what life was about because my mom told me enough to prepare me. She tried to give me age-appropriate information about the reality of what was going on. I appreciated her honesty, and it made me trust and believe her guidance. We developed a team-like mentality. If Mom couldn't do it, then I'd do it. If I wasn't going to do something, she had to do it. It wasn't like we had a lot of excuses. Mom went to work every day and showed me the value of being consistent.

She also never stopped looking ahead.

"You looked pretty good out there on the court," Mom told me as we ate burgers after the game.

"Thanks," I said. "I can't believe I missed that last shot."

"I can't believe you guys won by twenty."

Mom liked to talk with me about basketball, not really to share her thoughts on the games but more to hear what I was thinking. I look back on my childhood and am so inspired by how my mom parented me. She really pursued my heart and studied me in order to help me grow up well and to thrive as much as I could. While we were still in Missouri, Mom could see that I was not only passionate about basketball but also talented at playing the sport. Naturally, a single mom raising her only child would want to act when she saw an opportunity for her child to use her gifts to get an education, so she started to help me think about the possibilities of the future with basketball. My preteen self was eager and ready to learn and dream, so she helped me create a beginner's résumé that contained my grades, my interests, and my basketball stats that my mom kept track of. As the years went by, we would eventually add more to this résumé and include my summer tournament schedule. When I entered eighth grade, colleges knew who I was and were pursuing me! "You have to put yourself out there so you can be seen," Mom told me.

There it was again: My mom showing me the importance of putting yourself in a place where you have an opportunity.

By middle school, we both knew that I was a very self-motivated kid, very driven. Mom never had to drag me to school or church or basketball practice. I *wanted* to learn and study and listen and practice. Even back then, when I locked into something or felt passionate about a particular thing, I became extremely motivated to show up and do it. My mom had made it a habit to expose me to different things in order to figure out what I was passionate about and where I was gifted. We had a home environment that encouraged doing positive and healthy things, so I always felt empowered by my mom. I wanted to be my best at school and be my best in basketball and be my best as a child of God. So when Mom saw my abilities in basketball and my passion for the game, she came alongside me.

All right, she thought. *How can I help equip my daughter to move forward to reach her dreams?*

The résumé I put together and that we sent out was the practical side of this. Every year as I got older, Mom helped me be mindful of it.

"Hey, this is something you can add to your résumé," she would tell me.

She was just reminding me to think and plan ahead, not in some unhealthy or controlling way but rather in a natural and informative way of teaching. *This is what it's gonna take to get somewhere*, and she was showing me. So I was all about it, motivated to embrace the things that were going to help me get better and excited to seize opportunities. When coaches offered extra training or teams offered different programs, I showed up because I wanted to be there. I wanted to be better.

By the time I was in seventh grade, I had my top four or five colleges that we mailed my résumé to, just to let them know about me. "I'm Maya Moore, and here's my summer schedule."

It was fun to be learning and growing and pursuing my dreams. So we kept looking for opportunities that moved us closer to those dreams.

◆ ◆ ◆

In February 2002, another opportunity awaited my mom and me in Atlanta. Mom found a good job there, and since we had some extended family that lived in Georgia, she decided to plant us in Lawrenceville, Georgia, in Gwinnett County, a suburb of Atlanta. Mom made sure that if we were going to uproot again, we needed to move to an area that gave her the opportunity to work but also gave me the opportunity for a good education and competitive basketball.

On our final day in Charlotte, when we packed up everything to move, I did end up finding my cockatiel. I spotted him in a tree, looking down at us and chirping away. I called up to him several times, but he didn't budge. We tried to get his attention by waving and whistling and doing anything we could, but Kobe was staying put. This was just like saying goodbye to my friends—I was heartbroken.

You gotta keep on moving, Maya.

That was our mindset. Mom and I were a team, and we were on an exciting journey, a grand adventure. Yes, it was sad leaving Charlotte, but we were moving toward something even better.

By the time I was in seventh grade, I had been to four different middle schools, but it was worth it because we ended up landing exactly where we needed to be. Mom was intentional about putting me in the right school, so I enrolled at a middle school that fed into Collins Hill High School. Not only did it have great academics, but it also had one of the best basketball programs in the state at the time. Mom wanted to make sure I was established somewhere before high school so we weren't moving around once I started. She wanted me to have a consistent high-school experience.

During the first week of seventh grade after arriving in a new middle school in Georgia, the teacher told us we were going to do an assignment that required us to take off our shoes and put them on a table. *Oh great*, I thought in terror. *Kids barely know my name, and now I gotta do this?* I already stood out, since I was taller than the other students. As I unlaced the men's boot I was wearing at the time and plopped it on the table, I could see my classmates staring at it.

"Whoa," some boy behind me said. "Why's your foot so big?"

There were some giggles, but that was okay.

Just wait till basketball season.

Maya in seventh grade

Chapter Five

BLACK MAN IN A WHITE WORLD

(1997–1999)

(J)

"HOW OLD ARE YOU?"

The white guy standing at my cell door looked tough and weathered, his voice direct and demanding an answer. He had a long ponytail and gray stubble and carried a commanding disposition.

"I'm sixteen," I said.

His eyes grew wide. "Sixteen? What are you doing here? Why are you— Did you tell them you're a kid?"

"Man, they know. I heard 'em talkin' about it."

"Look—you're in here with the big boys," he said. "You got to grow up fast, kid."

It was the day after arriving at the county jail, and they had taken me and my bundle to a permanent wing housing around twelve to fifteen men. The majority of the day was spent in the housing unit, and inmates were allowed to enter and exit their cells any time during the normal hours of operation. As I entered my new environment with all eyes on me, I didn't show the fear I'd displayed in the holding tank. This time I strode in my street mode, cattin' with my chest out and a mean mug. I glared at the grown men and didn't look away even though I was still scared.

Whatever it takes, J. Don't allow what happened last night to happen again.

I'd heard things about people that went to jail and prison. If you're scared, bad things happen. Everybody knew it. So, as I walked in the pod toward my cell, I strutted and stared back at others and tried to show everybody that, yeah, I'm hard. I just didn't know for sure whether my front was a convincing performance.

Maybe this older guy standing at the entrance to my cell saw through my tough-guy act.

"Can you fight?" he asked me. "Can you hold your own?"

"Yeah," I said.

"Good. It don't matter if you win or lose. You better fight. You stand up for yourself, 'cause if you don't, people are going to take from you all the time. Prison is a violent place. Men will try to rape you, try to rob you. Men will try to bully you and just dog you out. So don't be one of those guys. You understand? Don't be one of those guys."

"Yeah, I understand."

He studied me as if to see if I was being honest, if I truly understood the situation.

"Kid—I'm not going to spend much time with you until I see that you can stand on your own. But I wish the best for you, and I'm sorry you're here. It breaks my heart."

I'd learn more about this guy later. Conrad was an ex–Green Beret, so he knew everything about the military. All the inmates respected him, and he taught me a lot of things while I was around him. This initial conversation where he gave me advice was something he continued to do, sharing the things I needed to look out for and helping me understand the reality of this place.

St. Charles County Jail was a maximum-security jail built in 1989 that held inmates who were either awaiting trial like me or who had been committed or sentenced and were waiting to leave. It also held state prisoners along with federal inmates. With a capacity of just under six hundred individuals, the jail was comprised of men being held for a variety of offenses, from simple misdemeanor traffic violations to first-degree murder. Although most inmates were released from the county jail within six months or less, there were others who were forced to stay in there for years. I was held in there for almost a year and half just waiting to go to trial.

It took two days before I needed to heed Conrad's warning. So far, I had been moving in a regular routine and starting to catch a rhythm. The only problem was that nobody wanted to talk to me and I couldn't sit with anybody. I got treated like a little black sheep. There was nobody to hang out with and no friend in sight. One evening at dinnertime, I'd gotten my meal and sat at a table. I was still getting used to the food, so I was hungry all the time. There were two cookies on my tray, and I'd eaten one, when I decided to go get some juice. When I came back to the table, I looked down at my tray and noticed it was empty. I glanced around at everybody else.

"Man, am I in the wrong spot?" I said.

Their eyes moved from mine to a big guy sitting at the end of the row. His name was Dirty Red, and he was a big guy, stout and obstinate and mean. I could see him chomping down on something.

"You eating my cookie, man? Is that my cookie?"

He just nodded without a care in the world. "Yeah, and you ain't gonna do nothing about it. You soft."

He could see that I was scared, and the reasonable, rational side of me didn't want to do anything. He was bigger and stronger than me. But a rush of anger came over me, and so did fear. I wasn't going to be soft. I *couldn't* be soft. I was more afraid of what would happen if I didn't fight. So I got up and walked over to him and fired off the first punch. I blasted him right in the nose. Soon we were wrestling and throwing punches.

You never get used to being punched in the face, your lip ripping against the top of your teeth, your nose smashed and bloodied, your jaw feeling dislodged. You never know if you're gonna get an elbow in the rib cage or a knee in the groin, or maybe someone biting your arm locked around his neck. Yet despite his fist connecting, I landed a handful of punches myself. As I struck a blow against Dirty Red's temple, I heard Conrad in the background. "That's right! Get 'im, youngster! Don't take that. Stand up for yourself. You be a man!"

That's exactly what I did. I dispatched Dirty Red and beat him up. The COs came in and broke it up, spraying us with Mace and throwing us back in our cells for seventy-two hours straight. After the time was up, I discovered that they had moved Dirty Red to a different housing unit. I would never see him again. The first guy to come up to me was Conrad. This time he carried a wry old grin on his face.

"Youngster, I wanted to see you stand up for yourself, and you did." He spoke like some sort of proud pop. "You're in the jungle, and this is the law of the land. You stand up for yourself, because if you don't, nobody will stand up for you. If you get beat up, you'll heal."

This was one of the things I repeatedly told guys, especially new inmates. Even after someone took a vicious beating and their face was swollen and bloody, I'd tell them that they were going to heal and that they'd be all right. What was the worst thing that could happen when you stood up for yourself? You'd get beaten and bruised, but people were going to know that you were gonna fight back. That's all that mattered in a place like this. You didn't have to be strong. You just needed to be willing to scrap and spar with anybody at any given time. You could never back down from a skirmish. If they saw you do that, they'd never leave you alone.

Of course, sometimes it took numerous fights before people learned what you were capable of doing. But word traveled fast.

◆ ◆ ◆

After being let out of my cell after seventy-two hours, there was a whole different vibe with the guys around me. It felt as if there was a collective affirmation, that the general consensus was *Okay, kid, you'll stand up for yourself. That's good.* Suddenly I could hang out with them and socialize. They let me play cards with them and began to get to know me. They also learned more about me through fighting.

There was only one TV in every housing unit, which required everyone to share. Luckily for me, no one really watched TV. So I was able to watch what I wanted. One of my favorite things to do was to watch cartoons. It was something that reminded me of being at home with Granny. Only a few weeks in at the county jail, I was watching one of my favorite cartoon series as a new guy strolled into the area. The bulky meathead stopped and noticed what I was watching on the television.

"We ain't watchin' no cartoons," he said in disdain as he walked to the TV. "We're watchin' the news."

"Hold on, man," I shouted as I stood up. "I'm watching it."

"Naw, we ain't watching that today," the guy said as he changed the channel.

"Says who?" I asked.

"Says me."

I used the remote control to turn my show back on, but he switched the channel once more.

"Man, don't touch that TV again," I warned him as I walked over toward him. "I'll fight you about this TV." Watching cartoons was the only way I could escape the harsh gravity of my situation. I was still a kid. Even in the lion's den, I couldn't go without watching them.

Since he was new, he didn't know I was being honest. "You ain't gonna do nothing," he said as he took a swing at me. I weaved and hit him with a four-piece combo, watching him crumple to the floor.

As I turned back on the channel I was watching, a guy nearby said, "You really ain't gonna watch the TV now!" He was right, because the guards came and put me in the cell for another three straight days. Seventy-two hours. I was bummed, too, because this was the last episode of my cartoon series I'd been watching. I never got to finish the show, either. But after this fight, I never had a problem with the TV again. I got to watch my cartoons, and more importantly, guys started to befriend me. Inmates treated me like I was a little brother to them, taking me around and introducing me to new people.

"Hey, this is young J here," they'd say. "He's solid. Real solid."

Guys told others that I wasn't gonna run my mouth, that I would stand up for myself, that I was loyal and smart, that I was a good guy. One older man even called me Little Tyson.

"Boy, you knocked him off his feet," he said about my argument over the TV. "Where'd you learn to fight like that?"

"My uncle taught me to fight," I said.

"You one of them Irons boys, ain't you?" the older guy asked. "Ain't your uncle Joe?"

"Yeah," I said about my uncle who once whipped five police officers with his bare hands.

"Man—y'all stand up for yourselves. That's right. That's what you gonna need in here. You have to stand up for yourself. You gotta be a man in here."

That was the constant theme I kept running into. Every day, some sort of skirmish or fight was happening. In order to survive, you had to engage, because if you didn't, people were going to take everything from you. Fighting kept the craziness away, and it also garnered a measure of respect. In jail, the majority of inmates didn't respect knowledge; they respected violence. This came from how much pain you could inflict on another human being. All I knew was that fighting seemed to keep me safe. I felt like I was living in an alternate universe, and I was willing to do whatever it took to stay safe. But I never enjoyed fighting; my heart ached more after every fight. It felt like I was losing a piece of myself with each punch I landed with bad intentions. Even if I won a fight, I was still losing. I was becoming a monster in the name of survival.

◆ ◆ ◆

A regular routine began to take shape. Getting up and going to breakfast. Reading the newspapers and going to play basketball. Watching cartoons. Going to lunch, hanging out with people, walking and talking and exercising in the wing. Dinner and then going out to the rec (recreation) yard again. Then it would be shower time, and after that, we'd be locked down. This was my life, the same life as all the other guys around me. This life was becoming my new normal.

I was able to talk to my grandmother on the phone, but I came to discover that calls were expensive. A fifteen-minute conversation cost around twenty to thirty dollars. We didn't know they were so pricey until Granny's phone line got shut down because I was calling her every day and she couldn't pay the bill. So I stopped calling as much and started writing letters back and forth instead.

Mail call became a precious time. Just the thought of having someone out there thinking of you and wondering how you were doing meant the world. Receiving a letter from anybody, whether it was Granny or a friend, gave me instant encouragement. Not receiving mail caused other men to sink into depression and lose the will to enjoy life. Having someone say *We're thinking about you and hope you're doing well* meant that I hadn't been forgotten about. Hearing what people were doing made me smile and laugh and remain determined to be a part of their lives again. *We're waiting for you to come home*, the letters stated. *Keep going.* So that's what I did.

Several months after I got to the county jail, I met my public defender. The first time I spoke to Christine Sullivan, she was encouraging and gung ho for me, telling me she knew I was innocent and that she was working hard on my case. I didn't trust her just like I didn't trust the cops or the COs or anybody around me. Why would anyone in their right mind trust someone they didn't know with their life? Yet at the same time, every few months, I got a call from her, and conversing with Christine was the highlight of my day. I started to believe she was helping me, that she was there for me, so I relished the hope she brought. I spent a lot of time talking to her on the phone and through correspondence in letters.

Everything changed after she had a meeting with the prosecutor a few months before my trial. Her entire demeanor shifted. She stopped talking and communicating with me, and when she did meet with me, she wouldn't look me in the eye. I could tell that she had stopped fighting for me just in her tone and her attitude and spirit. Energy is key to seeing someone's heart about any particular issue or subject, so I knew her heart had changed. She knew she could win my case, but they had tied her hands behind her back.

One day, Christine came to me and told me I should take a plea deal. They offered thirty years at first, and right away, I balked at the very idea. "I'm not taking a plea," I told her. "I didn't do this." At that point, I wasn't even aware of the concept of a criminal justice system. I just kept clinging to the notion that there were adults that were going to be in the courtroom and surely they would know that this was wrong and that I didn't do this. It was impossible for there to be any evidence to show that I did it, because it wasn't me. Another plea deal came, this time twenty-five years, then twenty, then even fifteen, but I refused to take any.

During this time, Conrad talked to me about things I should do and what to expect. Just like he had given me the cold hard facts about prison when he first came to my cell, the seasoned veteran also held up a mirror to my current legal situation.

"You're not gonna like hearing this, but you're going to prison," Conrad said. "'Cause if you can't get a lawyer, then you can't do anything. The public defenders are no good."

"Someone's gonna let me go," I told him. "I know I'm going home."

"No, you're not. They got you. They gonna jam you up. I believe you when you say you didn't do it, but these people don't care about that."

Conrad gave me my first lessons about the criminal justice system, about public defenders and trials. He also told me where the library was and encouraged me to go there. At that time I wasn't a strong reader and had no idea where to begin. All the legalese being thrown at me sounded like another language.

Conrad planted the first seeds of finding a path toward freedom on my own, and that path went straight through the library and all those endless pages full of stories and cases and examples and ammunition to be used in a court of law. He continued to teach me things until the day they took him to prison. Conrad had been sentenced to life without parole. I never saw him after he left the county jail.

"You need to think your moves through and plan ahead," one inmate told me as we sat playing a game of chess.

With so much dead time in jail, you had to find something to do. Chess was a great occupier. I had seen chess on the street and a teacher had once shown me the basic moves of the game, but I never knew about the strategies behind playing until I was in the county jail. The more I played chess, the better I became, and I ended up becoming a really good player. The game calmed me down and made me focus. A game demanded intense concentration, so I learned how to do this as I played.

Four or five different guys taught me different moves and strategies, helping me understand chess from different angles and perspectives. They allowed me to ask them questions and then gave me games to break down and study. I took these back to my room since I had so much time on my hands. As I learned the game and studied it, I started thinking about school and my former education.

Teachers always said I couldn't focus and I was stupid and blah blah blah.

The sad fact was that I believed them. But one day as I was playing chess, I received a great compliment from the guy teaching me.

"Man—the way you're picking this up . . . You're a smart kid. What kind of grades did you make in school?"

"They told me I was borderline mentally retarded."

The guy laughed at me and thought I was joking.

"No, for real," I said. "They told me and my grandma. It was in my paperwork."

Later on, I even showed him proof that they said this, and the guy couldn't believe it.

"Wow. You might want to get that checked out, like wherever you go after here, take a test."

This guy had been in prison several times, and every time he went, they made him take an aptitude test. I didn't plan on going to prison, but I was encouraged to get tested once I got out of jail.

There was something else I began to learn about. Right after I arrived at the county jail, my grandmother sent me an old Bible. When I was a little kid, she used to read from a Bible storybook with colorful pictures inside. I learned stories like Noah's ark and Jonah and the whale that swallowed him. I wanted to go to church, and Granny took me a few times, but she couldn't keep going because of her knees. As I became older, I lost interest in the church; the streets caught my attention after I got to know my cousin more and wanted to follow in his footsteps.

One day on the phone in the county jail, Granny brought up this subject.

"Are you reading your Bible?"

"No," I admitted.

"Well, you need to read the Bible. Whenever you're going through something, open it up. Read a Psalm and a Proverb every day."

"All right," I said.

I had been hearing stuff about God and the Bible ever since coming to jail, so I offered up a prayer.

"Okay, I'm here," I said to God. "I'm hearing all this stuff about you. I'll try."

I opened up the Bible and started skimming through it. I was still skeptical. I didn't believe God could help me, nor did I comprehend the valuable weapon in my hands, a weapon my grandmother had given to me. But Granny knew.

◆ ◆ ◆

It would have been nice if the only part of being in the county jail was playing chess and reading the Bible and hanging out with fellow inmates and learning about my case. Violence still lurked behind every door and dark corner. I learned this one day while taking a shower. As I was naked under the water, an inmate tried to sexually assault me, grabbing at me. I wasn't standing for it. I shoved him away and grabbed my clothes and went back to my cell to put my shoes on. He thought this was over, but I was furious.

Why would another man want to do this? Why me? Why try me like this?

We got into a fight, and this was a bad one. I don't even remember everything that happened—I blacked out during the beating I gave the guy. This fight didn't just get me seventy-two hours in my cell. This time I was charged with third-degree assault, which was a misdemeanor and would be added on to my other charges when I went to court.

◆ ◆ ◆

My trial began on October 19, 1998. My grandmother sat in the back of the courtroom watching. Right away, the defense made it clear how strongly they felt during the jury selection when the prosecutor stated that "the State is going to be asking for a very severe sentence in this case." After the members of the jury were chosen, James Gregory recounted the State's version of what happened. While I sat helpless in the defendant's chair, I felt like I was living in an alternate universe hearing a story about myself that wasn't true.

This confusing trial went on for two days. For all the detailed facts being presented, my public defender never called any of the alibi witnesses who could verify exactly where I was that night. During the closing statements, Gregory continued to claim I was guilty without having any evidence. Not only that, he went deeper into speaking about me as a human. My fate was sealed.

"That young man is a dangerous person," Gregory said about me. Later on, he stated, "Don't be soft on him because he is young. He is as dangerous as somebody five times that age."

The prosecutor didn't hold back on his judgment. "We need to send a message to some of these younger people that if you are going to act like somebody old, you are going to be treated like somebody old."

When the final verdict was read, I felt like I was Charlie Brown listening to his teacher going, "Wah wah woh wah wah." Nothing made sense to me. I heard numbers and counts and terms and years and instructions, nothing but "Wah wah woh wah wah."

"As to Count I, we the jury find the defendant, Jonathan Houston Irons, guilty of assault in the first degree as submitted in instruction number five. We assess and declare the punishment for assault in the first degree at imprisonment for a term of twenty-five years. As to Count II, we the jury find the defendant, Jonathan Houston Irons, guilty of armed criminal action as submitted in instruction number seven. We assess and declare the punishment for armed criminal action at imprisonment for a term of twenty-five years. As to Count III, we the jury find the defendant, Jonathan Houston Irons, guilty of burglary in the first degree as submitted in instruction number nine. We assess and declare the punishment for burglary in the first degree at imprisonment for a term of fifteen years."

All I thought was *Wait a minute—what'd you just say? Did you say guilty?*

When I got back in the elevator with my lawyer and the bailiff, I asked her what they said.

"Take it like a man," she told me.

It was only when I got back to my wing and talked to my fellow inmates that I learned they had given me a sentence of sixty-five years in prison.

Sixty-five years.

Arrested when I was sixteen. Sentenced at eighteen. That meant I'd be eighty-three years old if I served out my entire sentence.

My soul had been ripped from me for no reason other than being in the vicinity of a violent act and for being a Black kid in a predominantly white neighborhood. In my cell, I wept and remained in my bed, grieving and hurting and defeated. I stopped eating, stopped engaging with the guys, stopped breathing as far as I was concerned. Eventually my fellow inmates came around and encouraged me to get out of my cell. "Come on, J—come on out. Go watch some cartoons or something." So eventually that's what I started to do.

A convicted felon finding comfort in cartoons on television. It showed just how much of a kid I really was.

The big limestone walls loomed over me as I looked out my window on the bus rumbling toward the Missouri State Penitentiary.

I'm being driven into a nightmare, into a pit of pain and despair.

These large stone blocks that I'd be locked behind had opened in 1836, over 160 years ago. Some of the worst criminals in the history of our country were put behind these bars, and now I was joining them. The prison was nicknamed The Walls, and those towering structures produced terror in a convict's heart when he first saw them. It made me think of one of my favorite cartoons of the '80s, *He-Man and the Masters of the Universe.*

This looks like Castle Grayskull.

The scary-looking castle from the show became a popular toy with its large skull entrance and a drawbridge that opened up through the skull's mouth. It was the perfect picture of this prison I was entering.

As I shuffled with other new inmates into the prison with shackles on my hands and feet, the first iron door I passed through slammed behind us and caused us to jump. The hollow echo shook in this lifeless corridor. I felt every ounce of life and energy inside me sucked out. As we arrived at shipping and receiving, where they made us change our clothes and gave us the rules and information, I noticed the sign on the wall.

Welcome to Missouri State Prison.
Leave all your hopes and dreams behind you.

I'd stepped inside a home of suffering and agony, a place where the horrors were kept secret and silent and forgotten about. All lawfully and legally done. I spent the first night in my own cell, petrified and unable to sleep. People around me in the darkness screamed and hollered.

The approaching footsteps of the COs checking in on us throughout the night kept me on edge. If I started to drift to sleep, their flashlights through the bars of our doors would shock me back awake.

This was the worst night of my entire life, and it was only my first night in this hellhole.

God help me.

The Walls (Missouri State Penitentiary)

Chapter Six

A LIGHT
IN A PLACE
OF DEATH

(2004–2007)

(M)

THE BUS WAS LATE.

On the afternoon of the first state championship game I ever played in high school, after a day at school being excited and anxious for the big matchup, our basketball team stood in the parking lot of Collins Hill High waiting and waiting and waiting. Of all the days for the bus to be late, it happens now?

In my first season for the Collins Hill Lady Eagles, we had reached the Class AAAAA girls' title game undefeated at 32–0. The seniors on the team were attempting to win their third state title in the last four years, so I wanted nothing more than to help them get that. It had been an awesome season, playing with a great team and learning from one of the most legendary coaches in Georgia, Angie Hembree. I couldn't have asked for more in my first year of playing in high school. I felt a camaraderie with the upperclassmen and knew they respected me. We competed hard in practice and worked hard, but we also knew how to have fun, whether it was good times on a bus ride or during our pregame warmups. Now we were simply hoping to arrive to the arena on time to get to do those warmups.

"All right, let's do this," the coaches told us. "Any of the upperclassmen who have cars can drive. We'll just get everybody in vehicles and take everybody to the gym."

In the rush of getting in groups and climbing into cars and making sure nobody was left behind, two of my teammates who were driving collided with each other in the parking lot. No one was hurt, but it got everyone even more on edge. *What is going on?* I wondered. Why was everything suddenly going wrong before *this* game? Tensions were high, and both the players and coaches were stressed out and frustrated. While people were dealing with the accident, the bus finally rumbled into the parking lot. All of us climbed back out of the cars and got on the bus.

Our whole routine was thrown off for the night. We didn't get as much time to do all of our normal things during warmups and before the game. If anybody knows anything about athletes, it's that routine is critical. So needless to say, it just wasn't a good start to the night.

The game was held at the Arena at Gwinnett Center, a place I would become very familiar with over my career and find much success on its court. Tonight was a different story. We were playing Stephenson, who had only lost one game all season. They had a talented senior who was headed to LSU, and they had heard about our outstanding season, so they were ready and waiting.

It was a competitive game, but we didn't play our best. Just like the start of the day with the missing bus, things were kind of off for our team, with unusual things happening. Players not in sync, a point guard dribbling the ball off her foot for a turnover, strange sequences that hadn't occurred all season.

With 1:53 remaining, us trailing by 9 points, we drained a couple of three-pointers, sparking a 10–0 run for Collins Hill and giving us a one-point lead. But the game was sealed when the Stephenson senior stole a pass and drove down the court to score and retake the lead for good. As the final seconds evaporated, the score stood 69–62.

We were heartbroken. It was a frustrating way to end our season, knowing we could have played so much better. Coming into a great program like Collins Hill and seeing such great players, we wanted to keep that tradition going. I was devastated for our seniors to have this be their last game. We had been the favorites to win, and we had worked so hard and had such a great season, and now this. There were lots of emotions from all of us.

As I wiped tears from my face, I walked up to Coach Hembree, who had once again been a phenomenal leader that season.

"This won't happen again," I told Coach. "Not like this!"

The next three years, I stayed true to my word. The Eagles would not lose again to a team in the state of Georgia.

◆ ◆ ◆

I was a part of my first national championship team with AAU when I was fourteen, so by then I realized that I not only loved to play but that I could really compete with the best of my class. This game was fun, and I liked to win. Growing up watching the WNBA and women's college basketball, the dream was getting a scholarship and playing in college. So early on I wanted to continue to put myself in situations where I could be pushed as well as pushing myself.

There was such a great foundation that was set for me with many opportunities to grow and learn. Not just basketball-wise, either. The training I had in classrooms during high school prepared me for college. I had fun learning. The stress came as I navigated trying to balance everything, handling AP classes while trying to compete for championships, all while learning how to cope emotionally and manage my time. My plate was full, and I had to say no to and sacrifice certain things because I had to go to practice or finish a school project. I didn't give in to peer pressure easily because I had a level of clarity on who I was and what I wanted to be about; I got along with most everybody but wouldn't say I had best friends, either. My mom has told me I was very stressed during that time, and I won't deny this. I probably wasn't the most fun person to live with during those years. They were challenging, but they prepared me for life.

In so many ways, I began to experience life as a pro during high school because of all the things I was managing. It was a busy schedule with the national tournaments and the media and the rankings and the interviews. I was now being heavily recruited by colleges across the country and became ranked number one in my class. I've always felt that the recruiting process for me was as good as it could have been. I had already been thinking about college, looking ahead and researching programs, all with the assistance of my mom.

"What do you want in a college?" she asked me. "What do you think is important?" There were so many things we talked about, like the academics and the fan support for the program and the coaches and the players and the location and the surrounding churches. My mom was a great collaborator for me in thinking through all the possibilities and potential with life after high school. She had always kept the big picture in view while also planning out the details to move life forward. I learned the rules of recruitment, and my coaches were very supportive in helping me make sure I understood everything I could and couldn't do. When could I take this visit or that visit? We went on unofficial visits to the campuses I was interested in. By this time, I knew what I wanted, so we were very thoughtful about the entire process.

The top four schools I was interested in were the University of Connecticut, the University of Tennessee, Duke University, and the University of Georgia. I had done my research and communicated with some of them all the way back in middle school, so I was able to develop relationships with all four schools. It was fun to travel and spend time with the best programs in the nation.

My priorities never changed throughout the process, and my focus remained the same. Tracey Tipton, my coach the last two years of high school, recalled the twelve-day period during my junior year when college coaches could visit and watch me practice and work out. On the very first day, the coaches from both UConn and Tennessee showed up. Geno Auriemma and Pat Summitt are both legends in the sport.

"I knew that they had a history of not getting along so well and I was so nervous about how to handle that because it was my first time having to deal with a situation like that," Tipton told *USA Today*. "Maya did well with it; she couldn't talk to them anyway. You would've thought that it was her fellow students in there watching her; she didn't change anything about how she acted or worked out. She was always herself. Always."

It was an incredible opportunity to be able to choose any school that I wanted to go to. *Where could I be pushed?* This was the question driving me. I didn't want to go to a university where I knew I'd be the star. I wanted to go somewhere competitive, somewhere that would force me to grow and work hard. When I visited UConn and watched them practice, I knew that this was where I needed to be. It was unlike anything I'd ever seen.

I need to be a part of this.

After I graduated high school and got to UConn, our practices were what set us apart from everybody else. What I saw that day on the court while visiting them remained true. This was the bread and butter of what made UConn UConn. I wanted to be pushed and compete for a place and pursue greatness. They had great players and a super-competitive environment, so that was the place I wanted to put myself in.

As a highly recruited athlete, there isn't the normal pressure of waiting for an acceptance letter from your desired college. I had excellent grades, so being accepted was a straightforward process. I made my decision to attend UConn during my junior year in order to enjoy my last year of high school and to be able to focus solely on my classes and on basketball without the distractions of recruiting. It wasn't an easy decision. After making my commitment, I personally called each of the other head coaches of Tennessee, Duke, and Georgia just to let them know how much I appreciated the recruiting process but that I wasn't going to be going to their school. I respected them and the relationships we had built. I think the coaches appreciated the phone calls even though they didn't appreciate me choosing another school!

In April 2006, I organized a press conference to take place in the cafeteria of my high school to announce my college decision publicly. I was giddy as I printed out the logos of my top four colleges in the library at Collins Hill high school. I would set up these logo signs as props as I talked through my decision. One by one, I explained why I loved each school, but ultimately, I could only choose one. When I revealed that UConn was my choice, my mom and I simultaneously placed a UConn ball cap on our heads and the cafeteria went crazy. The day ended with me answering some questions from the media and, of course, celebrating with cake.

Once again, I credit the positive experience of recruiting to the preparation my mom and I had done, as well as the help of the great coaches that I had around me. Mom and I felt like pioneers, learning as we went. The truth was that we didn't know what we were doing. Looking back, the map of the journey seems like such a certain thing, but at the time we didn't know what was going to happen. We had never done this before, and nobody in our family had been a college athlete. It was a thrilling new experience for us. I was just playing as hard as I could, trying to be a good teammate and taking care of my body, then seeing doors continue to open.

It's the little things that make the biggest difference. Being excellent at playing your role in anything you do begins with the little stuff, and I learned that every year playing season after season of basketball. You have to stay consistent, focusing on the small details in each day that comes. Little things you learn in practice and little goals you set for yourself end up making or breaking you in games. Every single win during a season moves you to conference championships and national championships. Every winning season builds on the last, and every streak heightens with every victory added. But nothing can be built without showing up and being present for the big and the little things.

My mom was the first person to show me this. I learned from her that you don't have to be a superparent or get caught up in the pressure of it all. You try to do your best to show up every day. Like taking time to read to me when I was a little kid just so I could hear the words and hold the book and turn its page. She was the one committed to taking me to all those AAU basketball practices and games, the one involved in my education and where I'd be attending school.

Mom modeled for me one of the truest parts of what makes being alive meaningful. It is about investing in people and having faith that the love you impart on them will help make this world flourish. This love and investment fueled my path to pursue basketball, and I was going to give it my best by focusing on the little details day after day.

A legacy is built by investing in others. I was about to see firsthand the truth of what this looked like.

◆ ◆ ◆

Entering my junior year of high school, we had won sixty-three games and lost two. After losing the championship game my freshman year, Collins Hill won the 5A state championship the following year. Our only loss had been in the championship game at the Dell Curry Classic over the Christmas break. Our goal was to finish the next season undefeated.

During the middle of our schedule, we were playing Christ the King in the finals of the Nike Tournament of Champions in Phoenix, Arizona. This loaded team from New York featured another all-American and future teammate of mine, Tina Charles, and the winner of this game would be ranked number one in the country. The tight game had gone into overtime, and with 2:13 left, we were tied 71–71. Desperate to save a long rebound from going out of bounds, I lunged toward the ground and underhand hit the ball like a volleyball to a teammate. Then a whistle blew. One of the officials had assessed me a technical foul for punching the ball. It was a controversial call, and it meant I had fouled out of the game. They made both subsequent free throws and went ahead, eventually winning 79–75, all while I watched from the sideline. The officials would later confess that they misunderstood the rules that had been changed a couple of years earlier. Instead of being a technical foul, the call should have just been a violation and a change of possession.

Finishing with a career high at the time of 38 points didn't give me any satisfaction. We had lost in such a heartbreaking way. But this sparked our run to the state championship, and it fueled us the following year. Our goals were to win every game we played and to be the number-one-ranked team in the country.

Throughout all of this, I continued to see my godparents, Reggie and Cheri. Even though they had hated to see us move years ago, we all had fought for our long-distance relationship. They traveled out of state to as many tournaments as they could to come watch me play and spend time together as a family. Mom and I also went back to Missouri every other summer and enjoyed making memories there. This rhythm of life was kept throughout high school. I treasured my time with my Missouri family, Reggie, Cheri, and each of my godbrothers.

Around my junior year, I heard Reggie and Cheri talk about a young man they had visited in prison.

"Papa told us about this inmate he met at the Missouri State Penitentiary," Cheri said over the phone. "His name is Jonathan."

They shared a little about his story, how he was sixteen years old and arrested for a shooting and burglary even though there was no evidence to be found. The man who was shot had brain surgery and survived, but all he could say about his attacker was that it had been a Black male. Jonathan had been in the same neighborhood that night, and he also happened to be Black. Reggie and Cheri couldn't believe how Jonathan could have gotten so much time with no actual evidence of his guilt, and they were moved to help him out somehow. They told me they had begun to see him regularly on the weekends.

One day while our family was vacationing at the Lake of the Ozarks and staying in one big house, I came across Reggie and Cheri appearing to be doing some sort of homework.

"What is all this?" I asked.

Files and folders and paper-clipped pages were spread out all over the kitchen table. They resembled the pieces of research someone might have collected in pursuing their PhD.

"Those are Jonathan's case files," Reggie told me. "We were able to get the entire set of files that the public defender had."

"There are so many of them," I said. "When did this happen?"

"January of '97."

"He's been in prison for that long?" I asked.

"Fifty years," Reggie said, shaking his head in disbelief. "He got fifty years. And the more I go through the material, the more you can tell that he didn't have anything to do with the crime."

I sensed how invested Reggie and Cheri had become in Jonathan's story. Like them, I wanted to know more details, and I grew to realize just how real and tragic Jonathan's situation was.

"Jonathan was visiting friends, and multiple witnesses account for him being present," Reggie told me. "Not only that, they don't have one shred of evidence on him."

Numerous details didn't make sense, such as why there was no adult with Jonathan when he was charged, or why he had a bond for one million dollars. Reggie gave lots of other facts.

"There was a police report that said the victim could not identify anybody, and that report contradicted what he said later on," Reggie stated.

I felt both shocked and concerned about Jonathan's story.

"Wow . . . This is a sad situation," I told Reggie and Cheri. "Keep me updated. I'll be praying for him and for all of you."

◆ ◆ ◆

We went 31–0 my senior year at Collins Hill, winning our third consecutive state title. It was satisfying to fulfill our goal in going undefeated and bringing another championship to our school. It was not surprising, however. From the moment I began to play basketball, I've always strived for the next goal, always wanting to improve, always wanting to build on past accomplishments.

As my career at Collins Hill ended on a high note and as the personal accolades continued to pour in, I celebrated a chorus of memories from these past four years.

The first AAU national championship I was a part of winning with the Georgia Magic travel team the summer before my freshman year.

The moments after we won our state championship my sophomore year as I went and gave Coach Hembree a big hug as the horn went off. After working so hard the year before and losing, we had done it, and our coach was so elated for all of us.

The game-winning shot for the Georgia Metros with 4.6 seconds on the clock at the AAU national championships in 2005.

Being recruited by great programs and picking the right place I needed to go.

My undefeated senior season, ending my four years at Collins High with a record of 125–3.

They say that I ended my high-school career with 2,664 points, 1,212 rebounds, 407 assists, and 467 steals. The only way any of this could have happened was with the great foundation and support system I had at home. My mom remained committed to taking me to all the practices and the games despite how my jump shot looked when I started playing. I attribute my development to my nine years of AAU basketball and the amazing teammates, trainers, and coaches who taught me the fundamentals along the way. Playing against older girls helped me deal with tough competition. I was never coasting in my amateur career. I was always moving toward the next goal, toward improvement, toward doing my best and enjoying my team.

My mindset showed during an interview in my junior year of high school: "Every time you play anything, there's a chance that you can win. There's no reason not to compete no matter what you're playing."

◆ ◆ ◆

The summer before heading off to the University of Connecticut, Cheri and Reggie asked if I'd like to get on Jonathan's visiting list so I could go with them and meet him. I knew they were going regularly to see him, so I felt a peace about the trip since I would be with them. I didn't fully know what to expect, but I felt that I would be safe. I really wanted to meet Jonathan. He was part of their lives, so I wanted to step outside of my comfort zone and put myself in his world. I knew Jonathan and I had very different life experiences. But I wanted to learn more about him as a person; he was becoming family to us.

The weekend we visited Jonathan, I felt a combination of excitement and nerves. Here was this twenty-seven-year-old young man who sounded amazing, fighting for his freedom behind bars. I had never visited a maximum-security prison, so that made me a bit anxious, but knowing Reggie and Cheri were used to this gave me a measure of confidence.

After entering the prison and walking through the first set of huge metal doors that opened, I followed my godparents until a large clang behind me made me jump. Each time we entered a new section, the massive prison doors would slam and make me flinch. Every room we went through had cameras watching you as they checked your IDs. Then we had to walk outside, where we could see the high fences and barbed wire surrounding us. It felt strange because the stretch of grass underneath the open sky looked kind of beautiful, but everything else around it felt scary.

When we arrived at the visiting room, Reggie went over to an officer behind a podium.

"We're visiting Jonathan Irons," Reggie said.

"Okay. Sit at table four."

As we found the short table with short chairs, I noticed the vending machines. Only visitors could go up to them to purchase things for the inmates. They had food you could buy, like sandwiches, chips, soda, and other junk food.

As Jonathan entered the room, he had his grays on with a white shirt, and the first thing that struck me was how alive he appeared. He grinned as I greeted him and gave him a hug. Looking at him and listening to him talk felt refreshing. I wanted to get to know this man and hear about his life. He had this light around him, a light in a place of death.

How is somebody like Jonathan living in a jungle like this?

I wanted to be present there, to hear more about his life and the circumstances of his case and just to know how he was doing on this day. I found the conversation and visit enjoyable. I was very comfortable engaging with him. Anybody who meets Jonathan instantly falls in love with him because he's a very likable guy. Very genuine and present. I could see why Cheri and Reggie cared about him.

Looking back on that day and over our whole story, I can see God moving in all of our hearts. God was moving Jonathan's heart to have the courage to open up to Cheri and Reggie. For someone in Jonathan's position, being vulnerable and trusting people is risky because you don't know how long they're going to stick around. On the other hand, Cheri and Reggie had to let the Lord lead them into getting to know Jonathan and seeing him for who he truly was. All of us were just trying to move toward love and kindness, but we also realized this was a very broken situation and a lot of wrong had been done.

None of us knew what the future was going to look like. We just knew that things with Jonathan's case were not right, so we were going to keep trying to show up and continue to do the next right thing.

Jonathan (Big J)

High school graduation

Maya (eleventh grade) at a press conference announcing her commitment to play at UConn

PART TWO

Chapter Seven

FLOWERS IN THE DARKNESS

(1999–2000)

(J)

"PRISON IS A violent place. Men will try to rape you, try to rob you. Men will try to bully you and just dog you out."

I carried Conrad's words with me into The Walls and discovered just how true they were. If you don't stand up for yourself, you will lose everything you value. Bullying is an unhindered daily occurrence committed by prisoners and correctional officers. You can lose your life in a few seconds. I quickly learned my marching orders every morning. I was at war.

Get up, survive the day, then go to bed and start over again.

Going from the county jail to The Walls was like jumping out of a fish tank into an ocean. Or like being transported from an enclosure at the zoo into the jungle. Potential predators lurked all around you. For me it started with my first cellmate. After having that single cell in receiving and orientation, I was placed with a stranger who sized me up and wanted to try me, seeing I was young and assuming I was potential prey. But I had learned in the county jail that I needed to stand up for myself no matter the cost, so I fought him off and had to hurt him and make him know not to ever touch me. Predators avoid hunting difficult prey.

There was a good reason *Time* magazine once called the Missouri State Penitentiary "the bloodiest 47 acres in America." Months after arriving there in 1999, I witnessed this firsthand after getting my first job picking up trash. While I was working in the main corridor right off of the kitchen, some guy walked up to a prisoner named LD and stabbed him with a shank. Everybody knew LD. He was a big bad dude that you didn't mess around with. He fought off his assailant and then stood there leaking blood and looking to see if any COs were around.

"Hey, man, come here," he told me.

As I nervously approached him, I noticed his bloodied shirt and pants and the trail of red splotches over the floor behind him.

"I need some help," he said.

The most logical thought to an outsider would be to find a CO to get this man some medical assistance, but of course, logic and reason didn't reside in a place like this. Being wounded only put you in the hole, where they would wait for you to tell them who did it. There was no desire to actually help you. If you were sick, they'd just send you back to your cell, even if you had a broken bone. Most of the officers didn't care. You might see the doctor weeks later.

LD held on to his side but didn't exhibit any sort of pain as he looked at me and said, "Go find Hamburger John."

I rushed into the kitchen to find him. The nickname came from his job in the kitchen, but in reality, Hamburger John had been a really good doctor outside of prison. I'd heard that he had been convicted of murdering his wife and his wife's lover. He was like a medical MacGyver, someone with the ability to patch you up with homemade tools. Even some of the COs went to him. After I found the guy and told him what happened, Hamburger John gave me some gauze and tape to give to LD.

LD ended up becoming a good ally to me in prison. He was a powerful guy who I'd helped. In the years to come, I'd learn I needed every little bit of help I could get. There wasn't a lot of it to be found.

◆ ◆ ◆

Cells stacked on cells stacked on cells. Bars behind bars behind barricades. An entire world existed in The Walls, and it was one that nobody else saw except for those inside.

The Missouri State Penitentiary overlooking the Missouri River was the oldest prison west of the Mississippi when I got there in '99. I learned its brutal history through stories from older prisoners and from what I eventually read in books. A big reason why Jefferson City became the capital of Missouri was because of MSP. At the time, there were other towns wanting to be the capital, but in 1831, Governor John Miller of Missouri sold the idea of building a prison there. It was authorized by the Missouri legislature the following year and opened in 1836.

Imposing thirty-foot-high limestone walls surrounded the sprawling compound that the *Jefferson City News Tribune* once called "a city within a city." The gray stone barricades and drab buildings had expanded throughout the years through the sweat and toil of prisoners quarrying the limestone on-site. The first guard towers positioned along the walls were circular, like those of a medieval castle. They were replaced with square glass rooms that allowed guards to see better, but some of the original towers remained visible.

"A city within a city" was an apt description. There were around twenty-five buildings within The Walls. These included the housing units, like Housing Unit 4, or A-Hall, which was the oldest building there. It was the honor cell block, so convicts who demonstrated good behavior could stay there. There were "dungeon" cells underneath A-Hall that were once used for solitary confinement. Now those prisoners going to solitary went to Housing Unit 3, which also once housed the death-row cells. A small, single-story square building was once a gas chamber before it stopped being used in 1989. Over the years, forty people had been executed at The Walls.

My cell was the size of a small guest bathroom. Imagine a place where you couldn't open the door—a square room with a toilet, a bed or a bunk bed if you had a cellmate, and a little desk. Basically you were living in a bathroom with somebody you didn't know. Housing Unit 5, where I was first placed, had four floors with two walks per level.

Years ago when prisons began to use convicts to work in industry, MSP followed and ended up becoming one of the biggest manufacturing centers in Missouri. Even as far back as 1885, the prison had a major shoe factory, a soap factory, and a clothing factory among others. Over time, I would find myself working eight- to twelve-hour shifts in many jobs in some of those factories, earning twenty-five to fifty cents an hour. Right after getting to the prison, I was asked if I wanted a job, and I gladly accepted. I was on the yard crew, basically just picking up cigarette butts and trash off the yard. Even when I was outside on the street, I knew that working was key. "You gotta work hard," Granny used to tell me. "You take care of your family." I knew this was an opportunity for me to start working for however long I was going to be in The Walls. Not long after this, my boss told me I was overqualified for my trash-collecting efforts.

"Man, you need a different job," he said. "This is beneath you. This is for old grunts who've been here thirty years and can't bend over."

Right after that, I got a job in the kitchen, working in the dishwashing room washing all the trays and the pots and pans. One motivation behind getting this was so I could eat. I was able to pick what I wanted to eat versus just eating what they gave us. I also got a raise. My yard job was ten dollars a month; working in the kitchen earned me fifteen dollars a month.

The Walls had once been the largest prison in the nation, when it housed over 5,000 inmates. By the time the prison officially closed in 2004, there would be around 1,350 inmates living there. I wouldn't have thought that MSP would shut its doors on September 15, 2004, with the remaining convicts being bused out to the Jefferson City Correctional Center. Six years after I heard "guilty" spoken over me, I couldn't fathom I'd still be living behind these towering walls. But I held out hope that someone would realize they had made a big mistake sending me to this hellhole.

◆ ◆ ◆

The nature of prison is nasty and unpredictable. You could be walking around perfectly fine minding your own business when something happens. You may have made someone mad and didn't realize it until it's too late. There are people living in the same space as you who are literally sociopaths and psychopaths, individuals who legitimately should be locked up. People who can snap at any given moment, who can change moods with the flip of a switch. I learned that you had to live and move in anticipation of the worst. You had to be on guard all day long. And when the night came, you needed to be able to see someone's side-eye in your sleep.

You had to sense the violence that wasn't visible, that waited to jump out at you.

On the day when the two men came after me, I was ready. I was working in the kitchen, and these two dudes tried to jump me because they thought I was somebody else.

"You killed my homeboy," one of them said.

"Man, I don't even know you," I stated. "What're you talkin' about?"

"Oh, you know," the other guy said.

One of them attacked me with a shank, but just as he lunged at me, I grabbed his extending arm and cracked his wrist until I felt it pop. The homemade knife had pierced my side, but thankfully I kept it from going deep into a vital organ and killing me. As I took their knife in my hand, the tables had now turned, and I chased them off. I couldn't feel the pain until I started to calm down; I wasn't even aware that I had been stabbed. But a rushing tide of hot fire overtook my senses. It hurt to even breathe, walk, or stand still. It was all I could do to try to act normal while holding a dirty old shirt from the floor against my stab wound.

I needed to visit Hamburger John, this time for my own wound. I knew if I reported my stabbing, they were gonna lock me up in the hole and I might die down there. I knew they'd be locking me up for my own safety and security, but they'd also be asking who did this to me. I'd be stuck there until I told them, and if I did tell them, then it would make my life even worse because I'd be branded a rat or a snitch. If there's one thing you don't do in prison, you don't snitch on anyone. So Hamburger John stitched me up and gave me some medication for the pain.

Later on, the guys who attacked me realized I wasn't the dude they were looking for. They apologized in a small letter called a "kite" and even sent me some food through a neutral party, but at that point, the damage had already been done. The next time I saw them, I was going to get my hands on them and harm them in any way I could. Thankfully a fence separated us when I saw them again.

"Man, we good?" my assailant asked.

"No, man, we not *good*," I said. "You stabbed me. You almost killed me."

People were noticing that I knew how to take care of myself. Sure, I was only twenty years old, but that didn't matter. I was solid and strong and knew how to swing my fist, like another time in the chow hall. A guy cut in front of me while I was standing in line and taunted me, saying, "Man, what you gonna do about it?" I knocked him out, not because I was angry but because I was afraid. One thing you couldn't do in prison was let other people see that someone has disrespected or abused you, because if they did, it was like sharks smelling blood in the water. If one person bullied you or disrespected you and you didn't take a stand, the news was going to spread like wildfire and others would want to do the same to you, but worse.

But for me, the opposite happened. The word spread that I knew how to take care of myself, so I was encouraged to take part in these unofficial fights that the COs organized in the dishwashing room so I could keep my reputation. Instead of having dogfights, they got convicts to fight each other. Not boxing, but full-on bashing each other's heads in. Prisoners and COs would place bets. They were smart to bet on me.

◆ ◆ ◆

There was a racial divide in The Walls. It could be seen in gangs like the Bloods, the Crips, the Latin Kings, MS-13, Gangsta Disciples, Family Values, Black Fam, the Aryan Brotherhood, and several more. Then there were other groups of guys that just hung and mingled, no affiliation necessary, and I eventually became one of those guys. It wasn't a popular thing to hang out with people from other races, but I didn't care. I'd always hung out with white people and people of other races. This didn't change in prison. An Italian guy named Gary became one of my best friends. The guy was a firecracker; he was short in stature, but he had the heart of a lion.

Gary and I were in Housing Unit 5 when we met for the first time. We were with a bunch of other guys on the same wing and we spent every day that we could just clowning around. We'd have fun and do silly stuff, like throwing ice cubes and trash at each other. We didn't like each other at first, but then I saw his heart. He didn't run when faced with attackers; Gary stood his ground just like I did. He became a good friend at The Walls, and those are rare to come by. I learned that he was one of the guys who had life without parole, and at first, I couldn't wrap my head around such a serious thing. Life without is basically being told, "We're going to sentence you to prison and you're going to die there because you have a life without the possibility of ever getting out." It was crazy to even imagine.

Not long after I was sent to The Walls, a young white guy named Tru showed up on the yard. I'd gotten to know him from the county jail. He arrived at the joint scared and silent. He didn't want to hang out with me, telling me that prison was different, that there was too much of a racial divide. I understood but was nervous for the young guy. He needed a good group around him. I was still just getting my bearings around there, so I couldn't do a lot for him. Unfortunately, my worst fears for Tru were realized when I saw him hanging around Cool Sam.

Everybody knew that Cool Sam was one of the guys who regularly raped other men. They either take their time to sweet-talk you or they just take it by force with a knife. I approached Tru as soon as I could to warn him.

"Man, whatcha doing?" I said. "You know who that guy is?"

"Aw, J—he ain't nothing. He's my guy."

Tru didn't listen. Not long after that, I heard that he had gotten raped. When I saw him walking around with his head down avoiding everybody, I asked him what happened.

"Man, he got me," Tru said.

He didn't look at me as he spoke. I couldn't contain my anger.

"Okay—look. I'm gonna get a knife for you. We gonna handle this. He took your manhood. Listen—I'm with you. Okay?"

One of the first things you needed to do when you entered prison was to buy a knife before anything else, but I had no money to even buy toothpaste or deodorant. But it was now time to get one. *Tru needs my help.* I had already saved up $100 from the measly amount I made working, so I bought a knife from someone. It was a junky, rusty, ugly knife that honestly was more like a little bent-up ice pick. It didn't matter to me. I believed it would do its job. After I got it, I went to Tru and showed him.

"Come on, Tru. Let's go. Let's get him."

He just stood there, shaking his head, his face showing no emotion. "No."

"What do you mean 'no'? Man, he just raped you! I'm here with you. I'm standing with you."

Tru sighed. "I can't lie to you. I let it happen."

He was broken and had given up on life. A dead man buried underneath a long sentence.

"It's just too much time for me. I want the drugs. I don't want to live."

For so many prisoners, drugs were a way to numb the pain and escape prison for as long as each fix lasted. Drugs were everywhere, and some of the COs were the biggest suppliers of illicit drugs in prison.

"No, no, no," I started to say.

"Just leave me alone," Tru said. "I'm asking you, man. If you're my friend, leave me alone."

He walked away from me. It broke my heart, but I was smart enough to know I couldn't do anything for him. It was a good thing we didn't go after Cool Sam. Later on, I was playing around with the knife I'd bought just to see how sturdy it really was, and it crumpled at the slightest amount of pressure put against it. If I'd struck Cool Sam with that homemade blade, it would have fallen apart and I would have been forced to try to fend him off. He was a strong guy, too, so it would have been trouble for me. He would have easily dispatched me.

I ended up seeing this disturbing look on prisoners' faces time and time again. The blank expression of despair, the black hole of desperation. I came to see this place breaking the strongest of men. People assumed they were good, they were strong, they were equipped coming into prison, but then they walked through these limestone walls and they lost everything. Their hope, their health. Because ultimately, this place took our humanity. Some men died five or ten years into their sentence because of health complications.

For a long time, prison did take Tru's humanity. For over a decade, he lost himself to drugs and sex and helping other men rape guys. He tried to kill himself multiple times. But years later, a new man would walk up to me one day and tell me how he got his life back together. He got into a program for help and stability, and started going to church.

Tru's story wasn't over, however. And neither was mine.

◆ ◆ ◆

When I wasn't working, I spent my time in the lower rec yard exercising and getting into shape, preparing for a war or another riot. Most people exercised because it made them feel and look good. I worked out with the mindset of surviving and being prepared for any conflict. Some days, I would exercise for at least eight hours a day in my cell and in the recreation yard.

There was a hill that rose up from the yard, making the wall look particularly intimidating. Someone had painted a mural on the wall of Sonny Liston, a famous convict who became the world heavyweight champion in boxing years after he was released from The Walls. Liston wasn't the only notable person who spent time in the Missouri State Penitentiary. Notorious bank robber Pretty Boy Floyd spent four years in the prison, while James Earl Ray, the man who would later execute Martin Luther King Jr., managed to escape from The Walls.

One sweltering Sunday as I was walking across the rec yard, I saw Chaplain Steven Craft approaching me. Wherever he walked, he commanded respect. With my state-issued gray pants sagging, a red rag hanging from me, I was walking around like I was hard. But really, I was terrified. I had been at The Walls no more than ninety days when the chaplain came up to me and grabbed me by my collar.

"Young man," he said.

He had yanked me upright. "Yeah."

"Pull your pants up," he barked.

I did as I was told.

"Take that rag out of your pocket."

I took the rag out of my pocket.

"I see something in you, kid, but you're out here walking like trash," Chaplain Craft told me. "Come to the chapel. Come see me. I want you to go to church."

I'd never been in the chapel at The Walls. It was a small building made out of stone with big glass windows. I decided I would go check out the service they were having that day.

Stepping inside the chapel felt like leaving the prison. It was a relief to get out from under the oppressive summer sun, to be in a cool and clean place. Everything was neat and orderly, and it even smelled good in this chapel. Sitting down in a wooden pew, I watched how everybody acted respectable as they gathered together. I could feel a sense of peace brimming inside this building with the large stained-glass window above the altar. The two front doors opened as the choir came in with men joyfully singing familiar songs. I couldn't help but smile.

I like this.

I found myself singing along and remembering how much I loved to sing when I was little. The voices moved me. When the men onstage spoke and delivered a message, I didn't understand everything they were talking about, but I listened to every word. These were important men in front of us, guys like Chaplain Craft who carried themselves with dignity around the prison yard. Some of them were dangerous, but they didn't impose that violence on anybody else unless they needed to defend themselves.

This wasn't just a church service. It was a sanctuary. I started to go every week, and I came to learn a lot from these men. In time, many became mentors and father figures. At first, I was afraid of these guys and didn't trust them, but with time, I saw their hearts and their character. These were really good, godly men, ones who would teach me how to become a mentor myself.

People from the outside world came into our chapel to meet us, talk to us or sing to us, and give us a good word. That's how I met Mr. Flowers, a retired music teacher who had taught for decades. He volunteered his time to come in and direct the choir. You could see his kindness in the way he looked and listened to you. We immediately bonded as he encouraged my singing.

"You have to sing from your diaphragm," Mr. Flowers told me as he demonstrated on the piano in the chapel.

He showed me how to do vocal exercises and how to go up and down on the musical scale.

"You have perfect pitch," he said. "Do you know what that is?"

"No."

I was blown away, not because he thought I could sing but because a teacher had never used the word "perfect" in a conversation with me. He took the time to explain to me the basics of music, about what pitch meant and how melody and rhythm were important in singing. When I asked questions, Mr. Flowers listened and never let me feel ignorant.

For the first time in my life, I had a teacher who wanted to help me learn. More than that, Mr. Flowers was the first person who made me feel intelligent for the right reasons. After being imprisoned, I felt like my soul had been ripped from me. A man named Hugh Flowers helped to fill that void. I ended up spending more time with Mr. Flowers every Friday and Sunday. Little did I know he was training me to be a leader in the choir. He taught me how to lead praise and worship, how to go through the songs and sing in tune and understand their meaning. I learned how to direct my energy and presence on the stage, how to communicate with the guys. And as I continued to go to the chapel and learned from Mr. Flowers, I was inspired to get books on music theory and study them.

Mr. Flowers inspired me to believe in myself. For the first time in my life, I was given confidence that I was intelligent, that I had value and worth. I believed that I had something inside me that could be built, that could be used for something bigger than myself.

Not long after getting to know the kind music teacher, I started to sense one of my deepest desires. I knew I had needed the love of a father all my life, but I had pushed that desire away until now. In my heart, I wanted to somehow be his son, but I didn't know how to tell him. After losing my nerve several times out of fear of rejection, I finally opened up to him.

"Man, I love you," I told Mr. Flowers. "Will you be my dad?"

That bright smile was followed by his comforting laugh. "Yeah."

"For real?" I asked.

"Sure."

That was when I became a part of the Flowers family. I didn't know any of his family—not his daughter or son-in-law or grand-niece. All I knew was that I wanted this gentleman in my life. He not only instructed me on music and helped me realize my own intelligence, but Mr. Flowers gave me my identity as a man and a human being. He also lit a spark that turned into a huge flame, this burning desire for knowledge and wisdom.

My life matters. I know that now. I'm going to make something out of it, even in a place like this.

I decided if I couldn't go to a university, I could turn myself into one.

◆ ◆ ◆

There were only three places where I felt safe the whole time I was in prison. One was my cell, depending on my cellmate. If I had a good cellie, then I felt safe. Another was the chapel, where I went as much as possible. The third place turned out to be the library. There were two parts of the library—the law library and the leisure library. Both were in the same part of the school building in The Walls. On one side, you had a space dedicated to law books, while on the other side, you had nonfiction and fiction books as well as magazines and technical books. They also had a journalism department called "The Wall Speak Journal" located at the back.

I practically made my home in that library because it made me feel free and I got to imagine the world as if I was living in it. I'm very imaginative, so it was easy to visualize things in my mind whenever I was reading. This became an escape, but more importantly, the library became a classroom and a study hall. In a walled-in world full of violence and chaos, I could block out that insanity in a sea of books. There was never any violence or anything crazy happening in the law library. It was peaceful and quiet, and all the inmates enforced this.

"Shhhh—be quiet," men would tell others. "People are trying to study."

The guys listened to each other and respected this space. There were a lot of wise, smart, and intelligent dudes in the law library, men who truly were geniuses. They inspired me in my search for gaining knowledge, wisdom, and understanding.

One such individual was Maxwell, an inmate who was known as the "prison lawyer." He had read my case and knew my story. One day, he saw me in the library and started talking with me.

"Do you want to know how to get out of prison?" he said. "I hear that you're innocent, but you're not telling me anything."

That's because I don't trust you.

"Yeah, tell me," I said.

"The key to your freedom is in those books," Maxwell said, pointing to the law library.

He went and found a thick hardcover book, placing it down in front of me at the table. At the time, I was still barely reading and writing, but that didn't stop Maxwell from opening up the book and finding the right pages.

"Start reading that," he said. "It's an important case. From what I've read, this is the position you're in."

I stared at the header on the page.

U.S. Supreme Court
Brady v. Maryland, 373 U.S. 83 (1963)

After Maxwell left me alone with this weighty tome, I began to read. At least, I attempted to read.

CERTIORARI TO THE
COURT OF APPEALS OF MARYLAND

What the heck is "certiorari"?

I sighed. This wasn't going to be easy. But I knew what Maxwell was telling me with this book.

You got a choice to make. You can take this path, trying to learn inside here, or you can take another path out there with the rest of the guys.

As I continued to read, there were so many words that I didn't comprehend. "Petitoner" and "counsel" and "prosecution" and "extrajudicial," and those came from one sentence. There were names and numbers and quotation marks and footnotes and even strange symbols like §. Each line I read lulled me to sleep. I dozed off, and when I opened my eyes, I felt drool on the side of my chin. As I wiped it off, I noticed I'd drooled on the book as well. I just shook my head and rubbed my eyes.

How am I gonna do this?

I felt defeated and broken once more. When I first was arrested and in the county jail, I had been thinking that there were adults in the room and that, at the end of the day, someone was going to come and admit that a mistake had been made and let me go home. But by now I knew that was simply naivete and juvenile thinking. That day never happened. So my mindset had gone from *Man, what happened?* to *I gotta figure out what happened*. But this looked so daunting, so impossible.

There are guys who spend four years or even ten years going to law school in order to practice. I didn't even graduate from high school. What am I gonna do? Like for real?

I was a young guy with the weight of the world on my shoulders, but something clicked. Something deep inside me sat up and became determined. I knew part of this confidence came from Mr. Flowers, but there was a bigger strength that I didn't fully recognize at the time. Like everything I was learning, my faith was growing as well. At this moment, God breathed just enough wind into my sails to encourage me to keep going, so that's what I did.

Looking at the words that resembled a foreign language, I realized that, even though I didn't understand many of them, I did know how to use a dictionary. So I went over to the librarian and found a book called *Black's Law Dictionary.*

"Hey, I need that book over there," I said.

The guy brought it over to me.

"So what's this? Is this for Black people?"

"No, this doesn't have anything to do with color," he said with a soft giggle.

I nodded. "Oh, okay, thanks. Can you give me a thesaurus, too?"

I went back with my tools and continued reading the book. I read every line and every word, constantly stopping to break down definitions and to comprehend the meaning.

Brady v. Maryland was the first case of many that I read. I would have never guessed it would be the key to my freedom.

Hugh "Papa" Flowers playing piano

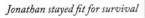

Jonathan stayed fit for survival

Papa visiting Jonathan inside JCCC

Chapter Eight

THE CRUMBLING WALLS

(2001–2004)

(J)

THE FIRST TIME I ever went to the hole was because a rookie prison guard gave me a direct order to attend the wrong recreational period. I spent a week in solitary confinement in an ice-cold cell. The second time was because I tried to help another inmate. I learned an important lesson on how to pick and choose my battles. I also started a war that would carry through the rest of my prison sentence.

In 2001, two years after arriving at The Walls, I had obtained my GED and was halfway through ITC, the Intensive Therapeutic Community. The military-based rehabilitative program taught discipline to young men and old men alike, addressing everything from life skills, emotional intelligence, leadership development, accountability, and proper self-care, to team management, drug addiction treatment, behavior skills, and conflict management. It was a whole other world that included one-on-one counseling and classes. I'd heard all these good things about ITC and thought, *I want to do that. I need some discipline and structure in my life.* I'd always wanted to be in the military, so I decided to investigate the program and see if there was a better way to live in a place like The Walls.

By then I had already built a considerable résumé for myself in MSP. For a kid growing up with no respectable job opportunities on the outside, I had managed to labor in a variety of tasks. After working in the kitchen, I became an ice man, someone who rode around in a big truck delivering ice from the plant inside the institution to all the housing units for the inmates. After that, I started my first factory job working in a dry-cleaning plant making twenty-five cents an hour. The furniture factory wanted me to work down there since I was strong, but it was a bad environment. "You have too much sawdust and horrible work conditions in general," I told them. "I can't even breathe around here." I saved up $200, then told the guys at the factory that I was going to go into this year-long program.

Saving up money was easy for me. I was resourceful. I learned how to live on $7.50 a month, the automatic assistance that all offenders are given whether they work or not. I'd buy my deodorant, a few stamps, a bag of chips, some paper, and a pack of tobacco. I'd roll cigarettes and sell them for two or three stamps; then I'd take those stamps and buy a little food and make it last. That's how I ended up putting a little cash away. When I started making $15 a month in the kitchen, I thought, *This is great!* Then I went to making $25 and $35 in the factories.

One day while I was in my cell, I heard a woman's voice talking to a CO.

"Where's Jonathan Irons at?" she asked.

Soon I heard footsteps and saw the woman named Robin who worked in our library.

"I want to give you a job," she said.

"Where?" I asked in disbelief. "In the library?"

"Yeah. You're always in the library, and you know what you're doing. It doesn't pay what you make in the factory—I know you are used to working there. All I can pay is fifteen dollars a month, but you can learn all you want to. I know that's why you're always in there reading and studying everything."

This was very unusual. Staff members didn't do things like this, being proactive and reaching out to inmates. Robin knew I was in the middle of the ITC program, so her offering me a future job was unexpected to say the least.

"I'm holding this position just for you," Robin said. "There are a hundred people trying to get this job, but I'm saving it for you if you want it. I'll give you a week to decide."

"You don't need a week! I definitely want it. I love the library."

She smiled. "But you have to complete ITC first."

So that's what I did. After graduating from ITC, I began working in the law library in 2001. Even though it didn't pay much, I still managed to save money, always putting a little away. I spent my time studying and learning and helping people. Being immersed in knowledge was liberating. I loved being in there. The highlight of every day was working in the library. I turned my job into a study hall, educating myself on everything from computers to landscaping and architecture and science and, most importantly, law. Any book I could read, I devoured. I was hungry for insight. Each day, I left my job bursting with newfound nuggets of wisdom.

Then, all of the sudden, my job in the library was taken away from me.

A couple of weeks before I lost my job, a friend of mine named Tim disappeared. Nobody knew where he went. As a law clerk in the library, one of my duties was to go and serve ad seg requests. "Ad seg" is short for "administrative segregation," which is a technical name for the hole. When you're in the hole, all of your rights and privileges are significantly reduced. So, if you're wanting to look at any files for your own case, you're limited to only seeing five a week while you're in ad seg. For contrast, while I was in the library, I might be able to look through fifty to a hundred case files per session. When these requests were made from guys in the hole, the librarian gave the files to the lead law clerk to copy. And since the caseworkers often didn't want to have to go down to ad seg to see the inmates, they asked people like me to deliver them.

One day on my routine, I passed by a cell and saw a familiar face behind the bars. I stopped.

"Tim—whatcha doin' down here?"

"I don't know, man. They snatched me up and put me down there. I've been down here two weeks. My mom was supposed to come see me but didn't ever come."

Tim used to be my cellie, so I knew him well and could see the hurt in his eyes.

"What's your momma's number?" I asked. "Give me her number and I'll call her."

When I was able to reach Tim's mother on the phone, she told me she had just tried to come down to the prison, but they told her he wasn't there. I was shocked.

"What? What do you mean? He's here. I just saw him. He's in the hole."

"What do I do?" she asked.

"Give me an hour, and I will go to the library. I'll do some research and find out who you need to call. I'll call you back in a little while."

I went to the library and wrote down all the information I could find, names and numbers for department heads and state reps listed in the Department of Corrections, as well as the director of Constituent Services.

"This is who you need to call," I said when I phoned her back. "Call up here, and then start calling all these department heads, because they got him in ad seg. They didn't follow the policy by giving him notice of why he's in the hole."

Never for a moment did I think I was doing anything wrong. I wasn't selling drugs or stabbing someone with a shank; I was just reporting what I believed to be a civil rights violation. Of course, I was reporting this on a recorded phone, but I didn't think that would be a problem for me.

Boy, was I wrong.

Two hours later, while I was working in the library, a couple of COs came to get me.

"Irons! Number one-zero-one-one-zero-four-five!"

I stood up. "Yeah, that's me."

"Let me see your ID."

I handed it to the CO.

"Turn around," he told me in an angry and loud tone. "Get up against the wall. Now."

They cuffed me and pat-searched me, then they took me to the hole, two cells down from the guy I tried to help. At the time, I didn't know why I was there.

"What am I in the hole for?" I asked the CO.

"You have to write to the warden or whoever you can. You're a writer—ask them."

So that's exactly what I did, writing to my state reps and the warden and even to the governor's mansion. They forwarded my letter to the latter down from the central office, so that's what must have made the warden officially respond. I still have that letter memorized, word for word.

"Due to your interfering with an ongoing investigation, you will remain in ad seg as is."

Sitting in my dark and confined cell in solitary confinement, I stared at the letter.

This dude thinks I'm a punk. I ain't no punk.

I knew enough about the law and policies about a prisoner's rights.

All right . . . I got you.

I decided to write another letter, this time to a state representative. I'd been in this nasty cage for thirty days. The stench was unbearable, and all you saw were either steel bars or stone walls. Yet despite being in this pit, I even managed to work on my case. One morning out of nowhere a guard began screaming out orders to me.

"Irons! Bunk and junk! Get your stuff! Let's go, let's go!"

"What's going on?" I said in disbelief, noticing it was only seven in the morning.

"You're getting out of the hole today. You should be celebrating."

Instead of celebrating, I was making sure to grab the most important things, like my legal work, hygiene items, and my ID. They took me to a new cell in 2 House, and later on, they gave me the rest of my property, which had been left behind in my cell when I got dragged to the hole. Someone came to my cell and took me up front, where I met with the state representative I had written to. She was an African American woman who spoke with power, great wisdom, and grace.

"I got your letter," she told me. "What they did to you is wrong. Are you in the hole right now?"

I shook my head. "No, they just got me out of there today."

"Okay, very good," she said. "I will talk to the warden."

It was encouraging that someone in authority was finally listening to me, but soon I realized this had been a mistake. Later on, I discovered that the warden got in trouble for not following the proper protocol when they sent me to the hole, and as a result of this, he started doggin' and harassing me. Correctional officers got on my case, showing up to my cell and tearing it up, tossing stuff out and putting boot prints on my bed almost every day of the week. I might be heading down the walk and a CO would yell at me to come over; then he'd search me. They no longer used my inmate number. Instead, they called me by my name, making sure I had a target on my back. They were trying to bait me, trying to get me to retaliate with my fists just so they could send me back to the hole and torture my mind in secret.

This warden's unending waves of covert and overt intimidation clearly communicated to me that he was seeking revenge, but he took measured steps to retaliate against me. Yet I did not react like an animal, with savage rage and aggression, a common inmate response in one of the most dangerous maximum-security prisons in the US. Although fear and anger boiled within me, I chose to intelligently respond with dignity and respect for authority. Because I had learned that even the greatest of kings must honor their own rules granting authority, I had become a formidable foe to the prison administration—the seldom-seen prison staff who had been given the power and legal immunity to make life-altering decisions behind the scenes, impacting prisoners for the better or worse. But studying history taught me that one can carefully and patiently defeat a ruling king with his own words or rules of authority.

I had done the right thing—reporting what I perceived to be a civil rights violation. I wasn't selling drugs or stabbing someone but rather stating that somebody had done something wrong. I had no idea if somebody had done it intentionally. The result was that I hopped into a hornet's nest. The warden got reprimanded for doing the wrong thing, and because of this, he started hounding me, and so did his CO buddies. This carried throughout my entire prison sentence.

I learned something from this. I realized that knowledge is power. Learning about the law and studying the rules of engagement gave me new weapons. *This is how I'm gonna fight,* I thought. *This is how I'm gonna win. Not with my fists but my faculties. I just need to be smarter about who I fight, and about when I fight and what I fight about.*

This sort of knowledge was transformative. But I also knew that you needed good-hearted people to be a part of the process, like the state rep who helped me. Otherwise I would still be stuck. I was educating myself, but I also needed leaders to be good leaders.

◆◆◆

Being sent to the hole for no reason was painful, but losing my job in the law library was a burden I felt I couldn't carry. I was heartbroken to learn they had taken my job.

I'm not going to be able to work on my case anymore! I thought, in a panicked state of mind.

I pleaded for them to give it back to me, that I needed it, but my desperate requests fell on deaf ears.

"You can't go back there," one CO told me. "You can't work in the library."

"Why? I didn't do anything wrong."

"You know too much, kid. You're dangerous. You're more of a threat than somebody who is violent because of what you know. You got a warden in trouble for retaliating against you."

This hopeless feeling stayed with me for a few days, until one morning when I woke up and felt some sort of switch being turned on inside me. I know now this was the Lord encouraging me and instilling something powerful inside my heart.

You've got everything you need, Jonathan.

I recalled how I had learned to write while attending my GED class, and how hungry I became for knowledge. During that time, one of my teachers told me I didn't have to work so hard.

"This is overkill, man," he told me. "You're an overachiever. You don't need to score this high. You don't need to do all these studies."

"Yes, I do. I don't know any better. I need to do this."

I ended up doing everything I could. I had learned how to research and how to write. I had discovered how to save money, since I knew it cost a lot of money to use the law library with all the copying you had to do. I knew the instructions on copying and filing and printing. The tools were in my hands, and I was going to be okay. My feeling of dread suddenly dissipated. God gave me this peace. He also breathed into me a desire to keep learning, to keep growing, to keep looking for more job opportunities and skills to acquire.

How do I do that? I'd wonder about a task I'd never done before. *I want to try that one out.* For the jobs that people said were difficult to fill, I went for them. There were jobs I fought for and scraped for. Each time someone said they didn't want to hire me, I defied their expectations and demanded to simply be given a chance. Soon I began to realize the most important thing about educating myself:

No one will ever be able to take my knowledge or skills away.

I could learn what I wanted to learn and be who I wanted to be. I could help others in a variety of ways.

One way was volunteer service as a hospice worker within the prison's medical unit. I cleaned up the hospital and helped with patients. There were men who died in my arms. I bathed inmates who couldn't bathe themselves and put lotion on their legs. One man had been in his bed for three days, wasting away from cancer and unable to move. When I first saw him, he was wailing, so I went up beside his bed and asked how he was doing. I realized he smelled really bad. When I pulled the cover back, I saw the bedsores covering his body.

"Where have the nurses been? Why didn't you say something?"

This was not like a typical hospital, however, and these were a different breed of nurses. In this place, most of them did not care. There were some that were helpful, but others were neglectful and negligent. After seeing the nasty conditions this dying man was suffering under, I brought him to the shower, where I bathed him, dried him off, and put some special lotion over him. His spirit changed, and he smiled at me. The joy on his face was his way of thanking me.

Helping others helped me because it brought a greater purpose into my life. Since I had learned to write, I wrote letters for guys who couldn't pen them for their family. I explained to their relatives what was going on and updated them with any news on the man's life. Over time, as I studied the law more, learning how to effectively read the journals and write and argue lawsuits, I ended up helping people with legal matters.

After showing my grit and earning my respect inside The Walls, a lot of older men came into my life and breathed love and wisdom into me. "You want to do the right thing?" they asked me. "I'm gonna tell you the right thing." They shared their life experiences, the wrong choices they didn't want me to make, the right paths they had chosen to go down.

One day, a big Black man named Johnny Mitchell gave me some invaluable advice. He used to box in prison back in the day, and his massive physique dwarfed mine. He carried his Bible everywhere with him like a sword. It was dirty and dingy, but it was his weapon.

"Listen, kid," Johnny said. "There are three types of people in this world. People who learn from the mistakes of others, people who learn from their own mistakes, and then people who just don't learn at all. Don't be the last one!"

◆ ◆ ◆

As much as I was growing, The Walls was falling apart. By 2002, the place was disintegrating, as a March 19 headline by the Associated Press showed: "Walls Crumbling at Historic Jefferson City Prison."

Several chunks of limestone had cracked and fallen off, shutting down a city street and causing repairs. A couple of months later, in May 2002, a large portion of the wall collapsed, forcing the prison to put up fences with razor wires and motion detectors. This might have been the final straw in deciding to go ahead with the building of a new prison, one that eventually became the Jefferson City Correctional Center, opening in 2004.

One of the worst places you could be in a decaying prison was the hole. Once I was sent to solitary confinement in the middle of winter, and the temperature was so cold that the water in the toilet had turned into ice. We asked the guards to turn the temperature up, but nobody listened. I was forced to collect newspapers from passing COs, who wondered why I wanted so many. "I like to read them," I told them, but I was really using them for insulation just to help keep me warm.

When you deprive people of their basic and fundamental needs, you put them in a dogfight for resources and respect. This was how the riot began at The Walls.

Missouri State Penitentiary was famous for its 1954 riot, where over 2,500 inmates were fueled by resentment over the terrible conditions at the prison and anger erupted. After convicts overpowered guards, they took the keys and freed their fellow inmates. The yard was flooding as men hurled rocks at the guards and lit fires that could be seen for miles. Four prisoners died during the eighteen-hour riot, along with many guards and prisoners being wounded. The total destruction caused $3 million of property damage to The Walls.

The 2002 riot began over a dispute about windows. In one building, the Blacks wanted to keep the windows closed because it was too cold, but the whites wanted to leave them open. The COs made it clear that they didn't care. They basically told the inmates as much. "Go ahead. Start a riot. We don't care."

The spark lighting the fuse began one day when people kept opening and shutting the windows. The tensions grew until some of the white guys took rocks from the yard and busted several windows out. A day after this, a couple of Black guys caught a cold, so a massive brawl ensued. Suddenly everything was chaos. I saw guys laid out on the floor in puddles of blood, COs popping off smoke bombs and telling everybody to get out of there. *Oh God, help me.* As I ran back to my building, I had this feeling that if I didn't get out of there, if I didn't keep going, I was going to die. As I kept moving through the crowd, violence was everywhere I looked. People jumping on somebody over here, a guy getting stabbed over there, somebody being chased with a bat. Someone coming at me. It wasn't simply Black inmates fighting white inmates.

In the mayhem and violence, at least two people lost their lives, and I knew one of them. I had worked with him in the factories. His skull had been caved in with a large stone. As I continued trying to make it back to my house, I stopped to help a different friend named Leroy because he was getting beat up by two prisoners. I knew him from playing basketball with him. He wasn't a bad dude, so I didn't know why they were jumping on him. After I helped him, we both ran in two different directions. As I made my way back to my cell, I had to knock down two guys. I didn't notice the color of their skin. I just saw rocks in their hands and knew they wanted to hurt me.

◆ ◆ ◆

Everybody's fading away since I lost my trial.

I sat in my cell waiting to call my great-aunt. She was the only contact I could call, the only phone number I possessed. It had been a long time—too long—since I last spoke to Granny, so I was wondering how she was doing. I had called numerous times but not reached anybody. My homeboys were facing their own problems with the law; Charles was on probation, so I couldn't talk to him. Even though my aunt Nikki and I weren't on the best of terms and she had told me she didn't want me to call a lot to keep the phone bill as low as possible, we were still family. She was taking care of my grandmother, so I needed to get in touch.

I no longer called more than once a month, since the conversations were so expensive. We had been writing letters back and forth, and Granny had come to visit me twice while I was at The Walls. It was a difficult trip for her to make with her knees. The first time she came to the prison, she didn't know what to expect, nor did she realize she could bring me food. The second time, however, she brought me a sixteen-piece bucket of chicken, and I devoured it.

"Dear Lord, are they feeding you enough?" she asked in a concerned voice.

"No, they're not," I told her. "And the food's not good. But this chicken's good, Granny!"

"Baby, whatever you need to do, stay out of trouble so you can get food visits. We're gonna fatten you up and feed you right."

I thought a lot about those visits and wished Granny could come again. We all need people in this world who are for us no matter what we're going through, whether it's fair weather or stormy days. I knew Granny was 100 percent for me. She was with me and for me and prayed for me and had my back.

I needed to hear her voice. I had to make sure Granny was okay.

When I finally managed to use the telephone, I called my great-aunt about three times a day for about a week, but she never answered. Thoughts of the worst began to creep in, but I didn't want to accept it or think about it.

Finally, after a of week unsuccessful attempts to contact my great-aunt, I decided to call my aunt Nikki.

"Sorry to bother you, but I'm trying to call Granny," I told her. "Is everything okay?"

There was a pause. A long and staggering pause.

"You don't know?" she said.

"Know what?"

"Momma is gone, baby."

She called my grandmother Momma.

"She's in the ground," my aunt said. "She's been there for three weeks."

A cyclone of shock rushed through me as I uttered a "What—" and stood there in complete disbelief. As my aunt continued to talk, I couldn't hear her words anymore. I couldn't hear anything around me. Without telling her goodbye, I dropped the receiver and watched it swing back and forth like a noose. I walked back to my cell and lay on my bed and began to cry. Grief poured out of me. I wept until I fell asleep.

I would later discover that my aunt had called the prison and told them to let me know that my grandmother had passed away. Naturally, nobody had bothered to relay this information to me. Granny had passed away and had been buried in a Wentzville cemetery for three weeks when I finally heard about it. I felt like part of me died with her. I couldn't go to the funeral, of course. The prison administration wouldn't have allowed that anyway.

When I woke up the following day, feeling like I had been lost in some nightmare, I thought about my grandmother again and began to cry once more. The tears flowed all day. I didn't get out of bed or move, and eventually night fell and I went to sleep. Two days after hearing the news, I spent the day in the same miserable way. At least I was going to until Louis came to visit me.

"Brother Johnny," he called out to me. "You can't stay in the cell like this. You gotta get in the shower."

Louis was a good man, one of my Christian brothers I'd met through the chapel. I wasn't listening to him, however. I heard the words but didn't really make sense out of them. I lay there on the hard thin slab of a mattress, staring at the gray wall and feeling defeated.

Why am I alive? I ain't got anybody. Don't nobody love me. Don't nobody want me.

Brother Louis walked into my cell and grabbed my towel, soap, and washcloth. I barely noticed as he took my boxers out of my storage box. Then he yanked my arm and pulled it.

"Get on out of this bed," he ordered. "Let's go."

I stood up in a daze and walked like a zombie as he led me out of my unit and then down the hallway. I didn't know or care where we were going. I assumed it was the shower, but I would have been fine if he was leading me to the gas chamber.

"We're going down the steps," Louis said as he held my hand and guided me.

The shower awaited at the bottom. I hated the shower. There were six showerheads in the open space, and you'd head down there after recreation where you'd be surrounded by thirty other men. Two people had to share a showerhead. You needed to keep your head up because you didn't want to see anybody else's particulars. Everybody knew the drill.

Keep your head up. Keep your eyes up. Step up to the water. Get your face wet, wash it, rinse it, then step back and soap your body down. Don't drop your soap! Rinse off.

The next person would rotate, and you'd keep doing this until you were done. Other inmates stood on the sidelines, watching and waiting. Facing you and staring.

Bad stuff happened in the showers. Now I was being led into this dreadful place. To my surprise, nobody else was around. *Thank God*, I thought.

"Man, you need to get a shower, okay?" Louis said as I just sat there to the side on the hard tiled floor while he turned on the water.

The steady stream of water began to run in front of me.

"Come on—wash up," Louis said. "You'll feel better."

As he left, I sat there for who knows how long. It could have been five minutes or an hour. Then I finally stood up and began to undress. I smelled my drawers and winced. I reeked.

How can I smell this bad?

I felt dirty and musty and funky. As I moved underneath the showerhead, I looked behind me out of habit to see if anybody else was around. I felt relieved seeing that I was still alone, so I took my time. My body began to loosen up, and my mind began to move out of the fog of grief it had been in. As the water splashed on my face, I cried once again, thinking of my grandmother.

I'm never gonna get back home, Granny. I'm never gonna be able to tell you goodbye. I am sorry I couldn't make you proud of me.

I always knew that if she found out I was selling pot, she'd kick me out. I knew and respected her decision. I tried to reason with her, that I didn't want to do this, that I didn't like doing it.

At the end of the day, she was right.

I should have never been selling weed. I learned from a bad influence, cut a corner, and soon became a bad influence myself. I was thinking I was doing the right thing finally making money, that I was fine, but she knew better. Granny always knew better.

As I finished my shower and began to dry off, I began to feel and sense things again. For the last two days, I had been in a conscious coma, in some dark cloud. I pictured Florence Bell Spears, her sharp eyes and her sweet smile. My grandmother had been my momma.

My momma and daddy and best friend.

I knew if I could depend on anybody that I could depend on her. Now she was gone.

As I made my way back up the steps, I found Louis waiting on me. When he saw me, he began to clap and tease me.

"Good job, Brother Johnny. You got in the shower. The water's free—you don't have to pay for it."

"Man, shut up," I told him.

He could see that I was doing okay now. I was still hurting and still heart-broken, but I was going to be okay. I don't know how long I would have stayed in my cell, paralyzed and helpless, but I knew my good brother helped me keep moving.

He also reminded me that I wasn't completely alone.

◆ ◆ ◆

On October 14, 2004, the Missouri State Penitentiary closed. For 168 years, it had held some of the most despicable people in human history. At its peak, it had been bursting with 4,900 inmates. When it was my time to be moved, one month earlier, I left on the third of many prison transport buses to the new prison. I was among the 1,355 inmates being transferred.

As I left that day, I thought of the quote carved into the front of the three-story Gothic-looking Housing Unit 1:

"He who converteth a sinner from the error of his way shall save a soul from death." —James 5:20

But that wasn't what they were trying to do at The Walls. This was a place of punishment and brutality, a property where you could be left alone to die. They unlawfully murdered people there, beating men to death. Prisoners killing other prisoners, COs executing inmates.

Very few in these walls worried about saving souls. But there were some. *Like Papa Flowers.*

As the bus drove away from this dark place, I reflected on what this prison meant to me. These walls housed a place of containment and confinement.

For those trapped inside its crumbling granite, prison had become many things to many people.

A harsh nursery in the jungle for the young.

A retirement home for the old.

A drug center for the addict.

A hunting ground for the predator.

A psychiatric ward for the mentally ill.

A concentration camp for the illegal alien.

A group home for the troubled adolescent.

It was a place to learn who you were and what you were made of, to discover if you really wanted to become a better person and refuse to let prison define you.

Far too few inmates came out better than when they had gone in. But not me.

I may be in prison, but I am not of prison.

A thought I would regularly repeat to myself and share with others. It meant that my body was still physically bound in the system, leaving one prison to go to another, but my mind and spirit and soul were free. I did not accept or embrace the imprisoned mindset.

This dungeon I was leaving had never been my destiny, and this attitude I carried with me would be the difference between life and death for me.

From Granny's memorial service

Chapter Nine

THE PETITIONER

(2005–2007)

(J)

"HOW LONG, LORD? Will you forget me forever? How long will you hide your face from me? How long must I wrestle with my thoughts and day after day have sorrow in my heart? How long will my enemy triumph over me?"

As I wrote a letter to Papa Flowers from my cell at Jefferson City Correctional Center, I thought of Psalm 13:1–2, which I had read earlier that day. I had taken Granny's advice and read a Psalm and a Proverb each day. I loved how the Psalms weren't just songs praising God but they were petitions for Him to intercede and laments about the darkness in this world. Storms continued to fill my heart. I still grieved my grandmother's passing, and I dearly wanted to see Papa Flowers, who had taken some time away from volunteering at the prison. It had been a year since I'd seen him, so I decided to reach out to him to let him know she had died. It was an opportunity to ask him where he was at and tell him I missed him. I wanted him back in my life.

Moving into JCCC meant I had cleaner surroundings, but the violence remained the same. Six months after arriving, an inmate got stabbed in the kitchen and died. Then there was the sex offender in ad seg who had raped kids and everybody knew it. People were hunting for this guy, waiting to get at him. He ended up in a cell with another inmate who literally beat him to death. The assailant was a sociopath, some guy in the hole who was Charles Manson–like crazy. These were the types of monsters I was living with. My new house still felt like the same hellish home.

As 2005 passed and every appeal I attempted got denied, I came to my wit's end. The feeling of hopelessness fell back over me. I couldn't sleep and didn't want to eat. I spent hours crying, my mind racing with frustration and anger. But I remembered my grandmother telling me something else:

"It's okay to pray, but when you pray, pray with your heart, no matter how you feel."

I began to reach out to God with an open heart, a wounded and broken heart that echoed those Psalms of petition.

"Answer me when I call, O God of my righteousness! You have given me relief when I was in distress. Be gracious to me and hear my prayer!"

The more I had studied the law, the more I had learned about petitions in the court. After reading the Bible, I came to see that Heaven was like a courtroom and the enemy resembled the prosecutor, standing up there accusing people. But God was the judge, defending me through His son, Jesus. I simply needed to write out my petition for God to read, so I began that year and finished at the start of January 2006.

Heavenly Father, I humbly come to you in the name of Jesus Christ. . . .

The words poured out of me, as I wrote them from a place of humbleness and thankfulness, not from pride and desire. I didn't hold back from the demands of my heart and from their calls to action. My prayer was spoken in specifics and stated in faith, with numbered requests.

Number one, I pray that you allow me to overwhelmingly feel Your love and Your mercy. . . .

I knew God was a chain breaker, that He could break down these walls the same way He tore open the prison in the apostle Paul's cell. So my petition pleaded for this.

**Number two, I pray that You deliver me,
exonerate me, and liberate me. . . .**

I spent hours working on my prayer, faithfully pecking away at it on the old typewriter my grandmother had bought for me shortly before she passed away. I would have to get it fixed twice just to get it to print out the prayer letter.

Number three, I pray that You keep me safe. . . .

From day one, I knew I had to fight for my survival, that I needed to work out to remain strong, that I could never back down to anybody. But ultimately my safety and well-being were in the Lord's hands, and I had to give over my life to Him.

I ended up with seven requests in my prayer petition. After I was finished typing up the letter and printing out two copies, I stuck one in my Bible and took the other to work one day. I had been toiling away daily in one of the factories, Missouri Vocational Enterprises, so I knew exactly what I needed to do with this petition. Psalm 28:1 seemed to confirm this very destination.

"To you, Lord, I call; you are my Rock, do not turn a deaf ear to me. For if you remain silent, I will be like those who go down to the pit."

Outside of the building I worked at was a smoke pit where inmates and COs came to light up and have a cigarette, so I walked over there and noticed that nobody was outside. This was highly unusual in the middle of the day. It didn't matter to me. I was empty and anxious and needed to give this prayer over to God.

As tears lined my cheeks, I sat there on my knees and read the prayer out loud. It wasn't a short prayer, so it took several minutes. Then I set the letter on fire, watching the bright yellow and orange and red flames crinkle up the paper and send the black ashes upward.

Lord, show me something. I don't know no other way but to trust You, but if You are who You say you are, then make this prayer matter.

A whole team of guards and correctional officers could have been watching me as far as I was concerned, but the smoke pit remained empty. Setting this fire would have gotten me sent to the hole. Thinking about it later, it was so unusual for nobody to be even walking through there. There was a peaceful quiet in this pit, making me unaware for a few moments where I was even at and what I was doing. It felt so strange. But this was the sort of pressure I felt every day, spinning on a continuous hamster wheel, running and running and feeling like I wasn't getting anywhere.

I was only twenty-five years old, having been arrested nine years ago. I had been in prison for nine years. My twenty-sixth birthday approached, another I would be celebrating in a prison.

God answered part of my prayer petition shortly after this, opening a door to not only the help and hope I needed, but to another life I could not even imagine.

"I cried to the Lord with my voice, And He heard me from His holy hill. Selah I lay down and slept; I awoke, for the Lord sustained me."

◆ ◆ ◆

Earlier in 2005, after Papa Flowers received my letter, he asked his daughter to reach out to me. That's how I came to know Reggie and Cheri Williams. At first, Cheri wrote a letter to me and I wrote her back, and we corresponded this way several times. Then Reggie first came to meet me in person. Reggie had been working for a long time at State Farm in underwriting and claims investigation, so when I shared my story, I could tell his investigative mind was interested. I came to learn that Reggie had prayed before meeting me for the first time, asking to see me in the way God saw me instead of letting any sort of filters about prisons and inmates factor into his opinion of me. I was still skeptical of people, believing that nobody would ever stay around for long. But there was something different about Reggie and Cheri.

Right away, Reggie began asking me all sorts of questions about the case, and I knew he had already done his homework online before coming to see me. When I told him they set a million-dollar bond for me, Reggie looked astounded.

"That's ridiculous," he said.

The more details I shared about my case, the more interested Reggie became. He admitted that he was a big fan of TV shows like *CSI: Crime Scene Investigation* that focused on the procedural forensics of a crime. The more facts Reggie learned, the more questions he had.

Just a day before my birthday in January 2006, I realized that Reggie and Cheri were an answer to my prayer petition. Inmates were allowed food visits three times a year, when visitors could bring meals, but they had to be scheduled in advance. I barely made the deadline to get my food visit, but I was given a couple of days' grace to make it happen.

When Reggie and Cheri showed up, I couldn't believe they came wanting to celebrate my birthday. It was a new thing for me; when I was younger, Granny had too many kids in the house to worry about things like this, but she did her best, working through intense knee pain and daily fatigue. That afternoon, Reggie brought his famous gumbo, and Cheri ended up making me a little cupcake out of a Twinkie, with Twizzlers representing the candles and a Starburst acting as the flame. They even had "Happy Birthday" plates we ate off of.

To say this was a blessing would be an understatement. I cried seeing all of this, this time pouring out tears of joy. It was one thing for Reggie to be interested in my case, but an entirely other thing for this husband and wife to be interested in me. They had sons of their own, so they didn't need another. But that didn't stop them from bringing me into their lives and their family.

◆ ◆ ◆

"O LORD, how long shall I cry for help, and you will not hear? Or cry to you 'Violence!' and you will not save?"

The questions from Habakkuk 1:2 resonated inside my soul. The prophet of Judah was frustrated about the Israelites and how they had turned away from God. Habakkuk had been crying out to God to change things, and he couldn't understand why God wasn't doing something about it. Why was God allowing all the injustice and violence around him? Where was His judgment? The Old Testament prophet shared an attitude similar to Jonah, disheartened about God's seeming inaction against the evil of the day. Jonah remained angry, however, while Habakkuk became humbled and praised God in the end.

Shortly after Reggie and Cheri became an important part of my life, God gave me the same answer He gave Habakkuk for what I needed to do about the injustice of my situation. It came in verse 2:2:

"And the LORD answered me: 'Write the vision; make it plain on tablets, so he may run who reads it.'"

These words spoke to me even though they had been written in a very different context. That's the beauty and mystery of the Bible—how different passages speak to you in remarkable ways. It was like the Lord was talking to me and encouraging me with a task: *Jonathan, you know all the details of your case. Even though others might know some of the facts, you need to write out everything that happened to make it easier for them to fully understand all the wrongdoings.* So I wrote a case summary, giving reference points for everything I was talking about in the files.

Write it so people can read it easily and then run to tell others about it.

I had already sent Reggie and Cheri the copy of the petition prayer I had burned before the Lord. I knew now they were an answer to my prayers, to this prayer, so I wanted to share it with them. I wanted to make it absolutely clear about all the facts in my case and about all the work I had done on it. They had been continuing to discover facts about my case, bit by bit. At first, all the details had been overwhelming, but they grew to understand everything. My case summary helped them have a road map that they could pass out to others.

One person they gave the summary to was a Black law student named Jamal, and he passed it along to another law student. Eventually we ended up meeting some people who worked at the Innocence Project, a nonprofit organization that helped to exonerate wrongly convicted prisoners like myself and worked to reform the justice system. Each person we talked with and every form I filled out helped us connect the dots a little further and provide a little more information or some more ideas. The Innocence Project provided a significant thing when they scanned in all of my documents and converted them to digital files, making them easy to manage and navigate and send to people.

The biggest assets to my case were Reggie and Cheri. I put together an affidavit to give Reggie the power of attorney for me. For a while, I had been trying to figure out how to physically retrieve my entire legal file from the public defender's office and the police department. I knew how to request them, but I couldn't go there in person to get them. So instead I requested the files be sent to Reggie and Cheri's house as long as he signed for them, but when I wrote to the O'Fallon Police Department, they never responded to my letters. Since I didn't put a certificate of service on them with the return receipts, the letters were easily swept under the rug.

Reggie began combing through my files, looking at all the facts. The visits began to happen more regularly, soon becoming a weekly occasion. Each time I saw him again, he had more questions to ask me and more outrage in his heart. Each week, his interest and excitement and frustration and anger grew surrounding my case. We spent at least three or four hours every weekend talking about my case and just strategizing. Going nonstop. Reggie soon had an understanding of the facts, but he still didn't understand the law, so I started sending him cases to read to give him the reality of the nature of what was going on with my situation. Just because he could see the facts and saw that I was innocent still didn't mean that all those facts could get submitted into the court.

It felt surreal and special to be teaching law to the son-in-law of the chaplain who first inspired me to study it.

The longer the O'Fallon Police Department refused to send us records, the more suspect their actions appeared. *They're hiding something*, I thought. Reggie and others agreed. After doing my research, I learned about the

Freedom of Information Act and our state's response to this, the Missouri Sunshine Law. This law stated that all records, meetings, votes, and actions related to governmental bodies were open to the public. These records were anything written or electronically stored by any government body, and they could be requested by anybody. A statement of purpose was not required.

In other words, *Hand over the files. Now.*

When O'Fallon finally responded to our request, they told us we could come down to the department and look at the files. When Reggie showed up, however, they didn't want to let him in, basically telling him he couldn't enter. He reminded them that they had said to come down.

"So what exact files do you want?" the police department asked.

"We don't know what we want to see until we actually see them," Reggie said.

After they continued to refuse to let him in, a pro-bono attorney helping me at the time called the attorney general's office.

"We will sue O'Fallon if they don't allow us to come in and look through those files," Reggie said. "We have a right to do this under the law."

Thanks to Reggie, I now had someone representing me in person, armed with the law and the truth. This time our request had teeth attached to it. The attorney general was forced to call down to O'Fallon and Reggie was finally told to go inside. When he walked up to the young lady who was the record keeper, she gave him a nervous glance.

"Are you FBI?" she asked.

Reggie didn't answer her question exactly. "I'm just here to look at the files," he said. "I'm here to look at the evidence, ma'am."

First, they brought out the 911 tape for Reggie to listen to; then they brought a box of evidence and let him look through that. Finally, the young lady handed him a blue manila folder with copies of the files.

"That's all I can give you," she told Reggie.

Armed with new information, Reggie took the files back home to delve into, seeking to find something that could help, some missing piece for the petitioner he was working to save.

Sentence by sentence, and statement by statement, Reggie studied every single piece of evidence he had obtained in the boxes and the folders, the transcript of the trial and every last brief, jotting down notes and cataloging the documents just to understand how I had been convicted.

"If I had been sitting as a juror in that trial, it was very confusing," Reggie said. "It was a lot of jumping around."

As an underwriter at State Farm, Reggie was accustomed to working on claims, so he had to know the policies backward and forward, making sure that people were doing what they were supposed to be doing. He had even done some investigative work looking into claims and making sure something was covered in a policy. I couldn't have handpicked a better person to be researching these details for me.

During this time of reviewing my case and reading everything he could about it, Reggie's goddaughter not only heard about me and the visits they were making to Jefferson City Correctional Center, but she also saw firsthand those notes and pages. Reggie and Cheri gave her details, so as with anything that might have been happening in her family, Maya Moore listened and learned about the incarcerated Jonathan Irons. Eventually she leaned into my story and made it part of her own.

We first connected over speakerphone when Maya was visiting Reggie and Cheri. They had been telling me about her game, so when I first spoke with her, I joked and talked some trash. Telling her she needed to work on her crossovers, just being silly. It was a friendly interaction.

The first game changer in my life came after Reggie reviewed the files he had received from the O'Fallon Police Department. He went through them meticulously just to make sure there weren't other files we didn't have. Everything looked familiar until he came across one item. It was a latent fingerprint report that Reggie had not seen before, one that looked completely different than the latent report that was in the public defender's office with the blue stamp marked on it. He showed it to a couple of people working with us. "Well, this is different," he noted, making sure he kept it in a separate folder.

All the many documents and pages full of debates and discussions and determinations and declarations and suddenly this. A report nobody had seen.

We mentioned it to the attorney we had working with us, but he was too busy doing other things, so the report just sat there for a while. But it stayed in our minds since it was different and could be of value at some point. We made sure to hold on to it.

The other game changer came when Cheri and Reggie told me that Maya would be visiting them in the summer of 2007.

"We want to bring Maya to visit you," they said.

◆ ◆ ◆

She's probably gonna be afraid of me. She's gonna judge me and think I'm guilty.

Like chains around my hands and legs, I carried these thoughts with me as I walked into the visiting room. I still hadn't gotten used to Reggie and Cheri coming all the time to see me, so I assumed their goddaughter was making a token visit. As I made my way to them at the table, Maya hugged me and looked directly in my eyes. She didn't look away, not for a second, and she spoke to me in a warm and loving way. Something inside my heart stirred because I wasn't used to this sort of kindness. This young lady with a vibrant smile and a head full of beautiful micro braids carried a humble confidence far beyond her eighteen years. Maya also brought this amazing sense of peace with her. The longer we spoke, the more I couldn't believe just how down to earth she was.

I could remember the first time I met Reggie, looking calm and cool and collected as he shook my hand and said, "What's up, dude?" As if we might be having a business meeting instead of meeting in a maximum-security prison. He asked a lot of questions about my case, and with each subsequent one, I was surprised about how much he already knew. When Cheri came on his next visit, she appeared far more uncomfortable. She was almost hiding behind Reggie's tall frame when we first met. In the back of my mind during those initial visits, I kept thinking the same thing.

They're not gonna stay around long. Nobody does. This is a bad situation.

Yet Reggie and Cheri had stuck around, investing more of themselves and becoming more knowledgeable about my case. They even introduced me to their family. I had already met their sons, and they had been telling me all about Maya and her basketball success. After Cheri sent me some articles, I came to understand just how great of a player their goddaughter happened to be. *This girl, she's doing big things*, I thought.

On that first visit with Maya, I expected her to be more nervous sitting across from a convicted prisoner in a maximum-security prison, more judgmental and skeptical of my case. I never expected her to be so humble and kind. The next day, Reggie, Cheri, and Maya came back to see me again. I felt more comfortable around her, so I decided to challenge her to a game.

"You wanna play checkers?" I asked.

"Okay."

"You sure?" I said with a grin. "I know how good you are on the basketball court, but I'm tough to beat on a checkers board."

"We'll see about that."

Despite some good-natured trash talking, Maya promptly beat me at checkers. Her friendly disposition didn't prevent her from being competitive. When we finished, I congratulated her.

"Let's play again," I said, assuming that I'd get another chance at beating her.

"No. I'm good."

I stared at her as if she was joking. "You serious?"

"Yeah. I'm not going to mess with a winning record."

I teased her but soon realized she was serious. She wasn't going to let me have another chance. In fact, that rematch to this day has never happened. She took that checkers victory to the hills and refuses to give me another shot.

What Maya did give me was more of her time and her interest. She genuinely wanted to know more about me. Not just about my case, but about me as an individual.

"How'd you grow up?" she asked. "Tell me more about your story."

Somehow, Maya didn't see me as simply Inmate No. 1011045. She knew enough from her godparents to know there was more to me than a set of numbers and a fifty-year sentence. More than anything else, she made me feel human, which in a place like JCCC was a very rare feeling to have and wasn't encouraged.

"You sure you want to hear it?" I asked her.

Her nod and reassuring smile told me yes.

The easiest thing I could have done was to start the story off with the bad stuff, the dark and unjust stuff that got me thrown into prison. But instead, I began to tell Maya about where I came from, about my great-aunt and our home, about the little boy who loved the outdoors and who felt loved by the elderly woman who took care of him.

That little boy was older now, but he still carried hope. He still believed that someday he would be exonerated and home free with his loved ones. Nobody was going to steal that hope and faith from him. Not ever.

Cheri and Reggie visiting Jonathan in JCCC

PART
THREE

Chapter Ten

A BIGGER
STAGE

(2007–2008)

(M)

MY CELL PHONE rang on a sunny September day as I walked toward the student union on UConn's campus to get a bite to eat. It took me a second to grab it out of my purse and see that it was an unknown number calling. I had received similar calls like this in the past week that I had ignored, but I decided to go ahead and answer it. A woman's voice began speaking in a recording that I only caught pieces of.

"—is a prepaid free call—at the Jefferson City—this call may be monitored and recorded—"

That's weird, I thought, clicking the call off and thinking about my next class.

After my first month at UConn, I was still figuring my way around campus and still excited about my new surroundings and classmates. I lived on campus in a dorm with my fellow freshman teammate Lorin Dixon. The transition had gone smoothly, especially since my mom had ended up moving up to Connecticut to a nearby suburb a half-hour drive away from campus. It was a win for both of us, since I could still have a sense of home when I wasn't on campus for holidays, while my mom could come to all the home games and be a part of the Husky family regularly. That half-hour distance gave me both a sense of support and comfort while also being able to have my independence and experience college life on my own.

Life had been busy since I'd graduated from Collins Hill in May. The day after I received my high-school diploma, I drove with my mom and Reggie up to Connecticut to start my summer sessions with the basketball team. UConn had two summer sessions, with the first starting at the beginning of June. Players took a couple of classes in the summer since it wasn't reasonable for us as student athletes to take a full load during a regular semester. Typically, we ended up taking four classes each semester and then two classes in the summer to keep us on track to graduate on time. For our first summer session, everybody on the team was required to come; the second session later in the summer was optional, and a couple of us had international USA Basketball competitions to play in, so we needed to be away.

So just like that, Mom and I moved out of our apartment in Lawrenceville and into a townhome in Connecticut to start a new life. I moved to campus a few days later and began my summer-schedule routine. Monday through Friday, we took a couple of classes while working out with our strength and conditioning coaches and playing pickup games.

For the second half of the summer of 2007, I had gone to Bratislava, Slovakia, with the USA U19 squad. A year earlier, I had been a member of the USA U18 national team, and we had won a gold medal at the championship game in Colorado Springs. Our U19 team did well, winning all nine of our games and winning a gold medal at the FIBA U19 World Championship.

As the first semester of my freshman year started, the coaches gave us a little time to get settled in and to have our classes get going before enduring five straight weeks of preseason training. This happened before official practices began. Preseason was brutal. You had to wake up at 5:00 a.m. for grueling workouts, all before heading out to classes later that morning. Lorin and I were still just trying to figure out the campus and where to go. Preseason was no doubt great preparation in getting us in the shape required for UConn practices.

Later that evening, I received another peculiar phone call from a strange number, so I picked it up and heard another odd recording that sounded like a robocall or maybe some sort of telemarketer before hanging up.

The following morning while I was in class, Cheri left me a message to call her. I had spoken to her and Reggie a few times since the start of school. Her voice sounded urgent.

"Is everything okay?" I asked after reaching her.

"Jonathan's trying to call you," she told me. "Have you been getting his phone calls?"

Now they made sense. "Are you serious? I had no idea it was him! I just kept getting weird calls and recordings that I didn't understand."

"That's how it sounds when you get a call from prison. Jonathan called and asked me again if it was okay to call you, and I told him yes. That you were expecting it."

"I am. I was wondering if he was ever gonna call. Shoot, now I feel bad! I'm sorry—I'll be sure to pick up next time!"

I was serious when I told him I was interested and invested in his story. I wanted to keep up with his life, so I would enjoy hearing from him. Jonathan later told me that a part of him felt like I was going to be too busy, that I wasn't going to think about him. *Go live your life,* Jonathan thought. But regardless of being busy, I wanted to keep connected with him.

In the same way that my mom and I didn't know what it looked like for me to be playing sports in college, I really had no idea what to expect with keeping in touch with Jonathan. This was a very new experience, and I had never had a family member or friend that was incarcerated. We eventually connected and laughed about me not picking up those initial phone calls. Our conversations felt natural and enjoyable, and they began a rhythm where he would give me a call every few months and we kept up with each other, developing a friendship. He was also able to write letters, so he occasionally wrote me as well.

The college experience was still brand-new to me, and I remained excited for the season ahead of me. Having someone else out there who was part of my family supporting me gave me an unexpected comfort. And I embraced it.

◆ ◆ ◆

There was a legacy with the UConn Huskies, one that began with our heralded leader, Coach Geno Auriemma, and associate head coach Chris Dailey. Going into the 2007–2008 season, the Connecticut women's basketball program had won five national championships under Auriemma, the first arriving in 1995. The list of extraordinary players he had coached included five Associated Press national players of the year: Rebecca Lobo, Jen Rizzotti, Kara Wolters, Sue Bird, and Diana Taurasi. Our home opener was against Stony Brook on November 11, and this season began with an unusual pressure.

Coach Auriemma admitted the pressure himself in an interview early that season. The last three UConn teams had failed to make it to the Final Four, so if we followed suit, this would be the first time in two decades that a Huskies senior would graduate without making an appearance. "It's a period of mourning at Connecticut," Auriemma told the media. "Some teams haven't been to a Final Four. What happened is we found ourselves rebuilding. Because when we lost Diana Taurasi, we lost four players: our best point guard, our best two guard, our best small forward, our best power forward. Trying to replace somebody like that isn't easy."

Taurasi was a two-time national player of the year, so losing her to the WNBA in 2004 left a big hole on the team. The coaches told us they were going to push us to do something that they hadn't done yet with this group, and we were ready. All the players felt good about our chances of bringing another championship to UConn, and Coach A felt the same.

"I think this is as close as we've been in the last couple years," he said.

For me personally, there wasn't any pressure in being "Maya Moore," the one arriving with the accolades and the winning streak, the 2006 and 2007 Naismith Prep Player of the Year, the so-called freshman "phenom." I was very aware that I was a freshman. This was a new environment, and my goal was to learn and grow. I wanted to listen and soak up everything I could while at the same time remaining confident and competing and doing what I knew I could do.

It came as no surprise that I watched the game's opening tip from the bench. Coach A preferred for freshmen to come off the bench and enjoyed being able to have some offensive firepower waiting to jump into the game. The years when UConn had to start a freshman usually meant they were a year or two away from winning everything. Even though I couldn't remember the last time I had been sitting on the sidelines when a match opened, I remained as excited as I ever had been, knowing when I stepped onto the court, I'd fire up my teammates with energy and intensity. That's what made this game fun and worthwhile to play.

Our team opened the game versus Stony Brook with a 9–0 run. I entered three and a half minutes into play and scored my first basket at the 14:32 mark, making a tough catch from a half-court pass lobbed by junior Renee Montgomery to put the Huskies up 21–2. The lopsided score never changed; we finished with a 98–35 blowout. I was pleased to record a double-double with 21 points and 10 rebounds.

Coach Auriemma felt good about our performance and confident about this team.

"I don't think we're a year or two away from winning," he told the media. "I think we can win the whole thing right now."

◆ ◆ ◆

23.

The number on my jersey already represented so much to me, yet I could never have imagined what it would end up meaning to me later in life.

For most of my youth basketball life, I wore the number 32, but when I arrived at Connecticut, one of my teammates already had that number, so I had a decision to make: Try to convince her to give up her number or change mine. So many great players had come through Connecticut, so I didn't want to take on one of the legends' numbers. Then I realized the reverse of my number, 23, was available and shared some good company, too. It was LeBron James's number at the time and had obviously been Michael Jordan's number, so I was set with 23. My new number even had a connection to a new habit I had started around my autograph. During my senior year of high school, I noticed one of my all-American friends had been signing her autographs with Colossians 3:23 underneath: "Whatever you do, work heartily, as for the Lord and not for men." I loved it! It was such a fueling truth for my spirit. No matter what I was doing, no matter who was or wasn't watching, I'd give my best with my whole heart because I knew it pleases the Lord, who gives me my breath and gifts. I thought this could be a meaningful message that I could share with people every time I signed something for them. Twenty-three was falling into place.

As the season progressed, I adjusted to the rhythm of balancing academics and basketball. One of the hardest things as an athlete at school was learning how to balance your time and your energy while still wanting to make friends and enjoy people. I had learned a lot in high school, so I felt prepared. Being at Collins Hill had been a similar experience as far as wanting to pursue excellence in the classroom and wanting to be great on the court, so it wasn't as much of a shock to learn how to balance my time when I started at UConn. One big difference I discovered was that in high school you had a lot of opportunities to make grades through lots of quizzes and homework, while in college you might only have a handful of opportunities. A couple of tests and a final exam, or maybe one project or a few papers. In college, you were really judged on the preparation and work you did outside of the classroom, so I was grateful I had already developed a good work ethic back in high school.

Entering my freshman year, I did something I had never done before. I had prayed for many things in my journey with God so far, but this time I had a super-honest need: "Father, I need friends." I asked God to help me find great friends as I entered this new season of life. Naturally when you're on a team, you have a built-in family already, so that was a huge blessing. But I still wanted to meet new people and make friends because our friends end up shaping our lives more than we know. As the semester unfolded, the Lord began to answer those prayers. There was a campus ministry that was becoming more established by the time I arrived at UConn, so I was able to connect with some athletes there and develop some really great friendships. There were weekly gatherings led by this ministry, and I enjoyed the consistent rhythm of connecting and building relationships with people who were sincerely seeking to learn and know God. There were even summer camp opportunities that some of us went to that explored faith and sport. It was at these camps where some of my longest friendships to this day were born. I can't imagine what life would be like now without these precious friends I made over those summers at camp.

When I was in high school, my abilities on the basketball court weren't the only things that developed and grew; I continued to pursue growing in knowing Christ during those four years. But I had more of a me-and-Jesus sort of rhythm simply because I didn't have a bigger community to grow with. Our church at the time was a long distance away, so it was challenging to connect. It was a pretty big church as well, making it easier to come and go without much notice. Mom and I always made sure we got a copy of the sermons we missed if we were traveling for basketball on a Sunday.

It was a new experience for me when I arrived at college and got involved with this sports ministry. These men and women allowed me to discover a Christian community for the first time outside of my family. I came to college already rooted in a transformative love for God and people, but I was starting to sense that there were greater growth opportunities for me in being more connected to others. I had never really known how to articulate my faith journey or how to share the beautiful reality of God with people, so as I learned from others ahead of me, I was given tools that helped cultivate my ability to communicate my story. My enthusiasm for ministry was ignited, and I was all about helping other fellow student athletes grow in their faith. By the time I graduated, I was able to help lead and co-lead small Bible studies for other athletes on campus.

I loved learning and growing, whether it was in loving people better or in the classroom or on the court. But my first season at UConn would remind me that growth could come with a lot of hardship and hurdles, and we discovered this in our eighth game of the season.

♦ ♦ ♦

In the first half while playing the South Carolina Gamecocks, our talented junior guard Kalana Greene was driving toward the basket when she drew a bump from a defender and dropped to the floor in pain. Kalana had to be helped off the court by our training staff. After undergoing an MRI, the news was devastating: She had a significant ACL tear in her right knee, ending her season.

Coach Auriemma wanted my role to evolve over time, but that had now changed. I suddenly found myself in a unique position of starting as a freshman at UConn.

I will have to step up for KG.

That's exactly what I was able to do. I stepped up and was able to become a big contributor and also a leader while at the same time continuing to learn and pay attention and try to focus on the little things that helped make our team great. I was glad my game was effective and that my shots were falling.

One month later, in a match with Syracuse, the unthinkable happened when we lost Mel Thomas, our tough shooting guard. The senior had been going for a loose ball when her knee buckled and she collapsed. Once again, a starter was gone due to an ACL injury. Mel was one of the funniest people on the team, always so full of energy with a smile on her face. She brought so much joy and enthusiasm to our team, so watching her go down and then see her senior year end like that was crushing.

Even though we were 16–0, our depth and margin for error were now much different because we could no longer rely on two of our best players.

Nobody can ever really anticipate or prepare for how long a college season can be, especially when you're a freshman. It's very tough, and it wears on both your body and your mind. That's one reason why the coach made it tough for us, and I thought that was good because it was preparing us for moments like these, the unexpected hurdles in the road.

That year we worked hard and endured many long practices. One practice in particular lasted three and a half hours. We had a flight to catch for a road game, but the coaches were trying to teach us something and we weren't getting it right. It was one of those days where we realized, *We're not going anywhere until we get this done!* Eventually we did enough for Coach's satisfaction and made our flight. This was the grind of that growing and learning year.

When I came to UConn, I had made it a goal of mine early on to try to go into Coach A's office at least once a week just to talk with him and see if he had anything he wanted to share with me. Even if we had a grueling practice or I was frustrated at him, I still went into his office, and every time I left, I always felt better.

"What's going on, Maya Moore?"

Coach usually called me by my full name. The perspective he had and the advice he gave and the encouragement he offered always left me feeling like I had my head on a little more straight than when I came in. I always appreciated that about Coach. His door was always open as well. He had been doing this for a long time and had accomplished a lot, so he didn't have to make himself available. But since he did, I tried to take advantage of that, knowing I wasn't going to be in college forever. I wanted to really learn as much as I could from him.

Of course, Coach Auriemma was known for not being afraid to speak what was on his mind. He was very direct, and I liked that because he was going to tell you what you needed to hear. I knew as a freshman I was going to make mistakes, like being out of position and not knowing where I should be or shooting too fast and rushing things. I knew how to take the yelling and the criticism; I knew they were meant for the good of me and the team. I just kept playing. If I made a turnover, I had to get back. If someone scored on me, then I needed to make the adjustment.

While being direct and vigilant, Coach A also had an incredible sense of humor. We laughed every day at something he said, whether it was aimed at someone else or at you. He always seemed to be making some witty or unexpected comment.

Coach A was one of the biggest influences in our lives during our college years, but so were the assistant coaches. I would go to their offices as well, and each one of them had their own wisdom and insight and things that they poured into us athletes. I learned so much from all of the relationships I formed those four years with coaches and teammates alike. The UConn culture was all about preparation, preparation, preparation. As someone who grew up being this way, I thrived in this culture.

At the end of the day, the coaches gave us a lot of responsibility to manage ourselves and maintain high expectations for ourselves. If there was a player that needed to be pushed, we as teammates took it upon ourselves to try to motivate her. We looked out for each other. I remember one morning before an early workout when one of my teammates had not shown up to the locker room yet. It was getting late, so we called her several times. She finally picked up the phone and raced down to the gym. She had overslept and missed her alarm, but we thought ahead and helped her, saving all of us from having to run extra drills.

This sense of responsibility and ownership was perfect for a personality and player and competitor like me. I grew a lot, learning from the coaches and leaders what it was like to create and maintain a winning culture. Not just that, but also a family culture. That's what made us so great. We had a sense of ownership of the team.

◆ ◆ ◆

After the last game of the season, where I'd already learned so much and grown in so many ways, I experienced one of the hardest things to go through as a young player.

Losing on a national stage.

We had gone into the NCAA tournament playing well. I had made history by being the first freshman ever to get Big East Player of the Year, and I was also the first true freshman to be named to the all-conference first team. Junior Renee Montgomery made First-Team All-America, and sophomore Tina Charles was playing well and becoming more dominant as a center. We were doing our thing—stepping up for our injured teammates and rallying around them.

Even though Rutgers had snapped our thirty-four-game regular-season winning streak back in February, we accomplished our goal of making it to the Final Four. We felt good playing Stanford next, a team we had dominated back in November, but it turned out that loss had fired them up to prove that they were better. While the Cardinal had indeed improved since we last saw them, the Huskies had been wounded, and we showed it this night.

This is the hard truth of competing at this level. You don't always have it every game and every night. Sometimes you find yourself in a zone as a player and as a team, where everything works and everybody remains in sync, but then there are games where you don't click the way you need to. This was one of those games. I gave it everything I had, but I was held to only 6 points in the first half and struggled from behind the arc. I was 3–11 from beyond the three-point line. Stanford played great, with Candice Wiggins exploding with 25 points and 13 rebounds. In fact, their performance resembled the way we usually played.

The Huskies were shocked by the final defeat of 82–73.

We knew we had done all we could that season with our group, but we desperately missed our two wounded starting guards, Mel Thomas and Kalana Greene. Coach A put it best when he said, "This is the one team we can't match up with without the two guys that were hurt." Back in the locker room, the coaches did a good job as always leading us in those locker room moments. Coach A remained authentic and honest as he shared his perspective, telling us what we needed to hear to grow as athletes while at the same time encouraging us. But he knew the truth of a loss like this.

"At this time of the year, especially in this environment, unless you win, there's really not a lot that you can say that's going to make any of the players feel any better," Auriemma told the press. "The one thing I will say is it's unfortunate that the season comes down to one weekend and it doesn't go our way. The other five months seem to have no meaning. That's why this is such a difficult game to lose. . . . All you remember now is what happened in those forty minutes. You don't remember all the things that led to getting here."

In those moments after the game, as we consoled one another and shed tears in the locker room, I felt so terrible for our Mel and the other seniors. Tears come when you invest so much and work so hard and bond so tightly as a team. We had invested in each other and in the season, so it felt devastating to go out feeling like we hadn't played our best. But these moments serve as lessons you will take with you the rest of your life. They will shape not just how you play on the court but how you prevail through any catastrophe.

In this moment of devastation, with a heavy heart and watery eyes, I had a reality check.

Get it together, Maya. The locker room is now open, and the media are going to come in and ask you questions about why you didn't win and how you're feeling and all the things that you don't want to talk about.

This was the big leap I had made from high school to college. Now my moments of grief would be followed by the media and watched by the masses. There we were, grieving the loss of the season and processing these things as eighteen- to twenty-one-year-olds, all while having to give answers and talk on a national media stage. But I had chosen to step onto that stage, so I had to learn how to put my emotions aside and be a professional. To hide the heartbreak, to harden myself. I felt uncomfortable with this whole scenario, but had to deal with this.

If you want to be in the big-time—if you want to be in this industry—this is what it's gonna take.

This was the cost of being in this place and this moment.

"Life's thrown a lot of things at us this season," Coach Auriemma said. "It took away two players. The fairy tale didn't have a happy ending. That's life."

◆ ◆ ◆

On the drive back to campus, we were welcomed with the love and support of our great Huskies fans. People waved to us on the sidewalks and applauded us from the street. A host of people stood on the overpass with signs that said what a great season we had and how proud they were of us. We have awesome fans.

Shortly after getting back to UConn, I went into Coach A's office. I lay on the couch in his office, crying and shaking my head and talking about how I felt like I had let the team down and hadn't played my best. We talked about me becoming a more dominant rebounder and improving my one-on-one defense.

"I have to be more confident playing the post. There's so much more I can do."

Like any great coach, he listened and helped me process things by giving his perspective and wisdom. I knew he had been here before and understood it better than I did, so I trusted his input. Coach A could see that I really wanted to do well, that I cared about this team and about my performance, so he challenged me in ways that I could grow as a leader and continue to invest in my teammates.

Before I left his office, Coach A told me he wanted to give me something. I think he realized I needed to be reminded of something. He handed me a piece of paper that had a quote with a blue-and-white background.

I held the picture and read the words.

"Perfection, admire it, aspire it, but don't require it." —Anonymous

I ended up putting that picture in my locker as a reminder of something Coach A said to us regularly: "We strive for perfection, but we don't require it." It wasn't realistic to think we were going to be perfect all the time, but if we aimed for it, we could get somewhere great.

I'm an achiever. It's how I'm wired. This quote was a good perspective for me. It is easy to be a perfectionist when you are very competitive and in a competitive environment, but that isn't the healthiest mindset to carry. I needed to be reminded to not let my desire to be great make me miss the joy of playing. We weren't going to win every time we stepped on the court. Every shot wasn't going to go through the hoop. Every play wasn't going to go our way. But the journey with my teammates was the real gift. There was value to be found even without a perfect performance.

My freshman-year basketball season was finished. I had come in not really knowing what to expect and leaving it open to anything good happening.

Praying for God to lead me and direct me. Some of the things that followed—the awards and the accolades and the numbers and the records—were surprising, but I knew we had to keep going.

We had more things to do.

Things the basketball world had never seen before.

Coach A and Maya

Chapter Eleven

THE STREAK

(2008–2011)

(M)

START WITH JOY.

For any sport, there is no guarantee to greatness. There are no shortcuts, no way around the grind. When you're in the midst of building something magnificent, you can be tempted to obsess over the goal and lose sight of why you're building in the first place. So how does a team pull off a winning streak that breaks all records before it?

Always remember why you love the game.

From the very first time I touched a ball and tried making baskets on that little toy hoop, I've relished this sport. The Merriam-Webster definition for "play" is "activities that are done, especially by children, for fun or enjoyment." I began my journey with basketball from a place of love and enjoyment of playing it, and I carried that spirit with me throughout middle school, high school, and now at UConn. My team was a fun-loving group, and this only continued into the following year. When you play sports, the game is at its best when you are playing because it's fun. At this level, you have to remember the joy of playing because there are tough things that come as the game becomes more of a business within our American culture. That's why I love the third part of Coach A's mantra as a basketball coach:

"Play hard. Play smart. Have fun."

As my sophomore season started, that's what we began to do. Throughout summer training and the preseason, we knew we were on a mission, hungry and vowing to win a championship. Our expectations were higher this year. We were energized to prepare even better knowing we had the potential to top last year.

Begin with love for the game, but look ahead to where you want to go.

I knew what I brought to the team when I started my freshman year, but nobody knew that other players' injuries would move me into a starting position that quickly. The sophomore season would be no different. I knew my abilities and saw this as an entirely new journey. There was no taking anybody by surprise anymore; I would never be called a "freshman phenom" for these UConn Huskies again. Whenever the moments came to step up and do my job, I would sprint into them. The goal remained to grow in order to help all of us become the best we could be.

Happiness wasn't just something I found in the swish of a perfect shot. Being at UConn was a dream come true. I was grateful to be attending an incredible university and having my education paid for by earning my scholarship. I was traveling to so many great and new places playing the game I loved. My family could watch me on TV. And thankfully, my mom was close by. Having her near really helped to keep me sane, especially when I needed to get away and just rest and hang with someone I've known my whole life. There was a comfort this brought, and a security I felt knowing she was always there. I wasn't distracted by homesickness or feeling isolated. Talking on the phone is great, but there's nothing like being able to simply know you could go home every now and then.

◆ ◆ ◆

Go ahead. Try new things. You're not going to be eighteen or nineteen forever.

I had always wanted to dunk in a game. I loved being able to slam the ball through the basket the first time I did it. Sometimes after practices, Tina Charles and I used to put on impromptu dunk contests. So, during one game my sophomore season, the moment arrived during a fast break. I found myself all alone down the court, and I knew it was time.

I'm gonna dunk. I'm finally gonna do it in a game.

I was a six-foot power forward, so it was quite a feat for me to jump like that. But I had enough bounce and knew this was the time. Of course, the classic head game began to play out in my thoughts just as I approached the basket.

Wait—for real—should I dunk it or not?

I decided to launch and go for it. The mind games continued even in the air.

Can I make it? How 'bout just a finger roll? Can I?

I went for the dunk. The ball bounced off the rim and fell to the side. I blew it! I missed the shot, and we missed out on two easy points. I tried to avoid eye contact with Coach A, but he soon subbed me out of the game. As he approached me on the bench, I knew he was going to scold me for being reckless. Instead, he just gave me some calm instruction.

"If you're going to dunk it, make it," Coach said.

Rather than calling me out for trying the dunk, Coach A was basically telling me, "Hey, I have confidence in you. Just go out there and do it." He was encouraging me while at the same time making sure I was still held accountable for my decision.

It would be a while before I tried another dunk in a UConn game.

◆ ◆ ◆

Find your zone.

There's nothing better than finding yourself in a zone and flowing with it, especially when the competition is trying to make it as challenging as possible. On our seventeenth win of the undefeated season, against Syracuse, I found a zone early and never left. They had entered the game with the goal to disrupt my play and get me out of my rhythm, but the more they tried, the more I kept seeing gaps and strong-arming my way toward the ball and getting open. I had lots of open looks, so I knocked them in. There was no dunking on this night, just a lot of three-pointers. So many that UConn set a school record with 18, and I made a team record with 10. The final score was UConn 107, Syracuse 53. I was able to capture 40 of those points.

I had reached 1,000 points in my career faster than any other Huskies player, reaching the milestone in fifty-five games.

There was no getting an ego on our team, and I don't remember anyone printing up "Maya Moore 1,000" T-shirts. But we did like to celebrate when amazing things like this happened. We had all been determined to play well, and our energy and chemistry combined to bring out the best of all of us.

The intensity and aggressiveness of this matchup came at a cost, however. We ended up losing our talented shooting guard Caroline Doty to an apparent knee sprain. And with six minutes left, Coach A received a technical foul for screaming about Syracuse's overly physical play.

We were devastated to learn afterward that Caroline had actually torn her ACL and would miss the remainder of the season. Our celebration came mixed with a familiar feeling of losing another teammate to a season-ending injury.

A reminder that being in the zone is really a gift, not a guarantee.

◆ ◆ ◆

Sing.

Anybody who knows me knows how much I love music. My teammates have heard my ability to create various musical beats at any given moment. Our team was constantly singing and being goofy. You couldn't tell us we weren't a music group instead of a basketball team. We were always singing, always dancing.

Music has always given me a deep sense of joy. I'm pretty intentional about what music I feed my soul and those around me. I love many styles of music, but I'm pretty picky about the message and spirit behind the music I'm vibing to. You could find me bumping artists ranging from Lecrae to Mali Music to Hillsong to Tenth Avenue North. Songs from these artists grounded me and reminded my soul of the most real and true things in life. While the beats made my body move, the themes kept my mind and heart right and still. All my teammates heard me daily singing in the locker room, whether it was a worship song or something we made up together.

This passion came to fruition on February 28, 2009. The UConn Huskies clinched the Big East regular-season title at our senior night with a convincing 81–50 win over Seton Hall. The most difficult part of the night for me came not in the game itself but in the pregame ceremonies. We were honoring three of our seniors—Cassie Kerns, Tahirah Williams, and our incredible leader, Renee Montgomery—so junior forward Kaili McLaren and I had decided to sing the national anthem for them. I hadn't sung in front of others since I was four years old, so I couldn't remember being more nervous before a game.

We brought down the house. At least that's what I remember.

As we finished the song with "and the home of the brave," our teammates rushed toward us and tackled us. The team celebrated a victory even before the tip-off.

◆ ◆ ◆

Understand your role.

As we won UConn's sixth NCAA championship and finished a perfect 2008–2009 season at 39–0, we celebrated the most for our captain, Renee Montgomery. Coach A admitted as the game approached that he was desperate to end her career with a title and was sick at the thought of not having that storybook ending for her. Everything this season started with Renee because she was our leader. She had come in with an unselfish attitude and an acceptance of the different roles teammates played. Our captain trusted us to make big plays, and she brought out the best in us.

The victory was particularly sweet for me since we were playing in St. Louis. I was delighted to win my first college national championship in my home state of Missouri. It had been quite the year for me as well. I had led the Huskies in scoring and rebounding, and had been awarded such honors as the Wade Trophy, the Associated Press Player of the Year award, and the Big East Player of the Year. Despite all of this, I didn't seek out the spotlight. Everybody had contributed to our undefeated season, and Renee was the example I followed.

"I can continue to make smarter decisions on court, certainly," I told ESPN. "Like a lot of the decisions I see Renee making. That comes with experience. And just continue to be a good leader. I'm probably going to step up vocally more, and I'm sure Coach will fill me in on what he wants me to do."

◆ ◆ ◆

Never forget what this life is all about.

On a beautiful April day in 2009, surrounded by my gorgeous teammates flaunting dresses and heels, President Barack Obama honored the UConn Huskies on the lawn of the White House.

"Under Coach Auriemma's leadership, this Huskies program has redefined excellence again and again," President Obama said in his remarks. "Six of the last fifteen NCAA Titles, five undefeated regular seasons, three undefeated championship seasons, two 39–0 seasons. But for this team, an undefeated season just wasn't enough—they became the first team in NCAA history, men or women's, to win every single game by double digits, which is just an unbelievable, unbelievable statistic."

The day was an incredible experience. President Obama invited us to the outdoor basketball court on the South Lawn and gave us our only loss of the season as he beat a few of us in an impromptu game of P-I-G. We blame it on the heels and home-court advantage. We were able to take a tour of the White House, and we saw famous rooms I had only read about. The way President

Obama and First Lady Michelle Obama honored us left us all deeply inspired. For me, I was moved to write to the White House shortly after our visit and expressed the impact Obama had made on us.

"The way he took the time to shake hands, take pictures, and talk to everyone showed his humility and genuine personality. The way he sacrificed some extra time out of his day to shoot a few shots with us made me remember what life is all about. It is about investing in people and having faith that the love you impart on them will somehow make the world better than it was. Thank you to President Obama and everyone who made this event possible!"

◆ ◆ ◆

Be honest and transparent.

Earlier that year, before winning the championship, an important friend in my life had shown his honesty and transparency. I was still in regular contact with Jonathan in prison, so he had decided to write my mom, wanting to be transparent with her about our friendship. Even though our friendship was just developing, he wanted to be respectful, since her daughter was corresponding with an inmate. The letter gave a revealing look into Jonathan's heart.

January 31st, 2009

Hello Ms. Moore,

My name is Jonathan H. Irons (AKA "Big-J"). Ma'am, first and foremost, I want to express to you personally that, even though we've never met, I have a great deal of respect for you and, if you don't mind, I hope that one day you will let me get to know you on a personal level. I have heard some good things about you . . . some of your remarkable struggles of the past, and your victories over various forms of adversity. The joy of overcoming is very sweet. I

believe that we both can relate to this truth. Furthermore, with all due respect, it is my desire to personally respond to your inquiries about me, the content of my character, and my intentions with this introductory letter.

Your concerns about me are well received by me. I welcome you to ask me anything you like and I don't mind you asking anyone about me. I think that it is wonderful that you are protective of your daughter and if you ever feel like you don't feel comfortable with me communicating with her, I will stop. I don't want to disrespect you or hurt you in any way. Time will show you who I am and what I am about. I do pray that you get to know me for yourself with an open mind. I don't bite, scratch, or shed fur on the carpet. But I do give big hugs, though! Ha! I may be big to some people in stature, but I am a teddy bear at heart.

Yes, I am a prisoner, but I am not of prison. My body is temporarily bound, but my mind and spirit are free. I am in prison for a crime that someone else did and God has sent me a team of people to help me prove it. Over 12 years of my life have been wrongfully taken from me, but God has used this experience to bless and strengthen me in Him, and soon He will deliver me completely. I am not ashamed to declare that I am a Christian, but I wasn't always one. I grew up in a poverty-stricken household, I became angry and bitter about not having my biological parents, and I grew up believing a lie (that was told to me that my mother put me in a dumpster while I was still a newborn). I am ashamed to admit it, but I used to be a gang member and did what juvenile delinquents do. Please don't dislike me because of my past mistakes. I was young, foolish, and misguided. But I don't mean to make excuses. I am just trying to shed some light on my mentality then. I don't drink alcohol, use or sell drugs, and I am no longer a gang member. Although I have been in fights, I have never killed anyone. I have never been a fan of alcohol and the only drug

I used back then was marijuana. I am serious about my future and I have an awareness concerning God's plans for my life.

As far as my intentions concerning your daughter, at the very most, she and I share a friendship and a Christian fellowship. I won't lie to you and say that I don't like her, because I do. Be proud, you have raised a strong, intelligent, beautiful, spirit-filled woman of God! However, having an intimate relationship with her is not my focus. In other words, I am not aiming to be her boyfriend, lover, baby daddy, etc. . . . I am focused on my relationship with God, working on my case, helping other people with their cases, continuing to educate myself and staying healthy. At this time, I am taking a college course and I am maintaining a 4.0 gpa in paralegal studies—while still being in prison. This requires great effort and focus on my part, but I am taking advantage of my time to prepare for the future. Every day I achieve progress.

I call her from time to time, maybe 3 or 4 times a month, but I make sure not to interfere with her college education and career. The greatest thing that she and I have in common is Christ. My interests with her concern her spirituality and her intellect, and her emotional well-being.

Furthermore, I am a leader, a helper and a giver by nature. I also believe in supporting myself. I have no children now, and I refuse to have a child out of wedlock. I also refuse to have children and not be there for them. I know what it feels like personally.

Like I said previously, with all due respect and admiration, to your daughter and in this letter, I don't want to disrespect or be at odds with you. If you don't want me to talk to her, I will make it my business to stop. You are her mother and I feel like you know what's best for her and her future. You could have chosen to have an abortion, but you chose to let her live and you sacrificed and struggled through the years to raise her and meet all of her needs. I really respect that about you. I haven't said any of this to charm you or offend you, I have just spoken from my heart.

With respect,

Jonathan H. Irons
#1011045
Jefferson City Correctional Center
8200 No More Victims Rd.
Jefferson City, MO 65101

When my mom let me read Jonathan's letter, I found it incredibly heartfelt and honest. It revealed how much he cared for me and how much he wanted to know and honor my mom. I was blown away and inspired even more at learning what he was about. Jonathan and I had an understanding that we were friends and really enjoyed developing this friendship, but we weren't pursuing a romantic relationship. I'm sure my mom had her moments of doubt because she knew Jonathan the least out of anyone in our family. I'm sure she was thinking to herself, *Lord Jesus! What is going on here? Lord—I do not like what's going on.* My poor mama.

God had a plan.

◆ ◆ ◆

Follow in the footsteps of greatness.

John Wooden once said, "Winning takes talent; to repeat takes character." We knew that heading into my junior year, but we would all truly see this quote come to fruition. Coach A had already won championships, so he knew the pressure put on UConn.

"Coach Wooden got the absolute best players in America every year," Coach A said. "We get the best players in America every year. That's what everybody thinks. The things we fall back on are, I'm sure, the same things that every successful coach falls back on, is that every day we try to live up to that potential."

Part of living up to that potential was not to get hung up on milestones and records, like the one he earned against Hofstra when we won 91–46, extending our winning streak to forty-seven. More importantly, Coach A became the eleventh coach in the history of Division I to win seven hundred games. Don't get me wrong—we celebrated hard when we did great things, but we remained grounded and focused after reaching our marks.

"I try not to spend a lot of time thinking about that, that sort of thing," Coach A told ESPN. "I guess that's what keeps me going in the direction I want to go."

In turn, this sort of leadership and attitude kept our team going in the direction we wanted to go.

◆ ◆ ◆

Be more than a basketball player.
Something easier said than done.

When I was named the 2010 *ESPN The Magazine* Academic All-America of the Year for women's basketball in the University division, I carried a 3.70 GPA in my third year of studies. I joined two fellow Huskies: Rebecca Lobo and Leigh Curl. For me it was a validation of the time I had spent working and the time I had sacrificed. I wasn't a person who could just listen in class, not study, and then get an A on a test. I needed to pay attention and take notes and master my homework. Thankfully, by my junior year, my athletic and academic and personal lives were all in a great rhythm.

Those infamous and grueling UConn practices that went on and on were thankfully shorter, maybe two hours at the max. This was in part because we were just cooking, being efficient, and taking care of our business. We were staying focused and growing as a team. And it was exciting to see some of my teammates enjoy the Bible studies that were going on and to be developing relationships with them where I was able to connect with them in a deeper way. It felt like we were grooving in so many ways, and the experience was very rich, since there were investments being made into relationships both on and off the court.

My relationship with Jonathan continued to grow. Sometimes he would be on the other end of a phone call giving me encouragement and supporting me and I would find my mind blown. I remember once being in complete disbelief about his caring attitude.

"You're in prison, so how are you supporting and encouraging me?" I asked him. "I'm supposed to be encouraging you!"

This was what a real friendship resembled: someone who was there for me during the ups and the downs of trying to balance my busy life and grow through my college experience. Jonathan, along with Reggie and Cheri, continued to keep me updated on progress on his case as well. My godparents would come to as many games as they could, and Jonathan would try to catch as many UConn games on TV as he was able to.

◆ ◆ ◆

Never panic.

At the national championship in San Antonio, UConn found itself playing Stanford and making history by halftime. The sort of history you wanted to forget about. In the locker room during the half, there was a mix of frustration and determination that champions carry when they aren't playing like themselves! Stanford led 20–12. *At halftime.* I had gone two-for-eight. Our team had shot 17 percent in the first half, playing the worst half of basketball we'd ever played. It would have been easy for all of us to start panicking, seeing everything slipping away. But we remained calm as we listened to Coach A. He wasn't yelling or scolding, but rather, he was asking us some simple questions.

"Is this the way we played all year? What did we do all year? Are we attacking? Where's the team we've been all season?"

All of us knew there was a lot of time left. We just had to stick with it and push through. We also needed to settle down. Just settle down and hit some big shots. Coach gave us parting words as we went back on the court.

"If we're going to lose, at least let's lose our way. Don't let this be our last defining moment."

There was no fear, no freaking out. We opened the second half scoring 17 of the first 19 points. There was a stretch when Tina got hot and started doing her thing; then I got hot and did the same. A step-back three I took from the top of the key gave us our first lead since our 5–0 start of the game. The Huskies ended up scoring 41 points in the second half as we won 53–47. I remember an announcer for the game saying it wasn't pretty, but it was perfection.

"It was a real testament to these kids and how strong they are," Coach A said about the game. "How tough they are, how resilient they are. There are so many things that could go wrong along the way. And it's just unexplainable to me that that many things could go that right for seventy-eight straight games."

Seventy-eight straight games. Are you kidding?

The feeling I had most was the feeling of relief. We had been setting records, and talk of the streak was happening before and after each game. This was when my mom coined the term "streak stress." That's exactly what it was, especially for our poor parents, who had to endure waiting and watching in the stands while we were trying to navigate the pressure of winning night after night after night. When the horn went off, I honestly felt like I could breathe for a moment.

People don't realize how hard it is to win when you're expected to win. Everybody loves the underdog, the big upset. Every game during the streak came with an added air of pressure, but we entered each game very prepared and extremely confident. Coach A taught us that, about how you only feel nervous when you're unprepared. I'm not sure if that was a quote from Coach Auriemma or Coach Wooden, or maybe both said it. They certainly knew it to be a fact. This was one of the keys of winning—knowing that we were physically and mentally prepared for each game. This took some of the pressure off.

Of course, going into my senior season, our team was going to look vastly different. Being prepared might not be enough.

◆ ◆ ◆

Step up and lead.

Looking ahead to my final Huskies season, I knew we had lost two of our most reliable leaders in Tina Charles and Kalana Greene. Junior guard Tiffany Hayes and I were the only starters coming back. Our team would be young, with five freshmen filling half of the roster spots. I was never afraid of being vocal as a teammate, but now my ability to lead by voice and example could be the difference in us sustaining our legacy. Being the youngest player named to the 2010–2012 USA national team in the spring of 2010 helped to toughen me up more for my senior season. I was able to play on the 2010 world championship team that summer in the Czech Republic, and the experience was invaluable. As the youngest member of the team, I got a little taste of pro international play and got my butt kicked a little bit from some of those veteran guards as I learned to become a small forward (also known as the three). I had played power forward most of my career in college, so when I had my chance to play some small forward with the pros overseas, I could tell this was a whole other level of play. There were a few screens where I simply got rocked. But I still did my thing on the offensive end, playing hard and contributing to Team USA winning the gold medal at the FIBA world championship.

Another incredible experience being on the US national team was to play with and learn from veterans like Sue Bird, Tamika Catchings, and Diana Taurasi. Diana was a fiery and legendary guard during her time as a Husky. She helped lead her teams to three consecutive NCAA championships, capping it off with her unbelievable senior year performance.

A fun fact is that Diana and I both share a birthday on June 11. We are different people, but we share a great passion for competing at our best. When asked about his two June 11 players, Coach A explained:

"One had the ball in her hands all the time and told you what she was going to do before she did it and then told you afterward, 'See?' The other one just goes about what she does without a lot of fanfare. The sameness is that they are unbelievable competitors. The two of them didn't think there was any play they couldn't make. And if the game was on the line, they were going to make it."

As I began a new adventure with my new UConn teammates, I quickly knew we had a long way to go. Coach A reminded us of that daily. This would be a new leadership challenge for me, but I was going to put all I had into figuring out how to help us be great.

◆ ◆ ◆

Ignore the numbers.

Along with the streak stress arrived the never-ending headlines and reminders of what we might accomplish in the media. "The legendary 88-game streak of John Wooden's UCLA Bruins still looms," wrote the *Wall Street Journal* in a November 2010 article ominously titled "The Team That Forgot How to Lose." *No pressure.* Each game extended the streak, bringing us closer to eighty-eight wins, just eight shy, just seven shy, and on and on and on. Coach A helped us deal with the pressure and the expectation as he navigated the media during the streak.

"The number is just a number," he said back in my junior year. "People bring it up. It's probably bigger to everybody else but us."

As our dominant 2009–2010 year came to a close, our coach explained what the streak felt like. "The problem is while you're in it, while you're doing it, all you're thinking about is the next one. I wish I could put it into perspective, but I can't." Then after we won another championship, John Wooden's record came up once again. "I don't think about eighty-eight," Coach Auriemma responded. "I'm not looking at it as a goal. If we're fortunate and it ever happens, I'll be astounded again like I am right now."

Another set of numbers began to be discussed with me during my senior year: breaking UConn's all-time scoring record, a record Tina Charles had set last year. For me, this wasn't even on my radar. I was more concerned about figuring out how to get our five freshmen to be effective communicators on defense every day in practice. I was always thinking about what we needed to do as a team, what I had to do for our team to win.

The streak and the records and all of that—we didn't have enough room in our heads to think about that. Our coaches emphasized this all the time, and our team believed in this way of thinking. We couldn't change our mindset as our streak record got closer and closer. We didn't want to let the potential of breaking records distract us. All of us just had to discipline ourselves to stay focused, to limit the contact we had with all the outside noise. The UConn program had taught me that ever since I entered the program, so it was easy to just stay focused on the little things every day. If we did this, then if we looked up at the end of the season, we should be where we wanted to be.

◆ ◆ ◆

Rely on everybody.

On November 16, 2010, we found ourselves down by 8 points against a number-two ranked Baylor with six minutes to play. This was the second game of our season. Seventy-eight of our last seventy-nine games had been won by double figures, so this was truly uncharted territory. At one point, the Huskies had been up by 15, but Baylor came back with the help of their dominating six-foot-eight center, Brittney Griner. I stood there on the court, looking at the score and time with a team that hadn't been tested like this.

We've never been here before. Can we do this?

The answer turned out to be beautiful. Coach A said it was a great scenario the way it played out, especially for our younger players. "I don't know that I could have written it better," he said. "They grew up a little bit."

Freshman guard Bria Hartley especially grew up as she scored 8 straight points in those final minutes, nailing a three to give us a lead of 63–60 with just over two minutes to play.

"I don't know there's been a bigger shot made in her life," Coach A said of Bria's three-pointer.

We proved a lot to ourselves on this night with a 65–64 scare from Baylor.

◆ ◆ ◆

It's okay to break down.

There had been an unconscious groove of playing and moving and winning during those two undefeated UConn seasons. But now as a senior, that groove was over. We were starting over with so many new players, which meant long and grueling practices where the coaches were trying to impart our culture of accountability to that freshman class.

Two-thirds of the way through the season with the weight of the grind and new leadership challenges, it all caught up to me and I had a moment of breaking down. My hyper-responsible personality was carrying too much. I was very invested in my young team, and the intensity that I was pouring out to help them needed to come out in tears. I remember spending time with my mom shortly after as she helped me process and encouraged me.

I was not superhuman.

◆ ◆ ◆

Credit all.

On December 21, we won our eighty-ninth straight game by beating Florida State 93–62. Fittingly, I had a career-high 41 points.

All I could think about was the selflessness and toughness of all these UConn teams, about their drive to become better. We were standing on the shoulders of so many past players, of a historic program and the legacy of amazing players.

"It takes a group of people who are highly invested, unselfish, who do more than just what's required, do more than work together on the court," I told the media. "We're a group of people who are constantly around each other and look out for each other and care about each other off the court as well. This is a family, and that's how we treat it. We hold each other accountable. We will confront each other when we need to be confronted. We argue just like sisters do, and we'll also go to war for each other just like sisters do."

A week later, we continued the streak to ninety games as we headed to the West Coast, beating the Pacific Tigers 85–42.

All I know is that winning one game or ten games or ninety games in a row is so difficult because of all the parts and pieces of the game that have to come together. There are ten players on the court, so you have to keep track of your four other teammates along with the five on the other side. This is why basketball is extremely difficult and why it's so great. There would probably never have been a streak if this was a two-player sport. All along, there were five of us out on the court playing and picking each other up and being a part of history.

♦ ♦ ♦

Keep moving.

Holding our ninety-win streak in hand, or perhaps carrying it like a weight on our backs, UConn traveled out west to play against Stanford, the last team to beat us. The pressure was still there, but so was the desire to continue. We wanted this win so bad, but so did the opposing team. Stanford wanted to break our streak.

It was a tough game with Stanford playing with an overwhelming defense, keeping me scoreless for the first seventeen minutes of play. As the end approached, the Stanford crowd sounded like they were losing their minds. As I said, everybody loves an underdog. We ended up coming up short, losing 71–59.

As the reality of the loss and the end of the streak washed over me, I felt numb with disappointment. The emotion of everything gripped me as the leader of this team. There were tears flowing and shock. Looking back, I know I was simply exhausted. Like he always did, Coach A helped give us some perspective and some needed words of encouragement and wisdom.

"I've never lost sight of the fact that it is just a game," Coach Auriemma once said. "It is a bunch of people trying to get together to accomplish something that individually you can't do by yourself."

The streak was broken and our world felt weary and beat down. But as the plane took us from California back to Connecticut, I was reminded of what was coming next.

I have to go to class tomorrow.

◆ ◆ ◆

Accept the accolades.

Senior night was always a thrill for our team, but this year was different, since I would be one of the Huskies honored. The ceremony held at Gampel Pavilion before the game was emotional. As I stood on the court between my mom and my grandfather, holding the bouquet of flowers that had been given to me, the announcer began to list off the accomplishments of my past four years.

Three-time WBCA Wade Trophy honoree . . . Two-time winner of the Wooden and Naismith Awards . . . Three-time Big East Player of the Year . . . Two-time AP National Player of the Year . . . 2009 and 2010 NCAA Tournament Championships . . . Huskies' leading scorer . . . Single-season scoring record . . .

The longer he spoke, the more I wanted to hide, so I put the flowers in front of my face. When it was all spoken at once, the accomplishments were overwhelming. I couldn't help my emotions spilling over as I began to cry, thinking about how hard I had worked and how much this Husky family meant to me. So I kept looking at my grandfather's contagious grin and his pumping fist, and that made me smile. My grandfather, more than anyone I knew, was the best at celebrating people. I knew for certain he was the happiest person in the building. I loved this moment because of what it meant to him and everybody else in my family. At the end of the ceremony, I embraced my coach and sent a big thank-you to everyone in the stands. I had experienced so many opportunities in this building and with this university. I had been part of such a special group of individuals who all helped me reach my potential in so many areas.

♦ ♦ ♦

Finish with gratitude.

There is no single ingredient and no singular game. Every player and coach matters. Every match means something. The goal remains the same: Play well and win. But when the streak was broken and the season ended on a loss in the Final Four, I had to be grateful.

"I've learned what it takes to lead, and motivate other people," I told the press after the loss. "We all have to do our part. Coach Auriemma has taught me so much about the game—moving, different ways to score. But also, how you have to be invested in your teammates, making people feel like they're valuable, encouraging them and giving them confidence to be at their best."

I knew there was no way to fully show my love and appreciation for my coach and teammates and for this game, but I tried to share as much as I could.

"I've learned so many different leadership qualities that can't be taken away like a game can. It's been an amazing four years. I'm happy I was able to come to Connecticut and do what I was able to do. I feel I've done what I could. And it's cool to have it recognized and appreciated by so many fans, and, I hope, the women's game in general. I hope people have fallen in love with the game more because of our team and the competitiveness and heart we play with. I'd like to appreciate the bigger impact."

Maya and UConn teammates celebrating their national championship at a Huskies football game

Chapter Twelve

THE SOARING FALCON

(2007–2012)

(J)

I CAN'T BELIEVE IT.

I stared at the document and read it over again for the hundredth time. It was the latent report that Reggie had found after retrieving my files from the O'Fallon police station. The form itself looked different than the latent report that had been in the public defender's office and authorized with a blue stamp, but more importantly he had detected something completely different in the details listed on the form. It was a breathtaking discovery.

The typed details were clearly specified.

List of Latents: Interior smooth glass of front storm door above handle position.

Results of Comparison: Identifiable x 2

Elimination Prints Submitted on the Following: Irons, Jonathan

Latents Identifiable to this Subject: None 10-29-97

Over and over, I studied that line. *Identifiable x 2.* At first, I was confused and didn't know what to make of this. At trial, they had said that the fingerprints they had taken all belonged to the victim, but now we had this form that confirmed that only one of them belonged to the victim and there were two unidentified. They had fingerprints belonging to someone else. This critical evidence proved that someone else did it and that I wasn't involved in any way. This was our smoking gun.

The problem was, we couldn't just get a court hearing tomorrow and plead our case. It was going to take time to get someone to listen to us. I knew that because I had already been trying for years to get somebody to give me a chance to do the one thing I had not been able to do at my trial:

Speak up for myself.

Back in 2001, when I was spending as much time as possible in the library at The Walls, I wrote and filed my first Rule 29.15 motion. My first post-conviction motion alleging "ineffective assistance of trial counsel." I still remember those exact words as clearly as I did when I initially read about them. That was my first attempt. I was excited. I just knew I was going to win because they were wrong. There are adults in the room, and the judges are going to do the right thing.

Nope. That motion got denied. They referred to it as "harmless error." You could have a constitutional right violated, but due to the finality clause, they could simply sweep it under the rug and call it a harmless error. "Yes, it's an error, but it's harmless. NEXT!" Never once stopping to consider they had just convicted an innocent man.

As the years passed and I learned more about law, I continued to file for appeals and I made numerous claims. I was also helping other prisoners write their appeals. Before it was all over, I ended up losing eleven appeals in a row advocating for myself. But I had success with many of my fellow prisoners' appeals and prison condition complaints. So much of what I learned was trial and error, and I also enjoyed researching myself to sleep every night. But experience was my best teacher. It brought intangible concepts within my grasp. I enjoyed the discovery process and the journey of each legal pleading

I prepared. The more I learned about law, the more I could understand how to apply it to my case. As I researched and led the reinvestigation of my case through years, I discovered a comedy of constitutional violations and trial court errors. The lessons I learned from those losses spoke volumes to me about the mountain of adversity I was struggling to climb. They would tell me that I couldn't argue "actual innocence" because I didn't have new evidence, but I would try to argue that I was innocent as much as I could in all of my pleading.

Even after losing all the appeals for myself, I knew I had one last appeal. But my heart stirred with hope because I knew we were armed with new ammunition.

The battle was just starting. It would be a long and arduous campaign.

◆ ◆ ◆

After meeting Maya the summer of 2007 and first calling her as she was starting school, I would phone her and talk with her for twenty or thirty minutes. Maybe even an hour if we had the time. I insisted on paying for all my phone minutes from my paycheck. I wasn't going to let her pay a cent. This went on for years. Whenever I would call, I could tell she was excited to hear from me. She would try to find quiet places on campus where she could talk to me, whether they were in an area on the stairs or somewhere in the student union. I couldn't get away from the noise in my background, so I would put the receiver on my chin while I held the phone in one hand and cupped my ear with my other hand just so I could hear her voice. This kept the noise down, though sometimes she couldn't hear what I had said since I needed to adjust the receiver.

Our conversations were fun and casual, and we spoke about everything. Just kicking it, being friends, sharing our journeys with God and talking about her game and issues in the community. Of course, I was updating her on the case, but at the same time, we would be cutting up. I made a light threat every now and then, telling Maya I was going to dunk on her, trash-talking and making her laugh.

One day during her freshman year, as I was keeping track of how her UConn Huskies were beating everybody they played, Maya surprised me on our phone call.

"You know—you really inspire me," she said.

I was floored. "What are you talking about? Why do I inspire you?"

"You're transcribing math books into braille for the blind," Maya said. "You're using code and learning computer skills!"

I had told her about the job I had in the Center for Braille and Narration Production. Another job where I could learn and expand my knowledge base.

"I just think it's amazing—your determination and your perseverance. All these things you're doing and how hard you're working with your case."

"Well, you know. Before Reggie and Cheri came along, I was the only one interested in it. Now I have a lot more help."

Maya told me it wasn't just my persistence that inspired her. She spoke about my light and my ability to be alive while I was going through so much.

The way she uplifted me reminded me of her great-uncle, Papa Flowers.

"I just appreciate how much you encourage me and how you listen to me with everything you have going on in your life," Maya said.

She's thanking me? Everything going on in my life?

I was amazed by her comments, but I wasn't surprised. I knew the family she came from, and the foundation that gave her. I knew her firm convictions and shared her passionate faith. But suddenly having Reggie and Cheri and Maya in my world and on my side?

It gave me hope that miracles could happen.

◆ ◆ ◆

"I've been doing some investigating on the computer," Reggie told me in a quiet voice in the visitation room at JCCC. "I found out some things about the lead detective on your case."

Our conversations about the case were only held in person and not over the phone, since we knew phone calls were recorded. I knew people had noticed Reggie and Cheri coming around and talking about my case. I still had a target on my back after trying to help out a buddy in ad seg. So conversations like these were kept as private as they could be.

"I started looking into all the people involved, doing searches on Google and making my own notes," Reggie continued. "I found some interesting things about Hanlen."

Detective Michael Hanlen had been the lead detective on my case and was one of the guys who picked me up in Troy and brought me back to the police station. While interrogating me by himself, he had only taken notes during the interview but hadn't recorded it, and later he stated that he threw these notes away. As the supervisor, he had to initial all the reports that had been submitted. For medical reasons, Hanlen wasn't able to be there at my trial.

"I found a personal website where he wrote on a blog," Reggie said. "How he's Irish, likes to go to Ireland, that sort of stuff. I was clicking on links and one led me to something about the St. Louis Police Department. It was called 'War Stories.' They're stories about things that really happened, and they're very interesting. I'm mailing you copies of them."

"Interesting? How come?"

Reggie smiled in a way that told me he had some more important evidence.

"It gave me a different perspective of him. He's not the type of person that really accepts authority above him. In one of the stories, he basically bragged about planting evidence on a scene."

The pages Reggie had printed out from the detective's blog confirmed what he said. The website titled "War Stories" was a compilation of different events and details that happened to Detective Hanlen when he was a police officer in St. Louis. Included were stories about him planting evidence at crime scenes to cover up misconduct and conspiring to create false evidence in order to obtain a search warrant. There was a history of failing to report the misconduct of other police officers and altering facts to protect fellow officers.

After continuing to investigate online, Reggie came across a lawsuit that had been brought against Detective Hanlen that was happening around the same time as my trial. A federal civil suit had been filed against him as well as other officers on the O'Fallon Police Department force for egregious police misconduct.

Like the latent report we had discovered, this piece of information on Hanlen had never been disclosed to my public defender nor myself prior to my trial. Like so many other things, it would have been critical to my defense.

◆ ◆ ◆

Sometimes I dreamed about Damien. He was an Alaskan malamute I had when I was a kid. My cousin named him and gave him to me. Damien was one of the strongest dogs I've ever had in my life. Not just physically, but emotionally and mentally. When I was in elementary school, I used to walk around everywhere—in the woods and in the backcountry. I never had Damien on a leash, but he still always stayed within a ten-to-twenty-foot radius of me no matter what. He would go out and scout for me, and if someone wasn't safe or tried to walk up to me, he protected me. Once, a couple of farmers tried to approach me, but Damien stepped in between us and gave them a threatening look. He stood there with his tail up, basically shielding me. Sometimes I wonder if God was protecting me through that dog.

Damien was my buddy. When I got back home from school, he would meet me at the front of the driveway. It was crazy how he sensed when I was coming. Whenever I left him, he would watch me walk off, then go back home and my grandmother would put him back on his chain. He would've run off to find me if he wasn't kept on that chain.

One of the few things I missed the most being in prison was taking care of a dog. In 2007, that changed with an amazing program they brought to JCCC. For a while, we had been hearing rumors that they were going to bring dogs into the prison, but we were always like, "Yeah, sure. We've heard this before." They did that a lot—telling you they were going to do all of these things for the prison, just wait and see, overselling and underdelivering.

All we could hear was "We got dogs coming, blah blah blah blah ..." But then one day the first batch of dogs arrived, and our minds were blown.

"Wait ... Puppies? For real?"

The program was called Puppies for Parole, and the first ones they brought in were weaned but still young puppies that needed our care. Their poop didn't even have a scent, and their breath still smelled like gravy. They all had parvo, however, and the virus was highly contagious among dogs. If puppies weren't vaccinated for it in time, they would die if they got it. You had to either sanitize everywhere where they had been or burn fabrics and other things that they had been in so they didn't give the virus to other dogs. All the puppies eventually died except for three of them. But they made an impact on all of us who took care of them, and the prison continued to bring in more.

I shared a brindle-colored puppy named Bentley with Gary, my cellie. We used to jokingly fight about who got to hold the puppy the longest. I never thought I'd see a dog again, much less take care of one. When they brought dogs back into prison, it brought something back to life inside me. Not only did I get to have a dog and take care of him 24-7, but I got to learn how to treat him and train him and take care of him in the right way. It was priceless.

The director that brought this program into Jefferson City Correctional Center had seen how other prisons had benefited from dogs being brought in and how it helped offenders reduce recidivism. It taught parenting skills and job skills, but more importantly it brought out compassion and empathy from inmates. JCCC was an extremely dangerous place, where violence happened daily to staff and prisoners. But when they brought the dogs to prison, you gradually saw a whole culture shift. Guys who were hardened and hard-core criminals who terrified people—the sort of inmates who wouldn't fight you but stab you—would go up to the dogs or the dogs would run up to them, and suddenly they would be using baby talk while playing with the animals. When the dogs showed up, COs began to see inmates in another light, and inmates saw staff (especially the ones who really loved dogs) in another light as well.

This is the beauty of dogs. Their arrival brought in a culture of seeing men's true hearts like never before. Guys who I was cool with, who I shared a measure of respect and honor with. When we saw each other groveling and caring and tending to these animals that needed our guidance, it made you love these other men. We grew deep, genuine brotherly love for each other. You cared for them as a real person. Instead of seeing other inmates and second-guessing something they said or did, you gave them the benefit of the doubt. It was so dynamic how Puppies for Parole changed the prison environment for dog lovers. But even non–dog lovers loved it because they began to receive benefits and reap the rewards of the program. For example, in order to raise money for the dogs, we had sales projects where we got items that normally weren't sold on the canteen, but since the money could be saved for the benefit of the dogs, the prison allowed it. So even inmates and staff who didn't like dogs could all agree that they were good to have at JCCC.

They didn't just let the dogs stay with anybody. In order to get to be in the program, you had to have an exemplary prison record. For starters, you couldn't be a sex offender. You couldn't have any assaults on staff on your record, and you had to have gone a long time without a conduct violation. In prison, that's an amazing thing since there's basically a rule for everything. They even have a catch-22 rule that basically allows them to get you for anything they want to. So, in order to have an exemplary record, you had to walk on eggshells and just decide that no matter what happened, you needed to be on your best behavior. That's the attitude I took every day I woke up.

Thank you, God, for this day. I'm in a bad place, but I'm gonna try to be the best I can. I need to be grateful for this day. This ain't my home. I'm just passing through here. But let me take advantage of anything I can today.

This mindset enabled me to live in a way that kept me out of trouble for many, many years. It gave me privileges like taking care of a dog. I wasn't an anomaly; there were other inmates who had that same attitude. But a good record took a lot of hard work and a lot of patience and prayer.

Another basic requirement for being in the program was that you really had to love dogs, since they were going to be staying in the cell with you.

Your cell became a kennel. Cells were already small enough; some people have filed civil suits about not having enough space in their jail cell. But we were like, "We'll take the dogs!" We had all shapes and sizes of dogs. Great Danes, pit bulls, little bitty terriers . . . any type of dog you could name.

For those of us in the program, we started watching videos and reading manuals about how to take care of puppies. We learned from each other and taught each other. And eventually they brought in dog trainers. The further I got into the program, the more I could teach dogs different things based on trial and error and the principles that I learned through dog training, studying them, and then just the literature that we had. We did all sorts of training, like service work training and therapy training and Canine Good Citizen training. Somebody bought a college course and brought that into JCCC, but by then we didn't need it.

For over seven and a half years with only a few breaks in between, I had a dog with me all day long. I acquired over fifteen thousand hours on record with the US Department of Labor of hands-on training with many dogs while also training other people to do the same with their dogs. I learned how to do that inside prison. Now people look at the things I can do with dogs, and they ask me how I'm able to do it. They think it's witchcraft.

◆ ◆ ◆

"Hey, J! Your girl is going down."

Halftime had just started for the 2010 NCAA women's championship, and UConn was losing to Stanford 20–12. I sat with close to twenty other guys watching Maya and her Huskies on two fifty-five-inch televisions placed in the middle of the room. Normally I watched her games on the thirteen-inch TV in my cell, but as the facilitator/counselor of the Intensive Therapeutic Community, I had asked for the televisions to be brought in so that the guys in my group could watch different sports games. This was a privilege of being part of the group, and an incentive for inmates to join the rehabilitation program.

"Maya only got two baskets," a guy said.

"Stanford's too tough," another added. "The winnin' streak's comin' to an end."

"Just you wait," I said with full confidence.

The inmates were off the chain and let loose with trash talk. They knew about my friendship with Maya and her family, so some of them rooted for her because they were my friends, while others rooted against just because it was Maya. The guys were giving me a hard time now, since it actually looked like UConn *might* lose, and they never lost.

"Everybody calm down," I told them. "She's gonna hit those big shots."

"A thousand push-ups says she loses," my buddy Jackson said to me.

Instead of wagering money, we bet push-ups with each other. If you won a push-up from someone, you could be anywhere in prison—outside or in the shower or the cafeteria—and tell the guy to do a push-up. He would have to drop down and give you one, no debating whatsoever. I had already won five hundred push-ups off a few other guys betting on Maya.

"You sure you wanna do all those push-ups?" I asked.

Jackson was serious, so it was on. Everybody watched how UConn made history in the second half with the most points ever scored in a half. As the Huskies roared back to life and went ahead, the guys who had been talking trash grew quiet. So quiet. Especially Jackson.

I had him doing push-ups for the next two years.

◆ ◆ ◆

Other than watching Maya beating up on other teams or catching a game with the ITC group, I didn't spend time watching sports or anything else on TV. Studying the law and becoming good at it is a cruel master. It requires a lot of time every day, and you have to make a choice. Either you can open up the books and expand your mind or decide to play ball or watch TV and remain ignorant. I chose the books.

Learning how to train dogs resembled how I went about studying the law. There was a caseworker assigned to oversee the Puppies for Parole program, and we had access to their office. That meant we had a television to watch all the instructional videos on and magazines and books we could access. All the instructions were right there. We also had instructors come in, and it's always good to learn from one, but nothing beats having the ability to have a hands-on experience and to study what you're learning on your own. Teaching yourself and allowing yourself to be taught how to train a dog was amazing; you couldn't go to school and get that type of knowledge. That's how I felt about my time going to "law school."

Every day I spent time picking away at my case. When I wasn't working, I'd be in the library finding little details of things that had gone wrong in my trial and investigation. Little blocks that I was stacking up. I wanted to know and reinvestigate everything in my case based on my new understanding of the law, so I went through everything line by line, looking up definitions and quotations and forms and statements.

After studying juvenile law, I discovered that I had been certified improperly. I had a misdemeanor on my record for tampering with a car, but according to Missouri statutory law, a juvenile can only be certified as an adult permanently if he is charged with and convicted of a felony. The charge that I was certified for was a misdemeanor charge. My grandmother and I had questioned this at the time, but my attorney only said she would get back to us on it. Two years passed while I turned eighteen waiting to go to trial. Nothing could have been done to correct this problem once I had been certified.

At my trial, the prosecutor had lied and said it was a gun charge on my record, but I never had a gun charge. He had swept it under the rug with that lie. At the time I had thought, *Why would the prosecutor lie about that?* Now as I pondered on that and continued to do research, I realized that me being improperly certified was illegal. The prosecutor hadn't wanted the judge to spend time going back and looking at that. He knew I had been improperly certified. At the very least, I should have been taken to a juvenile court and processed for this case.

I came to my wit's end when I realized the brutal truth: I couldn't bring in any new evidence. I had new evidence that would prove my innocence, but I couldn't talk about it in a courtroom. I had no lawyer that I could trust, and I learned from experience that judges don't listen to prisoners who are forced to represent themselves in court, especially when they are claiming to be innocent. I wasn't about to blow my last shot by representing myself in court.

Over the years, I also learned that I needed to be careful looking for another attorney, because there are some awful lawyers blending in with good ones that will pretend to care about your situation until you pay them. They will take your money and do nothing for you for various reasons. All I could do was keep digging away. Day after day, week after week, month after month. Questioning everything. *Why did he say this? What did she really mean? Why is it written like this? What does the law say about this?* Hoping, somehow, I would find the right attorney or team of attorneys.

We had been working with a lawyer for a while and given him the latent report that Reggie found, but it had simply gotten put into a file and nothing had really been done about it. After we started working with the Innocence Project, they connected us with law students. They had a program where we allowed students to pull down files in order to work on my case. The Innocence Project worked on my case for years, but they had limited resources and a lot of other cases, so it was difficult to get momentum with them. I went through three directors at the Innocence Project, and each time one left, my file would be closed. That meant I had to start everything over by filling out all my paperwork once more and starting at the bottom of the list again and then waiting to hear back from them.

I kept working and I filed a habeas petition for the illegal juvenile certification process. I had learned how to challenge my certification into adult court through the lengthy process of studying law. Habeas corpus is a right provided by the Constitution protecting against unlawful imprisonment, but it was an extraordinary procedure to file one. I had conversations with professors regarding it, and after writing my initial draft, I sent it to some professors to review. They were impressed with it, telling me that it resembled the work of a third- or fourth-year law student. One of the professors encouraged me to file it, saying I could wait for them to be back in session to have the students look it over, but at that point, I was tired of talking to students and being repeatedly interviewed by law students. So I sent out the habeas petition, but it got denied. It went all the way up to the Missouri Supreme Court, but in the end, it was rejected.

◆ ◆ ◆

Despite the jobs I worked in and the small amount of money I was earning and the skills I was developing, I was still behind bars in a maximum-security prison. Even though I felt like I had been adopted into Papa Flowers's family with Reggie, Cheri, and Maya, I still was on my own, living in a home full of sociopaths and psychopaths. There were people like me who were unjustly imprisoned, but then there were bad dudes who needed to be separated from the rest of the public. Then, on top of that, there were individuals with serious mental health issues existing among us. Prisons are full of people like this, and it's well documented because people have sued the Department of Corrections nationwide for keeping the mentally ill living with people who don't have those conditions.

I saw the danger of this being played out one day in the cafeteria. One inmate walked up to another and asked him for the cookie on his plate. "No, man, you can't have my cookie," the guy said as he just walked past him. The next day, the guy asking for the cookie came and stabbed the other guy. Killed him. It turned out the assailant had a severe mental heath issue.

Most of the time, the guys with untreated psychiatric conditions were spotted because their behavior weeded them out. But there were some who functioned at a higher level, knowing if they acted up and showed too much, they'd get a shot in the butt with Haldol, an antipsychotic medication that would keep them doped out for thirty days. They didn't want that, so they would act normal and greet the COs and do what they were supposed to do, but then when they got in a cell with someone else, they'd be a whole different person. They'd turn into a real-life Dr. Jekyll and Mr. Hyde. I had a couple of them I had to deal with over the course of serving time.

As an inmate, you literally had to examine and check everyone around you. You had to notice everything. You had to listen to every statement and watch every interaction until you knew who they were. Strangers needed to be tried and tested before you knew they were okay to be around. So, when you got friends in prison—genuine men you could confide in—it was like discovering treasure on a deserted island.

I was still in a dark place with evil people. And I was still being hounded by a staff that didn't want to see me succeed with my case in any way.

After seeing my habeas petition get denied, I felt defeated. Then, to add to this, I got put in ad seg for no reason. An inmate had been locked up playing with games on the computer, and a CO who didn't like me was put in charge of the investigation. He began to randomly snatch people he wanted to send to the hole, and naturally I was one of them. I knew now what to do—I appealed and fought for myself, filing the necessary paperwork that said I didn't do anything to be put into the hole.

Being in the hole meant I had lost my job and wasn't getting a paycheck. This was the money I was using to talk to Maya on a regular basis, and it went to the money I was saving for legal fees. They had said that there were all these things on my computer, so I told them to produce the record and show it, but they couldn't do it. They eventually admitted that the guy who got the violation never said that me or any others had anything to do with it, so I won my appeal and put more pressure on them. Because of the work I did, five other people who were locked up in ad seg were released and given their jobs back. Of course, none of us got back the income that was stolen from us.

◆ ◆ ◆

Something happened to me while I was stuck in solitary confinement that first time at JCCC, something I haven't told many people. Something that remains with me to this day.

The cell felt suffocating and sparse. Looking out my front door, all I could see was the long walk with all the weirdos stuck in their own cells. My bed was a concrete slab, and there was no mirror in the cell. A window above me was covered, so if I stood on the slab I could see a sliver of sky through the window slits.

One day, I stood looking up at the sky and talking to God.

"Lord, I'm struggling right now. Just encourage me."

As I stared at the blue above me, a falcon flew by. I smiled as I watched it soar and glide with such ease and freedom. Ever since I was a kid, I've always loved looking at birds. I enjoyed drawing eagles.

"Whoa," I said. "Okay, Lord. Thank you for this."

The bird flew off and I waited, but the sky remained empty.

Did He really hear my prayer? Did that just happen?

"Lord, thank you for that. But please send the bird back."

Sure enough, the narrow wings and curved beak once again appeared. The falcon turned and darted down, then shot up again. I watched in wonder.

I sat down with my mind replaying the image of the bird over and over again. My doubts and unease still remained inside me. Later that afternoon, the falcon hadn't left my thoughts. You don't have much to think about in the hole, so I kept wondering about it. *There's not going to be a falcon up there.* I eventually couldn't help myself. I stood back on the concrete slab and peered out the window. There was no bird.

"Lord, let me see this bird again. I just wanna know if this is really You, if You're really talkin' to me, if You're tryin' to encourage me. 'Cause I feel low. Lower than a bow-legged caterpillar."

As I stood there, with no exaggeration and in full honesty as I write this, a falcon flew right where I could see him.

"Come on, no!" I shouted out.

This was no accident, no fluke. God knew I was there. He was in control. He heard me. And He had a plan. But, oh, we humans can be so weak, can't we?

The next day, it rained, so I didn't think about looking up in the sky, yet the following day, I decided to once again push it. Was I testing God? Maybe? But I needed comfort. I needed confirmation God was hearing me.

"Okay, Lord. Show me two birds if this is You trying to encourage me."

Perhaps this was too bold of a prayer, but as Granny had told me, always talk to God and always be honest. Open up your heart and tell Him everything. So I did.

I climbed back on the hard concrete and stood on the tips of my toes, and I scanned the heavens. Dancing in the sky were two falcons, circling and swooping and living and breathing. The sight took my breath away. I began to cry.

"Thank you, Lord. Thank you."

Losing the habeas petition had left me discouraged and depressed. But seeing those falcons after praying to God helped me get the wind in my own sails again to keep moving. To keep flying higher.

You learned how to do a habeas corpus petition, J. The majority of lawyers don't know how to do it, but you learned how to do it.

It was the first time I had gone through the procedure, and I had learned the things I did right and what I had done wrong. My whole understanding was expanded.

You've reached the mountaintop, J. But you gotta keep flying.

The only person I told about the falcons was Maya. She doubted neither the story nor God's goodness. Instead, she summed it up the only way Maya could.

"Birds are a reminder," Maya said. "God uses everything from His creation to love His children. I feel like that was an intentional moment to be a continual reminder to you of what He did and who He is to you in those moments. Sometimes when you're feeling good, it's just a cool thing to look up and see birds flying. But sometimes you might be feeling low and really need that reminder that you're not alone."

Jonathan training a smart border collie named Roxie

Chapter Thirteen

THE ROLE
MODEL

(2011–2012)

(M)

IT HAD BEEN almost four years since I first met Jonathan at Jefferson City Correctional Center. Over the years, he had opened up and told me more about his time at MSP.

"The Walls sounded terrible," I told Jonathan over the phone after hearing his description of the prison.

We had been on the phone for an hour, and he had been sharing some anecdotes about his time at the infamous Missouri State Penitentiary.

"Yeah, it was a bad place," Jonathan said. "But you know—there was some funny stuff that happened there, too. So listen to this story—can you still talk for a few more minutes?"

"Sure."

"I gotta tell you about the old 'Walkie-Talkie Caper.' So, like I've said, there were some bad COs, but there was one who was a real terror. Name was Jones. So this was around 2001 or 2002, I think. This particular correctional officer, he would come in a prisoner's cell and just toss it. It's basically like somebody coming into your house and taking all your dishes, throwing them on the floor. And if you've made your bed, he's coming and snatching the covers off and then putting boot prints on your sheets. He'd do senseless stuff, coming by and going through your paperwork, saying, 'I'm looking for a knife. I'm looking for a shank.' All along he's just being cruel, getting a sick sense of power."

"He did this to your cell?" I asked.

"Oh yeah. Several times. So, one day, CO Jones searched this guy's cell and forgot his walkie-talkie and left it in there. And this was the best thing that could've happened, because it made all the prisoners united against him just because of how bad he treated us. It was a hot and miserable summer, and we just always felt like we were losing. It's the opposite of your teams—we felt like we never had a single win. So Jones left his walkie-talkie, and when he was gone, one of the guys living in that cell yelled out and told the rest of us what happened. The guys were like, 'Pass it down the walk 'cause he's gonna come back.' So everybody on the walk grabbed and reached out and passed the walkie-talkie down the walk."

I laughed and could picture where this story was headed.

"Sure enough, that officer and about ten other COs came back and searched that cell," Jonathan said in a tone that made me picture his smile. "They searched every cell on that wall, but they couldn't find the walkie-talkie. They didn't tear up cells, however, because the supervisor was with them and they weren't supposed to do that. That was illegal. So about two days later, we hear somebody calling out, '1049.' That means 'fight.' '1049 on the handball courts.' You see about thirty guards run to the handball courts. And then, about five minutes later, somebody said on the walkie-talkie, '1049 in the chow hall.' That whole group of guards, once they realized there wasn't no fight in the handball courts, they ran to the chow hall. And then again: 'There's a 1049 in the school!' Then they ran to the school."

"Are you serious?"

"Yeah. And then they heard '1050,' which means 'officer needs assistance.' So about a hundred COs—you just see them just running around on the yard trying to figure out where this assault happened because they said it happened right in front of the chapel. And like everybody in their cells were just bustin' out laughing. We had been through so much harassment with this guard, it just felt like poetic justice."

"So what happened to the walkie-talkie?"

"Nobody knows what happened to that walkie-talkie. That's one thing you don't do—you don't do no snitching and you don't tell about what's going on in there, so nobody knew what happened to the walkie-talkie. CO Jones thankfully ended up getting fired. He was already on probation for his conduct, so that was like his last straw. I will never forget that moment when they let us out to go to the rec yard. It was probably about five hours later in the evening, and the temperature had cooled off. Guys were stampeding out into the yard and everybody's spirits were uplifted. Even people who didn't get along were talking. It eased tensions for a short while. We banded together and got a win after a thousand losses. We finally got our national championship. It didn't last long, but it was worth it. It was worth it because that CO was a bad man."

"It's a good thing you moved out of that place," I said.

"Yeah—The Walls was the bottom of the barrel. JCCC has improved because of some of the programs being allowed to thrive there. I'd give JCCC on a scale of one to ten, one being a Guatemalan or South American prison and ten being like Club Fed, where you basically get to live on a resort and you're never in your cell. A place where you get personal visits with the best food—where they're just basically getting paid to babysit you for however long. Yeah, JCCC would probably be a three. And it's hard to jump to a four. The Walls was a one point five."

Jonathan paused and sighed.

"Those were some bad days back then."

◆ ◆ ◆

As I reflected on Jonathan sharing some of those memories of The Walls with me, I thought about where I was at in my life. My senior year was finishing and the WNBA draft was approaching and my future looked bright. There were so many things I had accomplished in my life, and playing for the Huskies had been more transformative than I could have imagined. But my fondness for the past has never taken the luster off my present. I shared this in an interview back in 2011.

"I never want to say that I had glory days. I like to think that every new year there's something great that can happen, something great will happen, whether it's a basketball thing or an off-the-court thing."

The month of April was a whirlwind. On April 3, we were drying our tears in the locker room after losing in the Final Four to Notre Dame, but the following night we were cheering on our guys as they beat Butler 53–41 and won their third NCAA championship. I was calling the agent that I still work with today to say I wanted to work with her. And then draft day came on April 11.

As the WNBA draft approached with all the buzz and opinions and predictions, I had been able to drown out the noise. UConn has such a great legacy of preparing players for the pros and I felt ready. All the individual awards and honors through the season had just been icing on the cake as I finished playing at UConn. I did a good job of staying focused and making sure I was the person and the basketball player I needed to be. By the time draft night arrived, I had done all the work I could and knew that the predictions had me going to the Twin Cities, so I was excited to see what happened.

When the Minnesota Lynx chose me as the number-one overall pick, I was thrilled to be going to an exciting team that had been an injury away from making the playoffs in 2010 and a shot away from making them in 2009. The Lynx were not a bad team. The worst teams in the league were supposed to get the best draft picks, but this year the pieces fell together so perfectly because of the challenges they had faced and the players they were adding. Under the guidance of Coach Cheryl Reeve, who was named head coach at the end of 2009, the Lynx had picked up Rebekkah Brunson and traded for Lindsay Whalen in 2010, then added Taj McWilliams-Franklin in free agency before the 2011 season. Seimone Augustus was coming back healthy.

This team had all the makings to be great.

The Minnesota Lynx had only made the playoffs twice but never advanced to the conference finals. Sports fans in Minnesota longed for some kind of success but hadn't seen any in a long time. Coach Reeve had been an assistant coach with the Detroit Shock when they won championships in 2006 and 2008, so she knew success and intended to bring it to this state. So did I.

"I know the fans here are desperate for something to cheer for, and that makes me excited," I said in an interview after the draft. "I like to make history. I like to do things that have never been done before. We did a lot of that at UConn. I might as well keep it up."

Joining this great group was another exciting milestone in the long line I liked to call my career; I looked forward to getting back to work and trying to accomplish more in the professional league.

Everything happened so quickly. One moment, I was finishing up my classes at UConn; the next, I was packing up my apartment so I could arrive in Minneapolis on time for the start of training camp. No rest for the weary. And *definitely* no time for a graduation party! These would have to wait. So I took a breath and kept moving.

Right away I was struck with the physicality of the game and how everybody was bigger. Part of training camp was just getting a feel for the other players and learning the offense. I wanted to observe as much as possible while jumping in when I could. We immediately clicked as a team and knew we had the potential to be special. Coach Reeve and the general manager had orchestrated a great combination of players. A powerful combination.

I was keenly aware of how God had allowed me to be drafted into a situation that players only dream of. I was a rookie amongst greats! A lot of times high draft picks went to poor teams, so the rookies had a lot of pressure on them to take over and be the star and carry the team. But that's never realistic and that's not how the league works. Everybody coming in needs time to grow and learn. That was the mindset I carried with me. I wanted to listen and to learn from these vets. I wanted to allow them to help me grow. At the same time, I wanted to do my job as well. I wanted to compete and do what I knew I could do. So entering my first year on the Lynx, I felt like I wasn't asked to do anything that I couldn't do, and that was because of the incredible veterans surrounding me.

This was another beautiful aspect to my career. God opened doors for me to be surrounded by really great people—coaches and players and family and friends—who helped me appreciate that the game is bigger than one player or coach. Having that modeled for me at a young age helped prepare me to navigate the spotlight the pro industry requires. I wasn't burned out by this sport; I was enjoying the excitement of this new chapter. And I had the solid foundation of my faith and family. My identity was even more firm in Christ than in the name I had gained as a basketball player. This foundation would be essential in helping me find my way on a new team and as a new face of a legendary brand.

◆ ◆ ◆

"I'm sorry . . . What?"

I was talking to my agent about companies interested in meeting with me to discuss an endorsement deal, and I couldn't believe what she had just told me.

"Michael Jordan is interested in signing me to his brand?" I said. "For real? Let's talk about this."

After playing my last game and finishing up our season, I was free to meet and talk with managers and companies about my future. I had met with different agents the previous fall and knew the one I wanted to work with when I was allowed to contact her. She had already been working and came prepared with opportunities. The first deal you make as a professional athlete is the shoe-and-apparel endorsement, so I went to New York with my agent to hear presentations from different companies. The Jordan Brand was one of them. I didn't have to think about it very long. It was an amazing opportunity.

"As a student of the game, it is a dream come true to align myself with a brand that has a rich history in sports," I said in a statement. "Like most kids, I grew up idolizing Michael Jordan. I'm truly motivated to take my career to the next level as a member of Team Jordan."

I was excited to be the first female basketball player on the Jordan Brand. I felt like a trailblazer knowing how this would bring more attention to women's basketball and basketball in general, along with more exposure to women's sports in the media. While the brand didn't have women's apparel at the time, the move made a lot of sense for both parties, a chance to do something new in our sport. I felt like it ended up being a big cultural moment for the game of basketball.

I got to meet MJ, and this new journey began. A few years into my career, we started a girls' all-American game with the Jordan Brand Classic. Eventually we got some women's apparel into the market and had some player-edition shoes created and did other things to bring some excitement around the cultural side of the game.

There's a funny sort of irony with this partnership. I'm not a sneakerhead like some players, yet I have access to the world of Jordan. Some of my teammates were big sneakerheads. Like Seimone. She's a huge sneakerhead. Learning from her and watching her engage in the sneaker world taught me a few things. I always tried to hook my teammates up when I could with different shoes. It's fun to be able to share that arena with the women's basketball world.

Being named the first female basketball ambassador for the Jordan Brand was both symbolic and substantial. The most visible athlete in the world saw something in me and elevated me to a platform where I could give back visibility to young athletes everywhere. I never could have imagined as an eight-year-old that one day I would be helping to change basketball culture, and that I'd be doing that in partnership with the man whose greatness changed the basketball world.

◆ ◆ ◆

Any time you have greatness around you, it's going to bring out your best if you really strive to be great. I came into a really great situation with the

Minnesota Lynx. The group of people that we had around was just phenomenal. The coaching staff kept great expectations for us and helped push us, while the players kept their egos in check and pushed one another. We had a group of vets who knew what it was going to take.

One of those vets I got to watch and learn from was Seimone, who herself was a number-one overall draft pick by the Lynx in 2006. The incredibly talented guard led our team in scoring as well as being a clutch defender my rookie year. As I transitioned from being a power forward in college to now being a small forward in the best league in the world, Seimone helped me to learn my new role, especially on defense. The challenge was adjusting to playing more with the ball in my hands and going from defending power forwards to now running around chasing bigger guards or sometimes even smaller guards. The team gave me the space I needed as I made this transition as a rookie.

There was so much to learn about the new rhythm of life playing in the WNBA. As someone who had been playing in the league since 1999, Taj McWilliams-Franklin was one of the leaders on our team who showed me what life as a pro looked like. I basically followed Taj around that season, just trying to learn from her because she clearly knew what she was doing. She was not just unbelievably professional but a lot of fun to be around, and she endured a lot of questions from me that year. Rebekkah Brunson was another player I watched and learned from. Both ladies were true pros who showed me how to carry myself throughout the routines and the schedules. Our team had a lot of fun. When you had personalities like Lindsay Whalen, Monica Wright, Seimone, Taj, and Rebekkah, you were going to have silly moments. This was our squad for several seasons. We had a lot of fun, and we worked really hard.

When I arrived in Minnesota, I knew the person that I was and how important it was to get connected spiritually with my community, and to continue to grow and be rooted in some capacity with my faith family. I had worked hard in college at staying updated with my church online and making sure I didn't go through a week without making that a part of it.

Even though I had a demanding basketball schedule and traveled a lot, technology allowed me to still soak in some great sermons. I knew how important it was to make church in some form a priority, because it was easy to let it slip away due to the busyness of life. It was like anything important in your life: You needed to make time for it. And I knew I needed to do the same in the WNBA.

I had developed some very close church family friends through my college ministry experience, so I strived to keep in touch with them and continue to grow those relationships. Just like I did with Jonathan, I kept long-distance friendships with people in my church family and my friends. I tried to get established with a church in Minnesota, but it was really difficult because our schedule was very, very rigid. If we had a shootaround or a game on a Sunday, I couldn't really gather or connect. Thankfully we had awesome chaplains that became so essential to our well-being and our rhythm as pros by being a consistent place for us to go for our mental and spiritual support as women. Over time, I became very close with our Lynx chaplains and the different chaplains they had in every city.

I believe it is so important for professional athletes to know they are more than just players for a team and a league. They are humans that have hearts and souls. It gave me great comfort to know that if we wanted that support from chaplains, whether it was on game days or not, it was always there. This helped keep me anchored and remind me I was more than just a basketball player. I remain so grateful for all the chaplains I knew. We would have Bible studies weekly or every other week when our schedules allowed, with our chaplains leading. They would be held at our apartments and whoever wanted to come could come. We started to get a rhythm of doing that. Over the latter half of my career, I always hosted the study when the chaplains came. One of my favorite parts of the basketball season was getting a chance to go below the surface and really connect with my teammates as people and to allow them to see more of what was going on inside me. This was how we were able to support each other and grow in a way that was different than on the basketball court.

◆ ◆ ◆

"Every year the goal is a championship," I told ESPN before my rookie season began. "That's what I expect. I go on to every team expecting to win a championship, especially with the amount of talent we have. I don't want to limit to the playoffs, I want to win a championship."

The goal whenever I've played a game is to win. It can be Ping-Pong or basketball or even checkers, as a certain somebody knows. It's not that I'm necessarily wanting to beat others, but it's more that I want to do my best and continue to grow as a player. Winning takes time and work and strengths and skills. It comes down to having the desire and trying to be the best you can be. It's also about being put into a position with a team and an environment that allows you to win. This was what happened when we won our first championship for the Minnesota Lynx.

After the great training camp, we realized our team had an awesome energy and chemistry, but it was still surprising to see our league-high overall record of 27–7. I felt like I had ups and downs throughout the season as I tried to get a feel for playing at a professional level, but near the end of the year, I started getting a rhythm. I wanted to do everything I could to contribute and provide a spark and a lift to our team.

We entered the WNBA playoffs in October with a dramatic three-game series with the San Antonio Silver Stars. After Seimone drained a late jumper and Lindsay deflected an inbounds pass with four seconds left, we survived Game 1 with a 66–65 victory. After losing our second game, we beat a very good Stars team and made it through the first round. We ended up facing the Atlanta Dream in the finals, and since we had a better record, we played the first two games at home. After two straight wins, we headed to Atlanta for a chance to sweep the series and become champions.

There was a poetic symmetry in that 73–67 victory against the Dream in Game 3 to capture a title for Minnesota. We were playing at the Philips Arena in Atlanta, a short drive away from where I had made so many high-school memories. A lot of my family came to the game, and we played great. I had won my first college national championship with my UConn team in 2009, and the Final Four was in St. Louis. So, after winning my first college national championship in my first home state of Missouri, it was sweet to have my first professional championship happen in my other home state of Georgia.

It was also awesome to see Seimone end up getting the finals MVP. We were all really emotional and so happy for her, since she had worked so hard to be dominant again after her season-ending knee injury. We were excited to finally give the Twin Cities a championship. Fans had been thirsty for some success, and they had supported us all season long. It was great to see them setting records in attendance, meeting us at the airport when we came back and flooding us with enthusiasm with a victory parade and pep rally. There was a lot of media attention. We all felt like we had taken a lot of steps forward with getting some energy and visibility for the WNBA.

◆ ◆ ◆

I've always been a role model, even when I was younger. You become one when you grow up as the oldest kid in a group of cousins. I've always had the mindset of a role model, so it wasn't a new concept as I became more recognized playing basketball. What had changed was the platform that I had, and the chance I had to be a role model to many younger people out there. With women in sport still a relatively new thing in our American culture, a lot of new opportunities were increasing for girls in sports. I felt that doors were constantly opening for me. Winning championships. College visits. Nike All-American. USA Basketball. Undefeated teams. Schools across the country knocking. College scholarship offers. The streak. Drafted number one.

With every door opening, I just kept grinding and working, trying to grow and mature. I wanted to use my wisdom and opportunities for God's glory. To always be prayerful and try to lean into what He was teaching me every day. My identity as a child of God was always the lens that I used when saying yes or no to opportunities. Taking these opportunities might have looked seamless, but at the same time, when I look back, I know my mom and I could never in a million years have predicted how our lives would have unfolded.

Once again, that path brought us to the White House. When President Obama welcomed the Minnesota Lynx to the White House to celebrate our 2011 victory, he described what our success meant to him and to the world of women's sports.

"As the husband of a tall, good-looking woman and as the father of two tall, fabulous girls, it is just wonderful to have these young ladies as role models," President Obama said. "There's something about women's athletics. They play the game the right way. They compete fiercely. And so they're just wonderful examples for my daughters and my nieces and for so many parents. So I want to say thank you to all of you. Congratulations."

It felt wonderful to be a role model for young girls. I just wanted to keep moving and honor God in whatever way I could, as I stated publicly.

"I'm not going to put a limit on what God wants, so anything He wants me to do is what I want to do."

Kathryn and Maya after being drafted into the WNBA
as the number-one overall pick in 2011

Chapter Fourteen

THE
MOMENT

(2012–2013)

(M)

IN A FOREIGN land, I held the red, pink, and white teddy bear in my hands and looked at the note accompanying it.

Happy Valentine's Day!

Jonathan

I couldn't help smiling as the bear with bright, inquisitive eyes beamed at me.

Why is he sending me a Valentine? We're not dating.

The gift was unexpected, especially since I was now living in Valencia, the third-largest city in Spain. Located on the east coast, the city had miles of sandy beaches and boasted over three hundred sunny days every year. I had arrived in January and was currently playing for Ros Casares Valencia, the Spanish professional basketball team competing in the EuroLeague. After a busy 2011 of finishing at UConn and joining the Lynx to win a championship, I was now looking at an even busier 2012. I had a chance to win four potential championships: the EuroLeague, the Spanish league, the WNBA, and the Olympics. I was taking one day at a time, adjusting to yet another new team and also a new environment. Thankfully my mom had come with me on my first trip overseas; we were living in a nice apartment in this quaint two-thousand-year-old city.

The basketball rhythm for a WNBA player was very exhausting, since we were essentially playing year-round to maximize our income and make it worthy of the work we put into this particular area of life. Overseas was really where we made our money. I've seen that start to change; there has been a lot of improvement in getting paid more for the world-class work and talent and product that we put on the court. But the reality of playing year-round was unrelenting, and then if you were a USA Basketball Olympic-level pro, that meant you essentially played three seasons every other calendar year. I had started to become more aware of this after becoming part of the US women's national team as a collegiate player. As the youngest player on the Olympic team, I became exposed to the pros and to pro life, to how they lived and what the rhythm of that next level looked like. So in 2011, I began talking through overseas contracts with my agent, having to figure out answers to questions like "What do I want to do?" and "Where can I go?" and "What teams are available, and what are they offering?" It was exciting as I began to enter this arena.

While I explored the opportunities I had in front of me, I also stayed mindful of my health and well-being. By the grace of God, I was very in tune with myself and my humanity as my pro career began, so I knew going from the full senior year at UConn into a very competitive first year in the WNBA that I was going to need a break. I sensed that going directly overseas after the Lynx season was not going to be good for me. I needed to be home and rest. To breathe. So I worked it out with my agent to negotiate a contract for my first year overseas to be a half season.

The way the overseas market worked was that the better a player you were, the more negotiating power you had with the teams. Even though I was a rookie and wasn't as experienced as the vets, I still had a good amount of negotiating power. That's how I got my half-season deal. Obviously, I didn't get paid as much as I would have if I had to play the whole season, but I was fine with that. You couldn't put a price on the blessing of being at home and finding some stillness in your life.

That Thanksgiving after my rookie season was the first I was able to spend in Georgia in the past four or five years. To call it a relaxing Thanksgiving was an understatement, as I celebrated the holiday with around forty family members at my new home in the west side of metro Atlanta. We had a wonderful time with food, laughs, and celebration.

The two-and-a-half-month break from basketball allowed me time for some physical therapy to get my knees back where they needed to be. I had endured patellar tendinitis for my whole career, ever since starting to get it in both of my knees during my sophomore year in high school. That's when I developed a routine of stretching and icing to try to help reduce that pain and make sure I was ready to play and train. I've always been diligent with my warmup and recovery routine, always stretching and making sure to get in the ice tub every practice. I felt like I was a little bit different in how dedicated I was about this; it wasn't as common of a thing as it has become now. But my regimented routines paid off.

Despite all my care and due diligence, the workload of college sports and summer training and USA Basketball took their toll on my body. I had awesome trainers at UConn who provided great physical therapy, but by the time I got to my senior year of college, I could barely drive for more than ten or fifteen minutes without my knees starting to ache from being in that position. After a very heavy senior year of carrying a lot and then going into my rookie year playing in the pros, which is another level of intensity and physicality and speed, I was still suffering from patellar tendinitis. What I really needed was rest.

As I went into my rookie year with my patellar tendinitis being pretty severe, the athletic trainers on the Lynx started working with me to help me to do different exercises to strengthen the muscles around my knees, as well as ice and other treatments. I managed to get through my rookie year and did pretty well. The couple of months off were going to provide some much-needed rest along with a physical therapy routine before I headed to Valencia in January 2012.

One particular highlight this break gave me was to host a free one-day basketball camp at a high school in the Atlanta area in December. Dubbed "A Very Maya Christmas," the camp hosted seventy-five middle school girls in the morning and then another seventy-five high-school students in the afternoon. The young athletes went through basketball drills focusing on fundamentals, competed in three-on-three matches, and participated in team-building exercises. I was able to interact with the kids and give a speech that hopefully motivated them.

It was gratifying to initiate an event like this with the support of my sponsor. I already knew that one of the best things about being a pro athlete was being an influence for kids, and with this break I had the opportunity to do something for these kids. It felt good to try to live a normal life for a while, to rest my body and spirit while seeing family and friends. Of course, the overseas life was calling, and I packed my bags and prepared to get back on the court.

When I did finally step out on the hardwood of the court to play with my new teammates on the Ros Casares Valencia team, I was almost in tears of joy because my knees felt so much better. I realized I had forgotten how it felt to play without pain. It felt freeing and exciting to play once again without having to endure the severity of my patellar tendinitis. I enjoyed the game even more despite playing under a coach or with teammates who didn't speak English as their first language. It was one thing to have your coach yell at you in English, but in Spanish it was a whole different world! Most of the time the coach would say a few things in English after speaking in Spanish, and since we had women on the team from Australia, Belgium, Hungary, and the Czech Republic, there was always a Spanish teammate there to translate if needed.

The entire experience of playing EuroLeague for the first time was a thrill for me and my mom. We lived in an apartment complex with the rest of the team, and it was a chance to learn more Spanish and Spanish culture. We could get around since I shared a car with another teammate. The vehicle had a manual transmission, but thankfully my mom had taught me how to drive a stick shift in high school.

Even though it was winter in Spain, the weather was beautiful. I went to the beach a couple of times, and despite it being cold, I was still able to get out and see it. There was a lot to see in Valencia. They have a really cool aquarium in the city along with many great restaurants. We worked hard on the court, but the experience was incredible. My mom didn't stay the whole time, but when she left to go back to Atlanta to look after the house, I spent some good time with my awesome teammates. We were super loaded with talent, with Spanish player Sancho Lyttle, Lauren Jackson from Australia, and Ann Wauters from Belgium. Once again, surrounded by supercompetitors, our team only lost two games the whole season and won its first EuroLeague championship game. I played well, stayed healthy, and enjoyed an amazing start to my overseas career.

While in Spain, I was able to watch church online and read a lot to keep my rhythm of spiritual growth. I also managed to keep in touch with Jonathan and others after I got a Skype number. When I first told Jonathan that I would be spending several months in Spain, he assumed the obvious.

"Well, I guess I ain't gonna be able to talk to you," he said.

"No, I'm going to get a Skype number," I told him.

"A what number? What is that?"

"Skype," I told him. "It's like a phone system over the computer."

"Oh, okay."

There was a seven-hour time difference between Missouri and Spain, but we still found a way to talk on the phone. Jonathan wrote to me and gave the letters to Cheri, who would end up emailing them for him. So our friendship continued. Of course, when I received the Valentine's Day bear, my heart felt a jolt of romance, but I wondered how much romance he intended me to feel. The more I thought about it, however, the more I figured he was just being sweet like a big brother.

It's okay. He's like family.

I had known him for over four years, and we both knew that we were good friends. I had been going back to Missouri a couple of times each year, and when I did, I visited him. Our relationship was growing, and even when I wasn't with him, I continued to see his character through our phone conversations and in his letters. I hadn't written to him, and he understood. Every time he told me he was going to call, he called. I tried to think through my schedule and give him a window when I'd be available, and Jonathan always came through.

There was a comfort in knowing there was someone else you could confide in despite everything happening in both of our lives. Jonathan would encourage me and motivate me, and he always made me laugh. He listened. He let me know pieces of his past, and he allowed me to take time in sharing mine. Things between us felt normal even if our lives were far from that.

At the core, we were two humans who had connected with each other and who found a common bond. Like everything in my life, I approached our friendship in a thoughtful manner, always trying to stay in the moment, open to where God was leading. Our respect and admiration for each other was growing.

It was only natural for our friendship to develop into something more.

◆ ◆ ◆

On July 3, 2013, I found myself in another pleasant phone conversation with Jonathan. We had been talking for the past hour about everything—his case, my third season in Minnesota, his life in prison, my life on the road. So far, the Lynx were 7–3. We were playing well but knew we needed to do more after last season. I still had a sour taste in my mouth about how we finished.

We had entered the 2012 season as defending WNBA champions and dominated to reach a 27–7 record. We made it to the finals only to lose to Indiana three games to one. It was hard to accept that we had been the best team in the league but still didn't take care of what we needed to do in the finals. Indiana played us extremely tough, and we felt like we couldn't put it all together. We wanted to use this as motivation to improve on last year, but I knew how far off a championship could be. We couldn't think too far down the road and get ahead of ourselves. We had to take care of each day. Our team didn't need to change things dramatically; we just needed to be who we were and crank things up a bit.

The period of 2012 to 2013 had been a blur. I had gone from helping to win the EuroLeague and Spanish league championship in 2012 while I was playing for Ros Casares Valencia, then ended up winning an Olympic gold medal with USAB in London that summer. We lost in the WNBA finals in October 2012, and then I went straight to China for my first year in the Chinese Women's Basketball League, where I played for the Shanxi Flame. We won the club's first WCBA championship, and I played out of my mind, scoring 53 in Game 1 of the finals in February!

It had been a grueling past year and a half, but winning three out of four championships was gratifying. But I wasn't finished. We weren't finished. The Lynx had unfinished business after last season.

I shared this with Jonathan as we talked, then changed the subject to my family. We never ran out of things to say to each other. One day, I had come and seen him at the prison, where we spent the maximum time of four hours together; then he had called me later that evening, and we spoke for two more hours. We just loved talking to each other, especially when we could be there in person enjoying each other's company.

There was something a little different about Jonathan's mood and vibe this day on the phone. He seemed extremely relaxed and comfortable, almost like he forgot he was enduring prison. The truth was that I noticed Jonathan acting more forward than usual, and I thought, *Dude's being real flirtatious. . . . Where's this about to go?* As he was sharing a story and reached an important part, he teased me with a joke that made my heart jump in my chest.

Hold up. That's not something a brother says to a sister.

This flirtation had not really been a part of our conversations before, so as Jonathan continued to talk, I had to interrupt him.

"Hold up," I said. "First of all, what was *that*?"

I was calling him out in a gentle and friendly way. I was at a point in my life where I was confident with putting the truth out there, especially with a close friend like Jonathan.

I repeated his comment and said, "Were you flirting with me?"

Maya Moore was putting Jonathan Irons on the spot. And he didn't shy away from it.

"Well, yeah," he said with his inviting tone. "That's what I said. And I meant it."

He was owning up to his flirting, so I had to be honest as well.

"Really? Well . . . I didn't hate it," I said.

And just like that, the relationship had changed. Of course, suggesting that we all of a sudden decided to jump into something deeper was the equivalent of calling a champion an overnight success. Most overnight successes take years of toil and trial and work. For Jonathan and me, our intentions had always been to be friends. No one was trying to matchmake us. Our relationship simply evolved into this moment. We had taken our time to get to know each other for years. For six years, we had stayed in touch and cheered each other on, so an intimacy started to develop. We got to spend so much time building a foundation of friendship and love, so a natural next step—if it was an appropriate place to go—was to make it the most intimate of relationships.

At the same time, both of us were realistic. We knew Jonathan was fighting for his freedom. There was always something in the works, so we were always kind of hopeful. Jonathan was always finding something to focus on to move his case forward, and that gave us hope for his future. But I knew we needed to talk about our current status.

"We're going to have to have a DTR," I said.

"A DTR? What's a DTR?" he asked.

"We're gonna have to have a 'define the relationship' talk , 'cause what just happened—we can't go back. We gotta talk about it."

For those of you who know me, this sort of response probably doesn't surprise you. I'm very good with boundaries and defining things, regardless of what area of my life they're in.

So we had that conversation, one where we basically admitted that we had feelings for each other and then asked the question of what we were going to do. What was the best way to move forward knowing what the situation was, because this was not normal. Jonathan was hesitant and so was I.

"This is a new path," I admitted. "I don't know what to do."

So we talked and figured out what to do.

There had always been a mutual appreciation and respect for one another, and perhaps the attraction was always there. Little by little over the years my attraction had grown. When Jonathan wrote my mom in 2009 to be authentic and tell her that he was corresponding with me and meant her no disrespect, I couldn't help admiring that. He was basically telling my mom, "I care about your daughter, but I am not pursuing her and I want her to be focused. If there's any point you're uncomfortable, I will stop talking to her." The letter also encouraged my mom to get to know him, to not cut him off before she really saw him for who he was. That was something that endeared me to Jonathan.

Over the years, I felt that I wasn't going to let myself go somewhere if I knew I couldn't go there. So for a while, developing a relationship with Jonathan always felt off-limits. As someone who is super private, the more I got to know Jonathan, the more relaxed I felt about our friendship and the more vulnerable I became. We had reached a natural place in our story.

So we decided we were going to find a way. We were hopeful. We didn't know how long it would take for us to truly be together, but we believed that one day it would happen. We said we were going to try to move forward and continue to be really good friends, focusing our time on our already awesome and growing friendship. But now with some flirtation sprinkled in. We could be more honest about more of the fullness of how we felt for each other. And we were going to allow ourselves to express it.

We weren't going to let this moment pass us by.

Maya and Jonathan on a visit inside JCCC in 2012

PART FOUR

Chapter Fifteen

MY
HEART

(2013)

(M)

EVER SINCE I was a kid, whenever I was excited about something, I became very motivated to show up and do it with all my heart. Anybody who knows me knows that whatever I do, I am "all in." I am a person of conviction and always aiming to be better. So when I got home from a championship season in China, I connected with high-caliber basketball trainer Idan Ravin and WNBA veteran Kara Lawson and spent several weeks in the spring building on my strengths, adding more skills to my game, and discovering my need to transform my nutrition. Eating cleaner and fine-tuning my on-court preparation routines elevated my game to heights it had never reached. We ultimately beat Atlanta Dream 86–77 to win our second WNBA title in three years. The season and victories hadn't been easy to come by, but that was what a championship was supposed to be. It was supposed to be hard, and when things got difficult, we came together and stuck with it and sealed the victory. We had talked about the things we wanted our team to do, but then we went out and did them.

The victory had been especially sweet because of where we played. Normally we would have been playing at Philips Arena, but because of a prior booking, our game got shifted to the Arena at Gwinnett Center. This was the place where I had played all my state championship games for Collins Hill and won the last three. The last time I had set foot in this building was when I graduated from high school. There were so many memories in this facility, so I was excited to be coming back there. Especially knowing that a lot of my family and friends would be there as well.

I finished the game with a fitting 23 points and was named WNBA Finals MVP. We hadn't lost a game in all seven matches in these playoffs, with five of those games being won by double digits. We came into the season determined, and our dedication had paid off. But under the surface, there was another passion I was determined to show up for. So on Christmas Eve in a hotel in China, I wrote Jonathan a letter for the first time.

Since we'd met in 2007, Jonathan had sent me several handwritten letters over the years. These letters were really rich and deep, and were the seeds that blossomed into our friendship and relationship. I had told him that taking the time to handwrite and mail letters back to him was going to be challenging for me, and he understood. But later that year, a company called JPay charged inmates and their families a high price to use their communication platform, so I was able to begin emailing Jonathan.

From: M M. CustomerID: 9112639

To (Inmate): JONATHAN IRONS, ID: 1011045
Date: 12/24/2013 4:07:17 AM EST
Letter ID: 73196050
Location: JCCC

My New Found Love,

I am ready to write. I know it's been a while for you and I appreciate your patience and your willingness to put your heart out there first. I see that as leadership and boldness and that comforts my heart to see that from you.

You are truly special, and I think anyone that gets to know you realizes that as well. Your anointing is very evident because of the light that God shines through you, and I know it will only grow brighter with the right nourishment and determination. I've enjoyed being a part of your journey and thank you for letting me have an intimate role in your growth as a man and son of our God.

One of the things that has always scared me about letting people get close to me is them discovering my heart and rejecting/harming it somehow. Thinking it's weird, crazy, not seeing its beauty, not knowing how to care for it and help it grow, or take it for granted and treat it poorly.

I have a handful of amazing godly couples and close girlfriends in my life that have shown me great & healthy love of my heart and allowed me to do the same for them, but I've not developed a holy relationship with a male where he has been let into a sacred part of my heart, body and life. I believe the Lord wants this type of male/female intimacy to be reserved at its best for marriage. You are the closest I've come in my life to seeing potential in having that type of relationship and that's a new, exciting, and scary place for me (as you know), but I'm so grateful for it!

I feel like I've been a great student of relationships and seek wisdom constantly on how God has lovingly suggested for us to relate to each other. I thank God that He has given me a cautious, yet open attitude towards trust in relationships because it's kept me safe from relationships that would not have been His best for me at the time.

I proceed with you cautiously because I want to see if your heart is like mine (I will describe what that is later). If I put up a boundary it's because I am not yet convinced that it's time for you to be there.

Other boundaries are because God says those boundaries are for our good and His glory (spiritual, emotional & physical boundaries).

I think you, more than the other guys have been able to see my heart, but not completely . . .

Like I promised, I go on to describe a more sacred part of myself, a part that was written for his heart only. Two heartfelt pages later, I end with the promise of something more.

There's so much more to say and see, but it felt good to put it on paper for you. I hope you've enjoyed this gift and just to make you smile this is only part 1 of this unknown amount of letters from me . . . more to come . . . until then,

Merry Christmas, MNFL, and always praying for you.

As I finished the email, I thought of how the letter began. I began the letter by actually admitting to him that he was my newfound love (MNFL)! The thrill and the rush of that reality made me feel more anticipation for love than I'd ever felt in my twenty-four years of life. So as I ended the letter, I wanted to show him I had gladly accepted his name for me, which he had used in our letters since the summer. So I wrote . . .

Love,

Your Dear Joy

Chapter Sixteen

THE MNFL
AND
THE MVP

(2014)

(J)

"I'D LIKE TO take this money that I saved up and pay for this expert to work on my case."

I sat in my caseworker's office, excited to be taking another step in my case, but I could tell from the expression on her face that she didn't share my enthusiasm.

"You want to do what?" she asked in disbelief.

"I want to pay this guy to help me investigate my case," I said. "He's an expert on eyewitness identification procedures."

One of the many things I had learned was that I needed an eyewitness expert to confirm my suspicions and to break down all the problems and errors that had taken place regarding my case, since the only eyewitness to the crime was not telling the truth. He was also the victim, and his identification was unreliable and riddled with inconsistencies even to a layman's eyes. There were issues with the lineup and the description of the suspect by the witness.

I had found a guy from the connections I had made, so I contacted him and asked if he would be willing to work for me.

I worked many jobs while inside prison, and one of the hardest yet most rewarding jobs was when I worked in a program that aided inmates with disabilities. It took me years, but I had saved a little over $1,000. I told the expert I could send a down payment and then continue to send him $200 a month since I made $225. He told me to only send $100, which was fine by me. It had taken me well over a decade to save up money for my case.

"Okay, Jonathan," my caseworker said in a tone of resignation. "Go ahead. Write your check."

As I filled out the check and put it in the envelope, a new wave of hope overwhelmed me.

I'm finally getting an expert to help me out. And DOC is gonna pay for it!

All this hard work with my case and knowing what to do and also earning money to help pay for it . . . I knew this was all going to finally be worth it. I was excited to see what would happen.

Unfortunately, a few days later, they came to get me and locked me up in ad seg. Nobody told me anything. They just put me in a cell without an explanation. All I was told was that I was being investigated, but I had no idea why. When you go to the hole, you're guilty until proven innocent.

This was the second time I had gone to the hole at JCCC. This stay would be a lot longer than the first, however. I'd be there for months.

(M)

As Cheri drove the car to Jefferson City Correctional Center, I thought about Jonathan being stuck in the hole the past few months and how long it had been since we had spoken to each other. Our rhythm had been for me to communicate windows of time when I was available and then Jonathan would call me, but early in 2014, I suddenly stopped hearing from him. I learned from Cheri that he had been put in the hole for no reason at all.

How could a man be wrongfully imprisoned in solitary while he was already serving a sentence after being wrongfully imprisoned? Jonathan told Cheri that he didn't want me to come see him since he didn't want me to see him like this and didn't want me to be upset, but I gave Cheri a message to tell him: "There's no way I'm not coming."

My most important priority for the next two hours was to encourage Jonathan and be with him and lift him up during this impossibly hard time.

Over the years, Jonathan has always done a good job of not burdening Reggie, Cheri, and me with some of the darker details of his life that would break our hearts. We knew a lot of what was going on with him, but not knowing the fullness of what he had to go through helped me to focus on the things I needed to focus on while I was playing basketball. This was how I lived and how I played: *Where do I put my energy so that I can fully do what I'm committed to?* If I was focusing too much on the heavy and hard things in life, I was going to break. So I knew during this visitation that I needed to block out the bad stuff and just be present with him and enjoy our time.

I'm coming to make you smile and to love on you.

I couldn't believe this awful situation Jonathan was enduring, but that wasn't going to change the fact of me coming to see him. I needed to show up and be present. I was very committed to doing what I said I was going to do and him being in the hole didn't change that. I wanted him to know that no matter what he was going through, I was there and I loved him and he wasn't alone. We were going to make the most out of the time we had.

(J)

The familiar crack of the locks turning made me stop reading the legal document and look to see who was opening my cell.

"Jonathan, you got a visit today," CO Ozanich told me. "I'm gonna let you shave and get a shower. Just don't say nothing."

"You serious?" I asked in shock.

"Yeah. Enjoy your visit. I can't fix why you're in the hole—I'm just a CO. The least I can do is this. I'll take getting in trouble, but just don't say anything. Don't make them do their job."

"Okay, okay," I said as I stood up and quickly gathered my stuff for shaving and showering.

There were some good COs in the prison, and Ozanich was one of them. This gesture of kindness was unnatural, but it was a blessing. I was glad to be able to clean up for Maya, but I hated her seeing me like this. There I was in a maximum-security prison surrounded by barbed-wire fences circling our buildings, with my hands and feet in shackles, making all sorts of noise shuffling down the hallway while a guard held a tether attached to my back. They called it a tether, but it was really a dog leash to keep you in control. I was brought to a small room, and they locked the door. I saw Maya sitting behind a clear window giving me a sad smile, but as I sat across from her, with the glass in front of us, the walls around us seemed to disappear.

Whenever I had a chance to talk to Maya or see her, I was no longer in prison. I felt free of my shackles and burdens.

"This isn't right," Maya said. "I hate this for you."

"I know it's crazy. They're doing weird stuff, putting me in ad seg for no reason. They're just taking me away from my case. Trying to discourage me from my work. But it's okay. I'm okay. We're gonna get through this."

(M)

We made the most out of our visit, and I was thankful to see Jonathan's spirit carrying some hope and light. He explained that all he had been told was that they were investigating him for having stuff on his computer that he wasn't allowed to have. Things like legal work. So how could they lock him up when they were only investigating the situation? His desk was next to a staff member who was there all day long, and there were two cameras over his head, so Jonathan asked them to check the cameras.

He also demanded that they show him the material they found on his computer. But nobody produced anything, and Jonathan just sat there waiting on word in the hole.

Right after leaving JCCC, I wrote in my journal about my visit with Jonathan.

Big J:

Post visit 4-5-14

Cheri brought me and left 10 mins later. We had a couple hours to talk.

Great convos.

Just left the prison and watched him being taken away in cuffs and a leash . . . broke my heart to see him treated that way.

Loving him has helped me emotionally connect with loving Christ in that I feel the pains of seeing an innocent man punished, etc.

I feel prepared and ready to move into another level of fighting for him:

—increase prayer (me and others)

—spread the word (to family, friends, basketball audience)

I'm in a place emotionally where I know the Lord can help me get over any fears I have in being involved in these next steps. I feel they (Jon, lawyers etc.) know what they're doing.

He emphasized he doesn't want me to do anything that will hurt my career. That was sweet.

As I walked out of the prison the sunlight blinded me and I couldn't even look straight . . . God's overwhelming warmth and glorious will had this covered and is and will be shining so ridiculously bright because of this.

(J)

"Fear not, for I am with you;

be not dismayed, for I am your God;

I will strengthen you, I will help you,

I will uphold you with my righteous right hand."

Isaiah 41:10 gave me comfort as I read the passage out of the Bible that Maya had sent to me in prison. This was my most treasured possession that I took to the hole with me. The Bible my grandmother had given me started to fall apart in 2013 with sections missing. I couldn't use it anymore. The only Bible I saw in the chapel was an old Gideon Bible with the archaic text of the King James Version, and I just couldn't connect with it. I didn't have any commentaries for the Bible, either. I had prayed to the Lord asking for a Bible, and that's when Maya started telling me about her ESV Bible. After researching what ESV meant, I found it was the English Standard Version, with its text a literal translation done in contemporary English. I hated asking Maya but I knew I had to, so I eventually asked for her help.

"I need a Bible," I told her. "Will you help me?"

"You want a Bible? Of course I'll help you. Which one do you want?"

I told her I wanted the ESV, and she said it would be no problem. She just needed to know how to send it. I thanked her and treasured that Bible. It was with me for some very dark and hard times, including this long stint in solitary. I read it over and over again. I loved how the ESV translated the passages of Scripture; it brought God's Word to another level of life for me, and it provided such comfort. And it was durable, too. It wasn't broken and beat up like the one I thumped to death.

I still have that Bible Maya sent me to this day.

(M)

During our White House visit on June 12, 2014, to celebrate the Lynx's

2013 WNBA championship, President Obama joked about my sixth trip to the nation's capital.

"You did not only go 26–8 in the regular season, but you also swept the playoffs—a perfect 7–0," the president stated. "You won it with all-star talent, from Seimone to Rebekkah Brunson, hometown hero Lindsay Whalen. You did it with fellow all-star and finals MVP Maya Moore, who has now been here so many times I've lost track. I mean, basically there's like a Maya Moore wing in the White House. And when she comes, we kind of—we've got all her stuff here; she's got a toothbrush."

Everybody laughed at the comment. This definitely remained an honor to be welcomed to the White House by President Obama. I had gone three times while at UConn, once with the US Olympic team, and now two times with the Lynx. As the president finished his comments, he welcomed someone else to the podium.

Me.

"So today, of course, our job is to congratulate this outstanding team standing behind me, the 2013 Champions, the Minnesota Lynx," President Obama said. "Good luck with the rest of your season. And I understand—I don't know, Coach, if you want to say something. I think Maya, who basically feels like she owns the place, wants to say a few words."

As the room erupted in more laughter, Coach Reeve said, "I defer to Maya."

There was a reason I was talking today.

"Man, what a birthday treat," I said. "Thank you to my teammates—"

"Happy birthday," President Obama said. "I didn't know that."

"Yes, it was yesterday. It's all week, don't worry."

More laughter.

"Malia and Sasha do the same thing."

I smiled at the president. "It's reduced down from a month; now it's a week."

This was becoming the President Obama–Maya Moore comedy show.

"I just can't speak enough about this team behind me," I said. "It's really just been an awesome three years, going into my fourth year, and even before that. The foundation that was being built with Seimone, Coach Reeve, Shelley,

Jim, and all the other captains. But every year it starts at Mr. Taylor's house, our awesome owner. . . . We have our annual dinner at their house where we all come together. And as the rookies got to see, we're really a family."

I continued to pour out my gratitude to all the people making this moment possible, and finally ended it on a lighthearted note.

"So I think we can continue to make this an annual trip, and I want to see that room you're talking about."

Leaving the White House, I felt so empowered and believed in. But later as I sat in my hotel room waiting for the phone call I knew wasn't going to come, I thought about my beloved Jonathan trapped wrongfully in a place that didn't believe in him.

(J)

As I wrote Maya the letter, I wanted her to know the reality of our situation and where I was coming from.

I held Maya in my hand. It was an open hand, held up as high as I could reach. *I'm not gonna hold you hostage. I'm not keeping you trapped.*

My reality burned right in front of me. I was in this fire—this all-consuming fire—but I hadn't been consumed in my mind and my heart. I wasn't going to let Maya feel these flames, so I lifted her above them.

I'm not telling you what's going on down here with all the craziness. And, Lord, is it crazy.

I wanted her to be held up high in case something went bad. She needed to be safe in case I got scalded or seared. Our interest in each other couldn't keep her imprisoned.

Only one of us was incarcerated; the other needed to be free to live her life. This letter was giving her an out.

(M)

As I held his letter in my hand, the irony of the stamp at the top corner made my heart break even more. The stamp pictured an American flag that said *Freedom Forever*, while inside this stamped envelope were the heartfelt handwritten words of a man who had been *wrongfully* thrown into the dungeon of the prison he had *wrongfully* been held in for over half his life.

I took a moment, breathed, then opened it.

The first thing I noticed was the beautiful rose drawn in ink in the middle of the page with his words penned around it.

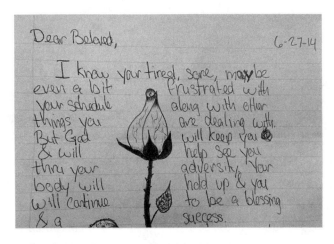

Once again, Jonathan was lifting me up while he was being held down. I read the precious words as I wiped my tears.

> I know that special appointment you have was given to you, because you have a message to share that will help make the game better. And with your position, seek to leave it better for the next generations.
>
> I also want you to know that I miss you & wish I could hear from you. But know that I am not upset & don't mean to pressure you. Get your rest and stay focused on your career as well as your ministry. We'll talk again.
>
> I know my situation hurts your tender heart. Please let me know if all this is too much for you. I love you & I care about the condition of your heart. I want you to be happy. I don't wish to put my burdens on your heart. It's heavy enough for me.

I know your time is limited so I will keep this short. Stay focused on the prize.

Love,

Your MNFL

I knew the answer to his comment of this being "too much," so I wrote him back with my thoughts in an email.

MNFL,

I think about you every day & throughout the day, I carry you in my heart and the Lord helps me do so. I know you asked me if our relationship was too much for me to handle. And my answer is YES, it's too much for all of us to handle BUT that's why we depend on our GOD for He holds us all up. In other words, I'm not going any-where! I'm already in too deep (in a good way) & I'm committed to helping share your burdens as we daily give it to the Lord. He is our strength and our hope! Thank you for caring so much for my heart despite all of the reasons you could use to only think about yourself. Your thoughtfulness and perseverance is such a beautiful and strong display of Christ at work in YOU! I am ever so proud of you!

I'm sorry for not writing you more than I feel I should have over these last two+ months, but it comforts me to know from your letters that you are still being encouraged by the Lord and being used by Him. What a mighty God we serve and you give me hope and encouragement in how you keep fighting in God's strength.

Despite my silence, I have been journaling and thinking about you. I hope you enjoy some of the attached notes I've written over the last few months for you.

(J)

Dear Beloved: I hope you are taking full advantage of your downtime and getting some good rest and relaxation. God knows your body, mind, and spirit needs it. I know that you feel a little lonely at times on the road, but know that I'm thinking of you and I'm praying.

My world here is harsh and painful. Yet God amazes me with joy, growth, wisdom, even in my darkest moments . . .

The pain of my current circumstances drove me to this day where I wasn't sharing God's provision of grace like I'm called to, but that changed about two months ago. I think we're all seeking God's peace and rest, but it's wrong and selfish to keep it to myself. God has been using me and flowing through me. I have been using my gifts to bless others, writing, praying, and sharing scriptures and faith experiences. I've been making stressed-out brothers laugh when they feel like crying. I've been helping them in their cases and helping fighting injustices. And now I've been sharing my food and supplies with others and much more. I find that I get way more joy, peace, and rest when I let God use me to steer my fellow men. I still have my dark moments but they have less sting when I'm focused on being a service to others who are experiencing the same hurts. I'll end this for now. I love you and I just want to tell you I was missing me some you.

Love,

Your MNFL

(M)

There are moments that allow you to pause and briefly reflect back on the journey you've taken. The afternoon before the playoffs were set to tip off, I was presented the WNBA MVP award for the 2014 season. Laurel Richie, the league's president, presented the award with kind comments and a summary of my season that even surprised me.

"My sense is that you came back this year on a mission and really to make an impact on your team," Laurel stated. "I know you did a lot of work in the off-season. And I think we're seeing the difference here. You came back and were named a captain of this championship team. You started the season with a hundred and thirty-five points in your first four games and with a team challenged by injuries; you went on to play in every single game this season. By the end of the season, you led the league in twenty-three point nine points per game. You set a new league record of scoring thirty-plus points in twelve games and thirty-plus points in four consecutive games. And along the way, you achieved a career-high and a franchise-best forty-eight versus last year's Atlanta Dream Finals matchup. You completed the season with the honor of being the only player in WNBA history to score in double figures, literally in every game. That, to me, is truly amazing. But it wasn't all about offense. Maya set new records on the defensive end as well, with eight point one rebounds per game and one point nine steals per game. . . ."

After being introduced, I walked up to the podium filled with gratitude and grace.

"Thank you, Laurel, for that awesome summary. These are the things that I generally don't think about. It's overwhelming to think about everything that's gone into achieving this award, and, you know, I've always been a person that has tried to keep a perspective of where my help comes from, and there's no question, first of all, it comes from the Lord, and I've always tried to be honest about that with people that ask. And from that source, God's blessed me with so many great people. . . . And I've always tried to give everything that I can in every situation. . . ."

It was impossible to name each of these people, but I tried to single out individuals such as Taj and Rebekkah and Lindsay and Seimone, as well as crediting my coaches and the league.

I had given my all this season, carrying more of the load for the Lynx, since so many of our starters were injured throughout the course of the year.

I was forced to step up in order to produce more points and play more minutes. Naturally it was hard work, but I was able to finish strong. Achieving MVP for someone on our team was usually unlikely since our starting five shared the load so well. That's one of the reasons the Minnesota Lynx were so dominant, reaching the finals six out of my eight seasons. No one player had to carry too much or tally up a huge stat every night, which meant it didn't really set any of us up to get the MVP, but that was okay. We were more hungry to have a Lynx player win a finals MVP.

As I spoke, I had to thank everyone, especially my mom, my first and biggest fan, as well as my family. I chuckled at the thought of the start of our adventure as I looked over at my mom.

"Would you have thought twenty years ago as a five-year-old running around just full of energy in Jefferson City, Missouri, that we'd be standing here today? I definitely couldn't have dreamed that up. I just think of my family members all over the country that just love me and support me, no matter what."

There was one in particular, one very few people knew about. And even though he had no way of watching this press conference, Jonathan was still there with me. Smiling and cheering and making me feel valued as a person and not just as a player. From the outside, it looked like the best statistical year of my career. I had shouldered more weight than ever trying to help my team succeed, but under the surface of my success, my heart was breaking thinking that Jonathan was still suffering in the hole. I had become good at compartmentalizing simply because I had to. One moment you're visiting the love of your life in prison and seeing him feeling so low; then the next minute you're asked to get up and go be a hero in your job. I couldn't really feel the fullness of everything Jonathan was dealing with. If I had it would have broken me.

(J)

I knew I was in trouble the moment I moved from solitary confinement to the two-man cell in ad seg where I would be waiting for a regular cell in the prison to open up. In a sense, the double cell was an upgrade from being alone, but not in the hole. Men got raped and assaulted all the time in double cells in ad seg, and some even lost their lives. They had an emergency button in the cells, but if someone pressed it, nobody was going to come. That's because people pressed it all day long. You were on your own in a double cell, forced to deal with whoever they stuck you with.

As I've said, there were legitimate psychopaths inside Jefferson City Correctional Center, and I ended up with one of them. I had only shared a cell with one other truly disturbed person, and that had been a guy named Randell who was an old creepo with mental health issues back at The Walls. My new cellie in the hole at JCCC was dangerous. I knew guys like him from being in the ITC program. All rough and tough and sizing me up as prey. For two days, he was feeling me out, all while I spoke calmly to him and tried to be respectful.

He must have thought that I was kind of a soft guy who couldn't stand on my own, because he just kept going and going with disrespectful comments and sexual suggestions. Then one day he grabbed on to me, making crazy comments and attempting to rape me. I put him down in the double cell. I didn't kill him, but I took him down and spoke the truth.

"All right. Look. You got two choices. Either I'm gonna continue to beat on you till you submit and get out or you get out right now."

The guy wouldn't go. And I didn't want to beat up on him anymore, so I stopped. That night, I slept real light; my time at The Walls had taught me how to do that. I barely slept, skipping in and out of sleep and listening to the guy's every move and breath. All I was thinking was, *Lord, get this man out of my cell.*

The next day, the guy tried to get me to have sex with him. He hadn't learned his lesson. I approached him. "Look, man, I mean it," I said as I flinched at him. "I will hurt you now. You need to leave."

He knew I was serious, so he finally began to beat on the door, screaming out, "CO!" The corrections officer came in, cuffed the guy up, and did the same to me; then he moved the psychopath out of my cell and brought somebody else in.

When I saw Cheri the next time she visited, she noticed my swollen chin from the altercation.

"What happened?" Cheri asked me. "Have you been fighting?"

I didn't want to tell her, but I couldn't hide the truth. "Yeah."

"What was it about?"

"Cheri, stop asking questions."

In the end, I told Cheri and Maya about what happened, not going into detail but simply telling them a summary. I didn't want them to know about all the crazy stuff going on at JCCC, about the wickedness of the world I was in. All I was going to do was make them worry about me more and have them be in a constant state of anxiety. I knew I could handle myself if something like this happened. I knew the Lord would get me through these things. And He did.

Maya wasn't the only person who had mastered compartmentalizing. I had to push the dark stuff away. You had to do this in prison. Your mental health and your survival depended on your ability to push away all the crazy stuff. To push away the pain and focus on the goal or the objective of the day at hand. As I said before, sometimes the objective was just to get up, survive the day, and go to sleep and start over.

(M)

The way the 2014 Lynx team competed to the end was truly inspiring despite losing to the red-hot Phoenix Mercury in the western conference finals. I had started the habit of taking notes after games to evaluate what worked and didn't work. But before I could review that season's notes, I would be joining the US National Team as we prepared for the FIBA world championship in Turkey.

"Country calls," I told ESPN. "Quick turnaround—put some closure to this season, pack up our lives in Minnesota, and then head to the East Coast (for training)."

My next letter to Jonathan would be emailed from Europe.

9/19/2014

Bonjour mon amour!

I am sending this little note from Paris!!

(J)

"Irons!"

I was sitting in the double cell with a new cellie who didn't want to attack me, and we actually got along pretty well. One of the COs who really liked me and was a sergeant at the time had walked by my door to do his security check, and after seeing me, he doubled back and glanced into the little window in the door with a grin on his face.

"What's up?" I said.

"What are you doing down here?"

I just shook my head. "Come on, man, you got a computer. You can figure out why I'm here."

"For real—what's going on?" The sergeant was genuinely surprised. He knew me well enough to know I didn't belong in the hole.

"Man, I don't know."

The sergeant left security check and went back to his office to check on my status. He returned a little later to my cell.

"There's nothing in the computer," the CO said. "They need to tell us something. If not, I'm going to get you a job. You can be a walkman." A walkman is just another name for a janitor. This was a highly desired job in the hole. It meant you could get out of your cell, get extra food, a shower every day, and even use the phone from time to time.

I finally had another job. I was able to pick a coworker, so I picked another friend of mine in the hole and we helped serve trays and things like this. We also basically cleaned up ad seg. If you don't clean ad seg, it turns into a biohazard. It's just a horrible and nasty environment. So we put on biohazard suits and cleaned the hole from top to bottom. As a reward, the

CO told me I could use the phone as long as I wanted to. The first chance I got I called Maya.

"Hey, what's up?" I said to her.

"Oh my gosh—how are you calling me? Are you okay?"

I knew she was hoping I had gotten out.

"I'm still in the hole. But I got a job."

As I told her about the CO letting me work, Maya was relieved to hear this news from me. We hadn't spoken in a long time. I had just finished writing her a long letter—something like thirty or forty pages long. It was good to hear her voice. To be reminded that she was still there with me.

(M)

Our prayers were answered, and Jonathan was eventually released from the hole. This meant I could finally go see him in person, no shackles or glass window between us. After each WNBA and overseas season, I did what I needed to do to make it to Missouri to go spend time with Jonathan in the prison. These were sacred and treasured moments in time. Reflecting on all we had been through that past year, I wrote to him shortly after our visit that fall.

10/24/2014

Hey My Love,

Even though I just saw you, I still miss you so much. It seems like too long already and I think of you & pray for you daily as usual. I hated saying goodbye to you when I had to leave and the look in your eyes was too much to bear so I tried not to look back at you for fear of being overwhelmed with sadness, grief, and frustration and vulnerability. But even though it's so hard for us both to say goodbye for the moment, I'm so grateful for the hope that we both have in the goodness of our God!

I ordered one of the books and CD we talked about for you today. Hopefully you will get them soon. I can't wait to talk about the written & lyrical content of the book & CD together.

It's been a rough first week here in China. To keep it short, the WCBA has added 8 more games to the regular season, changed the format of the entire regular season, & made it harder for foreigners in general, but the Lord is sovereign and will have to daily fill me with patience and wisdom in each circumstance. Hopefully I'll be home, at the latest, early March.

I have your long letter here and it is such a treat to have a piece of you here with me. I treasure your thoughts and the time you take to write to me with such honesty and open hearted-ness.

Well, I will write again soon and in the meantime enjoy the gifts and know you are loved and missed dearly.

Keep your eyes on Him My Love,

Your Dear Joy

(J)

I had worked hard to become well-versed in the grievance procedure and how to litigate and write up my complaints and provide evidence, prove evidence, and string together persuasive thought patterns. And some people hated this fact. I discovered that the same warden I had angered back at The Walls when I tried to get a guy out of the hole had been the one who started this whole thing. The retired warden had a hit squad, and CO Heck was a major player in it. Since I had been connected to him in a past investigation, he had stepped off this case so I couldn't accuse him of getting revenge. Instead, they put another investigator on it, who I later discovered was the warden's friend. All along, I kept asking to see the investigation report and to see the evidence, but they told me they weren't giving it to me. In the meantime, they changed the policy of sending money. They reduced the amount of money you could send out and made it more difficult to use the money you earned in the prison. They also refused to let me have a paying job. Employers who knew me told me that they tried to hire me but got blocked by the higher-ups.

One of the worst things about my time in ad seg in 2014 was that they had taken all my research journals full of notes I had on the case, so when I got out I asked for them back, but they refused to give them to me. They destroyed my journals. It was part of the case, so the journals had been collected. They told me they gave me notices explaining this, but I got nothing from them. No documentation. No explanation. Nothing.

This was what I was up against while fighting for my freedom in a prison inside the prison.

Chapter Seventeen

LITTLE MOMENTS

(2015)

(M)

Life on Earth is possible because of the smallest details being in their designed place . . . don't mistake the small things of your days as unimportant . . . life happens in the little details.

I POSTED THIS online on February 23, 2015, during my third season of playing basketball in China. I never spent a lot of time on social media, but every now and then I engaged or shared something close to my heart.

This post on Twitter and Instagram foreshadowed a year where small details made a difference and little moments mattered.

◆ ◆ ◆

A poem.

Jonathan was more than just an inmate unjustly imprisoned, and I recognized that the first time I met him at JCCC. Over the years, I had seen his many talents and abilities in the job positions he held and his work on his case. But I also discovered an artist who expressed his love and affection in remarkable ways. We shared our art with each other, with Jonathan writing poems and drawing pictures for me and with me sharing songs I had written with him.

Pieces of Jonathan's poem from Valentine's Day 2015.

> *. . . On my love you can depend.*
>
> *I'll always be your faithful friend.*
>
> *On this road less traveled we will walk hand in hand.*
>
> *For the Lord's way is the greatest plan. . . .*
>
> *. . . Kiss me tender. Love me true.*
>
> *Forever I desire you.*
>
> *Rising in love with you. . . .*

◆ ◆ ◆

A picture.

The love Jonathan and I shared was not conventional, so we had to be creative. As if the poem he sent me wasn't enough, he also drew a picture of Cheri, my mom, and me for Valentine's Day. Cheri scanned and emailed it to me, and I kept it as my screen saver while I was in China.

◆ ◆ ◆

A heart.

Of course, I couldn't let Jonathan have all the fun.

Oh, you gonna write me a poem? Well, I'm gonna make you a poem . . . in the shape of a heart despite JPAY's janky formatting options!

I think we were in a little bit of a competition. A *love* competition.

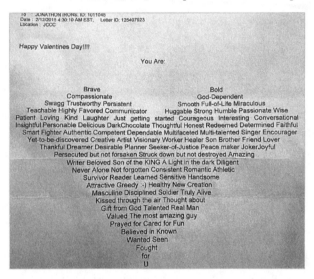

```
TO  : JONATHON IRONS; ID: 1011045
Date : 2/12/2015 4:30:10 AM EST,   Letter ID: 125407923
Location : JCCC


Happy Valentines Day!!!!

                            You Are:


                Brave                               Bold
             Compassionate                     God-Dependent
        Swagg Trustworthy Persistent       Smooth Full-of-Life Miraculous
   Teachable Highly Favored Communicator   Huggable Strong Humble Passionate Wise
 Patient Loving Kind Laughter Just getting started Courageous Interesting Conversational
Insightful Personable Delicious DarkChocolate Thoughtful Honest Redeemed Determined Faithful
  Smart Fighter Authentic Competent Dependable Multifaceted Multi-talented Singer Encourager
    Yet-to-be-discovered Creative Artist Visionary Worker Healer Son Brother Friend Lover
      Thankful Dreamer Desirable Planner Seeker-of-Justice Peace maker JokerJoyful
         Persecuted but not forsaken Struck down but not destroyed Amazing
          Writer Beloved Son of the KING A Light in the dark Diligent
            Never Alone Not forgotten Consistent Romantic Athletic
               Survivor Reader Learned Sensitive Handsome
                 Attractive Greedy :-) Healthy New Creation
                  Masculine Disciplined Soldier Truly Alive
                    Kissed through the air Thought about
                     Gift from God Talented Real Man
                      Valued The most amazing guy
                        Prayed for Cared for Fun
                          Believed in Known
                            Wanted Seen
                              Fought
                               for
                                U
```

◆ ◆ ◆

A nickname.

不败女王

That what was they called me in China as I played on the Shanxi Flame team. It meant "Invincible Queen." But even though we won our third consecutive Women's Chinese Basketball Association title in March, this season was particularly challenging. I wasn't feeling invincible.

The start of the season had been bumpy, since a series of rules had been implemented, forcing athletes from overseas to get working visas for the first two weeks. Our team had a slow start before we finally got momentum in the second half of the season.

One of the worst parts about being a pro was the constant travel. Living out of a suitcase and figuring out how to keep in touch with loved ones became exhausting. The games I played in China were very physical, and the environments weren't always the best. Some of the courts were slippery, and some gyms were freezing. Staying healthy was always a challenge.

I still always had Jonathan to make me laugh. Sometimes on a Skype call when the connection would be horrible, we would have to literally scream at each other on the phone.

"HELLO!"

"HELLO!"

"HOW! ARE! YOU! DOING!"

"WHAT???"

"I! SAID! HOW! ARE! YOU! DOING!"

We had to laugh because there was nothing else we could do. Both of us were living in environments that weren't our homes. Even with these phone calls—if you could call them that—we were forced to be creative.

◆ ◆ ◆

A sneaker.

Inspired by Jonathan's "Rising in Love" Valentine's Day quote, I created a "Rising in Love" Air Jordan 29. It was so special to me that I never wore it.

Rise in Love Air Jordan Shoe (Psalm 121)

◆ ◆ ◆

A wave.

When he could, Jonathan watched my games from the thirteen-inch TV in his cell. That was his window to the world, as he said. He was able to live vicariously through me whenever he watched the game. So during the All-Star game, I decided to send him a message. It was during an interview when people in the crowd were chanting my name and cameras were pointed at me and I was being asked the regular sort of questions after a victory. As the interview came to an end, I smiled at the camera and then waved.

Later that night when I called Jonathan, he told me he was able to watch the game.

"So did you see me wave?" I asked.

"Yeah, I saw you wave," he said.

He didn't get it.

"No, no—did you see me wave *at you*?"

Jonathan paused for a moment, and then in a quiet and surprised voice he asked, "You waved at *me*?"

He couldn't believe it, and later on he told me that when he got off the phone, he was floating with joy. Jonathan lived in a heartless place, yet his heart was full, all because of a sweet little gesture.

◆ ◆ ◆

An injury.

All injuries have a measure of mystery to them when you're competing. I think we do what we can to try to prevent injuries, and we have more science and understanding of the body now than ever before as far as injury prevention. But still there's a humility that comes when you're competing, where you don't really know what's going to happen every time you step out to play or train or move in life. I can't say that I have a full understanding of why my career didn't involve more major injuries, but I tried to soak up everything I could from my trainers when they would tell us how to take care of our bodies, whether that was nutritionally or how to warm up, how to cool down, how to recover, how to land, how to jump, and how to move. Some athletes have natural habits that lend themselves more toward not being as injured, depending on the sport they play and how physical it is.

Over my college and WNBA careers, I only missed one game, and that happened during the 2015 season with the Lynx. Thankfully it was by choice. Late in the season during a game, Sylvia Fowles and I were both going for an errant shot and collided, including Sylvia's elbow and my nose. Even though I broke my nose, it didn't require stitches and could have been worse. I played the next game, but at the end of the season, the coach wanted me to rest leading into the playoffs. Besides this, I missed no games and literally only missed one practice in college because of a strain, and even then, I was crying about missing that!

It's remarkable to have played for as long as I did and not to really have missed any games. In some cases, there's nothing you can do when an injury comes. I definitely tried my best to be physically strong. Having more of a finesse game than a physical game also increased my chances of not being injured through physical contact with someone else. Sure, I had a lot of tweaks and strains and sprains, but I always tried to get on top of them so that they didn't develop and become something more. I was always in the training room, and I think my trainers appreciated it because it was going to prevent me from developing something worse.

I kept a picture of myself from the week I broke my nose. Maybe as a reminder that I'm not as invincible as some think.

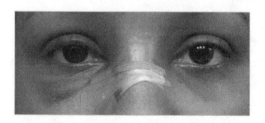

◆ ◆ ◆

A shot.

On October 9, 2015, we were playing the Indiana Fever in their building for a crucial Game 3 of the WNBA Finals. The series was tied 1–1, and the game was tied at 77–77 with 1.7 seconds left on the clock. Lindsay Whalen waited on the right sideline of the court to inbound the ball.

1.7 seconds . . .

For the first three quarters, I hadn't found my normal rhythm, having sat on the bench for nearly all of the third quarter after getting my third foul. But I made up for lost time in the final period, scoring 12 hard-earned points in ten minutes. The sixteen thousand–plus Indiana fans roared with all they had against our final effort to score. The referee blew his whistle and handed Lindsay the ball, and I took off running to mid-court.

Maya Moore . . . Always running.

As a defender ran with me, I changed directions and faded toward the top of the key. There wasn't a clean look to Sylvia down low, so Lindsay lobbed it in my direction.

1.7 seconds . . .

I caught the ball, gave a shot fake, took an escape dribble right, then pulled up for 3 with only 0.3 seconds left on the clock. I watched as the ball dropped down through the back of the net. The next thing I knew, I felt the rush of my teammates wrapping me up in the excitement at what just happened.

For a moment, I had somewhat of an out-of-body experience. As the refs checked to make sure I had made the basket before the buzzer, the arena was draped in silence. It was almost eerie how quiet the place became. The win was confirmed.

"That was pretty, pretty close to not making it," I said to the media after the game. "It was just a basketball move, and I was able to get it off."

We finished strong and became champions again in Game 5 in front of eighteen thousand fans in Minneapolis.

◆◆◆

A love.

A quote from one of Jonathan's many pages of letters he sent me sums up how we "dated" one another:

I have never loved anyone like I love you. Yessss, I am absolutely crazy about you and all that you are my beloved. Although we have our circumstantial limitations right now, we still creatively find ways to express our love to each other. I believe that God created humans to be creative lovers, too. I am truly blessed by how you make me feel.

Our lives existed worlds apart, yet we leaned into those little moments where we could be creative with one another. This inevitably sparked so many special and unusual moments of displaying love that we couldn't have ever anticipated. The challenge of our situation created such a depth of meaning. Everything—every word and moment and snapshot and smile—meant more. So like those 1.7 seconds in Game 5 of the finals, we made them count.

Chapter Eighteen

LIGHT IN THE DARKNESS

(2016)

(J)

I FOUND SOLITARY confinement the most forbidding aspect of prison life. There is no end and no beginning; there is only one's mind, which can begin to play tricks. Was that a dream or did it really happen? One begins to question everything.

These words Nelson Mandela wrote in his autobiography aptly described the place I had once again been sent to in JCCC. Ad seg, the hole, solitary confinement . . . The most fitting name for the room I sat in was hell. Ad seg was meant to break you. They put you there and forgot about you, and they hoped when you finally got out you had forgotten about yourself as well.

This time in the hole, they almost succeeded.

After all these years, the warden and the COs were still dogging me, pulling me in and out of my cell all the time, locking me up in solitary. At the start of 2016, I got tossed back in the hole for no reason at all. Once again, I received no explanation. Nothing. At first, I had been thrown in an ice-cold cell in the dead of winter where I felt like I was going to freeze to death. Then they moved me to another cell. It was a little warmer, but it was still the size of a bathroom, and I couldn't get out for any reason.

This didn't stop me from writing to Maya. The last time I had spoken to her she was in China using Skype to connect with me. She had sounded tired but didn't confirm this. Instead, she asked about how I was doing. I hadn't been able to talk to her since being put in ad seg. Cheri had told me Maya got some sort of bug while overseas.

My Dear Joy,
2-15-16

I received word that you were sick with some type of flu. I have prayed for you & hope you get well soon. Due to my current circumstances, I receive info slower than usual. But I nevertheless do faithfully receive updates.

I am frustrated with the games being played with my life. I am kicked like an empty can by people I never see. Yes, I am frustrated, but I have my hope in Christ & His word has brought me daily provisions of comfort. Yes, I am battered by the storm, but the Lord has me safe & secure in His mighty hand. But I have expressed to the Lord that I would prefer less painful circumstances. Our good, good Father is in control nevertheless.

I haven't heard from you in a while. I hope & pray that all is well with you. I hope you think of me even in your busiest moments. But I hope that I cause you no pain & I hope that if I do cause you pain, I hope that the pain doesn't cause you to give up. Here is a moment of silent vulnerability: My Dear Diary, losing you is one of my greatest fears. Other than the Lord, our Heavenly Father, you are the only one I've told this vulnerability. But I know how loyal, dedicated, true you are to me. But beware of those little foxes (Song of Songs 2:15). Don't let the enemy destroy our garden or plant those little seeds of discouragement. He'll try, trust me. When you feel the enemy, remember my words, my actions, my heart & remember that our good, good Father loves us & is for us. Yes, "Rudy" comes in many ways, shapes & forms.

I will end this letter for now. I know that you are resting & will be very busy soon. But I hope to hear from you soon.

Love,
Jonathan

I smiled thinking of the "Rudy" in my letter. Whenever we were talking on the phone, a voice would come on right in the middle of our conversation with a recording. "This is a collect call from a correctional facility and may be monitored and recorded." One time when we heard this interruption, Maya said, "That was *rude*." I laughed.

"Yeah, that's right."

"Rudy just interrupted our flow," Maya said.

"I like that," I told her. "I'm going to call her Rudy."

Rudy was part of the enemy, and she came anytime she wanted to no matter what you were talking about or how you were feeling. It was fun to joke about this. God knew I needed something to laugh about in prison. Maya told me she found it amazing how I always found ways to laugh, even in the hole. But I needed something to make me smile. Especially since I hadn't heard from Maya in a while.

Two days later, I decided to write her again.

Dear Maya,   2-17-16

Well, I am feeling pretty sad right now. This is the first year that I haven't received a "Happy Valentine's Day" letter, poem, or simple message from you. Yes, I am being sensitive. I'll admit that I'm all on my own. What does this mean? Are you tired of everything including thinking of me?

Maybe I am just being selfish & inconsiderate of the weight you carry upon your shoulders. In relationships, people sometimes forget to consider the burdens of another because of the pain that he or she may feel. I don't like pointing the finger, but I am hurting nevertheless, my Beloved. If you need time to get things in order, take your time. I am no stranger to pain. Pain has somehow managed to provide proof that I have a tender heart. Sometimes the pain is too much for me to bear, but somehow I keep going, thank God.

I love you, Maya. I am sorry that I cannot be out there with you. If thinking of me less helps you to better cope, then I am in full support. I know that you try not to think about those things that hurt you deeply.

Always love,

Jonathan

◆ ◆ ◆

1011045 – JONATHAN IRONS
Location: JCCC-007702 – 0D204
From: M Moore
Sent: 02/25/2016 10:34 AM CST
Subject: Hear my Heart

My Love,

I felt the weight of your last two letters and I feel terrible for letting you down for those three weeks. Long-distance communication can be a challenge for me and I realize my silence felt to you like a lack of care and I'm so sorry for being a part of you feeling that, but know that I think and pray for you every single day. I also struggle with fear of failure and I want to do things really well every time I do them, so if deep down I don't feel like I can offer something I think is awesome, I will wait to do it. In this case, I didn't have what I thought would be a meaningful Valentine's gift for you so I didn't send anything small by letter or through Cheri & Reggie.

Please forgive me for my poor communication during a very hard time for you. I wasn't there for you in the way you needed for those long 3 weeks. I want you to be okay so badly and it's been a constant ache in my heart since I heard the news of your recent injustice. My heart had a huge rush of release when Cheri said that you had been moved and are now in a warmer location. And I also sent some extra funds the other day in case they are allowing you to now purchase things (which I think they are if I understood Cheri's update correctly).

The timing of connecting with you over these 3 weeks has been out of sync with me transitioning from China to Atlanta to getting healthy, to hosting my best friend and preparing for USAB Training camp, but all the while I was thinking of you. . . .

I had planned on fasting after I got home from overseas and after I got healthier and pretty much over my cold, I started a 21-day fast. I've been fasting for about 10 days now and you are a constant theme of the focus of my fast. I'm eating food just not delicacies, I've cut out certain TV shows and I'm going to bed earlier, and once a week I'm going 24 hrs no solid foods. Just overall sharpening my habits to be more in tune with our beloved Lord. I've added in some time in the mornings for prayer and meditation and I'm memorizing Philippians 4:4–9. I've been trying to get my soul in a more peaceful place since coming back from China and ending a pretty tough year of 2015 of feeling worn down, by sharpening my spiritual habits. So that's why I'm fasting. . . . I want to be better for the Lord and for those he's placed around me. I'm really focusing on Phil 4:8 and it's been a cool journey so far. . . .

Lastly, I realize because of how close we are, like you said in your letter, that we are more sensitive to each other, which means hurt can happen more easily. I appreciate you sharing your feelings and being vulnerable with me, it takes a strong man to do that and I admire that in you so much. Yes, it was painful to read about how much it hurt you for me not writing and I hate this whole situation of it being this hard to communicate and the timing of it and just the fact that you were hurting makes me crazy, but God's love for us both and for you is greater than it all. I know we can bounce back from this crazy time and I LOVE YOU MORE AND MORE EVERY DAY. Be assured My Love. I will be on alert for my battle with perfection and I will keep my eyes on the joy of overcoming this fear with you (not on guilt, amen) as I stay close to your heart one small note at a time!

I love you,

My Sweet One.

YDJ

◆ ◆ ◆

My Dear Maya,
2-29-16

We only fail if we give up on our love, on each other and our future. I have counted the cost deep within the private places of my mind. This is my conclusion. You are worth all the pain and sadness I feel for missing you. For me, I will proudly say that it is far better to experience being hurt with you than being hurt without you.

I won't pretend that not hearing from you for so long didn't hurt as I explained in my last letter. But the fact that you can hurt me so easily is a testament as to how much I love you. No one can take God's place, but you are not in competition with God. He has allowed me to give you my heart to love, hold, to protect and cherish. But he didn't say that you needed to be perfect, dear beloved. I don't want perfection. I want you. Let me say it again. I want you. I want your heart, your mind, your body and your flaws, too. . . .

I don't want you to live in guilt about missing Valentine's Day, even though I was hurting. I held no grudge. You were forgiven well before it happened. True love covers a multitude of sins. I love you, baby. Although I was longing for your words, the Lord was with me and continued to give me assurance even in your absence, as he did. But I still feel your presence despite the pain I felt. As of now, let's not discuss this further. And you have nothing to make up, but I will let you make it up to me by just being you. . . .

◆ ◆ ◆

After spending several months in the hole, I had been moved to 6 House, which was the place you'd be held in ad seg before being released back into the regular population when bed space opened up. It was a double cell, but thankfully I wasn't with a psycho like I had been two years earlier in 2014. This time I had a young kid as my cellie. He was all of 150 pounds soaking wet with a head full of long dreadlocks. I knew I'd be getting out of there any day now, and in a couple of weeks, Maya would be coming to visit. But sadly, everything changed.

A couple of COs came to our cell and told us they were going to search it, so they put us in a holding tank, which basically was a cage twelve feet tall, six feet wide, and six feet long, built like a chain-link fence but sturdier. There was a chuckhole where you could reach in and put on handcuffs. We waited in the holding tank without cuffs until they finished searching our cell.

"Hey, man, we're about to take you back to the hole," a CO told me.

Right away I knew what they were doing. They were playing the same games they always did, being mean-spirited and messing with your heart and mind. One of the ways I think they teach how to break people is to grab them and let them think they're *never* getting out, then to grab them again and put them in another place, giving them a false sense of hope like they're *finally* gonna escape the hole. Then they grab you again and put you *back* in solitary. They keep doing that till inmates lose the will to fight. I knew that was real because that was how men in prison broke other men, how they raped and dominated them. They made them think they could get away, that it was going to be okay in the end. They even let them tell the COs. But in the end, these targeted men realized the COs weren't going to do anything for them.

As I stepped over to put one wrist out in the hole for them to handcuff, I felt like a volcano full of rage about to erupt. They knew they had to use two cuffs on me because I was too wide and muscular at the time. As I heard the one cuff latch, I realized I'd had enough.

I'm not going without a fight. They don't have to make up reasons to take me to the hole anymore. I can't take it anymore! I will give them a reason and earn it this time.

I snatched my left wrist out and turned around.

"What are y'all doing?" I yelled. "You're just gonna free case me in ad seg too? Okay. I'm gonna give you a reason to take me to the hole. Come try and get these cuffs."

For a moment, I lost control. I was tired and beat down and angry and confused. Fury filled me as I dared them to come get me. My young cellie hid behind me.

The COs didn't move. They could see I had gone to a very dark place, and they didn't want no part of me. They knew I had lost my mind. I was going to hurt one of them, and then they were going to hurt me in return.

They had driven me to this point.

Another CO I knew showed up and walked to the side of the holding tank.

"Johnny. JI! What happened?"

"I don't know what happened—you tell me!"

"Are you selling drugs?"

I let out an angry laugh. "What? No! Absolutely not!"

"Well, it's something to do with that."

This CO knew me well enough to know I had nothing to do with drugs.

"Look, JI. Just go to the hole and we'll figure it out. Just give me the cuffs. Don't make this any worse."

With every ounce of self-control I could muster, I put my hand back in the chuckhole. He double-cuffed me knowing I was yoked up and ready to go. I was 250 pounds of lean, mean muscle and a dangerous problem. They took me back to the hole, and that's when I found out the situation with the drugs.

"Hey, man, did you come down with that young dude?" my neighbor in solitary asked me.

"Yeah."

"They said they found some heroin on him."

I clenched my fist and sighed. The prison made me guilty by association with my cellie's drugs. An association I had no control over.

Another false accusation. When's it gonna stop?

"I don't know anything about that—this is crazy!" I said.

"Then you need to get word to him," the guy told me.

The anger still raced through me as I tried to calm down.

I would learn that the young cellie I'd been with had a friend who had just gotten out of the hole, they put him in the cell next door to mine, and he hadn't even gotten his property back from ad seg yet. No one got their personal property for at least two hours after being moved. When you go to solitary, they take all the possessions you own. Later that morning, the COs opened our door so that my cellie and I could go to the medical services building. After I caught up with the rest of the crowd of inmates going to medical, I looked back at my door to make sure it was closed. I noticed my cellie slide a thin magazine under his friend's door, next to ours. It barely fit under the door. But he seemed to not care that he was violating an institutional rule.

It is common knowledge that passing items can get you into big trouble, especially with so many cameras around.

Thinking he got away with it, he turned and sprinted back to the group just as we walked out the door to medical with a CO as an escort. After we came back from medical, the COs told us to return to our cells immediately.

About an hour later, all of our doors opened for lunch. We had to walk to the chow hall every day for breakfast, lunch, and dinner. But they brought your meals to your cell door in ad seg and handed them to you through the small chuckhole. After being in ad seg, it felt good to walk to the chow hall for meals each day, even if I didn't eat what they were serving us.

My cellie and his friend were in front of the group leading the way to chow hall. One CO called over my cellie's friend for a routine daily pat search. Once the CO felt the bulge in his sock, my cellie's friend sprinted hard up the walk from the COs in pursuit. But he stopped after about twenty yards, realizing there was no escape and cameras were everywhere outside of our cells recording our every move. They found two or three grams of heroin in his sock, so they locked him back up. Two hours later, they came for this guy's friend and me.

After eighteen-plus years of being in prison, I was about to discover I had reached a new low.

◆ ◆ ◆

Lord, have you forgotten me?

Years and years and years.

Picked up after getting off work at McDonald's and thrown in jail overnight and never told why. Released the next day without a word. Charged for a vicious crime I didn't commit. Arrested and questioned and treated and tried like an adult when I was still a kid. Imprisoned inside The Walls with true-life monsters, with people who ate people, with mass murderers and serial rapists and robbers and everything else that went boo at night and growled in the dark. Forgotten about with people who didn't care about other people and treated as subhuman. Battered after fighting an unjust system both inside and outside the prison. Battle-scarred from the years of stuff like this happening.

I sat in the hole, knowing Maya was coming to see me and living for that and realizing it might not happen. All the people around me were mental-health patients, beating on the walls and hollering obscenities. It was so loud I couldn't even hear myself think. A constant, chaotic "RAAAAAAAAARRRRRRR" filled the wing like poison gas as I just sat there without hope.

You never got used to the hole. The air reeked of body odor and urine and fecal matter. Everything was dirty. Even the bedding they gave you was grimy. A thick layer of dust covered the floor, so you couldn't walk on it with even your socks on. You had to walk around in your shower shoes. The first thing I always did when I got to solitary was clean my cell out. But now in this pit of madness, I finally felt defeated. All I could think about was how I was robbed again of my privileges, stripped of my job, and my chance to see Maya was gone.

I'm making a rope.

I started tearing off threads of my worn sheet, fashioned it into a rope, and tied it up. I even tested it to see if it would hold my weight. I had learned how to make a rope out of a sheet in my early days of prison. This was how you got stuff like stamps, paper, and food—you tied things together and then inmates would drag the items down the hall cell by cell. This time, I had to make my rope really thick, and then started putting it up through the water sprinkler. I didn't tie it in a loop, but I formed it and just stared at it. I stared at the rope. This was my way out. I couldn't take the pain anymore.

They had broken me. Now maybe they were gonna bury me, too.

Before I could do anything else, I passed out in a deep sleep.

◆ ◆ ◆

A deep, long sleep.

I now know this was the Lord saving my life, because when I woke up the next morning, I was different. I could see everything around me more clearly. It was quieter in the wing, and the colors were brighter. My desire to live had come back, and I was myself once again. Regaining my strength, I came up with a plan.

I started fasting.

Fasting is a humble way of cutting out food for a period of time to better connect with God. I needed my Heavenly Father now more than ever, so this was the step I took.

The COs called it a hunger strike. I did this for literally a week, not eating any of the food they tried to give me. This confused and scared them enough that eventually they called me out and took me back into my caseworker's office, taking off my cuffs. I immediately got suspicious.

I don't want any part of this.

"Oh, no, y'all trying to set me up," I said. "Ain't no camera back here!"

"No, no, J. We know you didn't do this. We know. We just have to work things out. You have to be patient. You know how slow things are."

Yeah, I know. Eighteen and half years slow.

The DOC was slow to move everything except when taking your money or putting you in the hole. But I listened to my caseworker and waited. And they eventually came and got me out of the hole about two days later.

◆ ◆ ◆

Remembering and reliving these dark moments in 2016 is painful and embarrassing. I never want to talk about the pain and the negativity without emphasizing the joy and the success of what happened in the journey. There were bad things that happened—unjust and inhumane things—but there were also good things happening, too. A love story unfolding in the belly of the beast is a beautiful thing.

Maya told me this once about the bad stuff.

"Be honest about the dark. But the truth is, the light is greater than the dark. It's true. It's our story and it's our lives."

From the moment I stepped foot in that first holding tank with those grown men staring down at me, my greatest fear was dying in prison without anybody ever knowing the truth about what happened with me. Then I met Hugh Flowers, who introduced me to Reggie and Cheri, who introduced me to Maya.

What Hugh really introduced me to was hope.

My hope wasn't in Maya and her family; my hope was in God. But I was thankful for all of them because they pointed me toward God. I'm so thankful that my loving Father brought their light into my dark world, and that they came alongside me to fight a system that was designed for me to fail. I might have been living in the system, but my body, soul, and life belonged to the Lord.

I was able to see Maya for that scheduled visit to JCCC, and even though this visit almost didn't happen, a way was made for her to be there with me that weekend. But really, Maya was always there with me in prison, in my cell, in the hole, anywhere. I wrote to her later that year and expressed this in a letter.

> I have been thru some hard times and you have been there with me when I needed you the most. You have been my faithful gift. Your love for me has not diminished. But we have only grown closer. Even in spite of the pain you have experienced, you have held on even tighter during some of our most difficult moments. Receiving mail from you always blesses my heart. But you quenched my thirst for your love every time you wrote to me while I was in the hole. It warmed my heart that you were able to share with me your feelings about what I was going through. In truth, you were with me and felt pain from my circumstances too, because of how much you love me. In spite of the pain you felt, you stood by my side no matter how limited our interaction was at the time and no matter how much it hurt you. Your dedication and loyalty to me has been unshakable. I see you, Baby. Yes, I feel your love. It is overwhelmingly wonderful. These are just a few of the ways you have creatively shown me how much you are in love with me. You may not fully understand this yet, but God

has equipped and prepared you to be able to remove burdens from my life, and your mere presence eases the pressure I deal with daily.

From the very moment I met Maya, she had been a pure light to me. The love we shared was a precious gift from God. Step by step, day by day, and year by year, we were thriving and overcoming all obstacles. We were trusting God and depending on Him rather than relying on our own understanding. The way I saw it, we had a great advantage. God was illuminating our path with gentle instruction, protection, and provision. Even though some days were filled with darkness, we were creating and living a great love story that would shine light on injustice while bringing glory to the Kingdom of Heaven.

PART
FIVE

Chapter Nineteen

WIN WITH JUSTICE

(2016–2017)

(M)

IF I MISS THIS SHOT, *our season will be over and I can go home.*

My mind really struggled with this thought while I was playing in China for the Shanxi Flames. I was globally known for competing at the highest level and had faithfully led my team to *three straight* WCBA championships from 2012 to 2015. But this year I decided to only play half the season, to take less money and take more rest at home. It was always challenging living on two different continents, especially during an Olympic year that would be taking me to Rio, Brazil. I had known I needed to play overseas if I wanted to maximize my earnings while I still had the talent, but playing in Shanxi for my fourth year in a row made me wonder if it was worth it.

Winning meant I had to stay in China for another three weeks. Of course, I did my best, but I hated being tempted to not want to win because I wanted to go home. It was so counter to the spirit of playing the game and was just so disheartening to battle.

This would be the beginning of the end for me in China. Each season had a unique expression or manifestation of what I was feeling inside. I called

2016 my weary season. One example of this was that when I went over to China at the end of 2015, I started to get terrible acne. My whole face broke out; I looked like I had a disease. I began to get really nervous when it didn't clear up by the time I got back to the States. *I can't start the WNBA season with my face looking like this! I can't just put on makeup and go play.* I went to a dermatologist and ended up on antibiotics and two face creams, and thankfully it cleared up a bit before the 2016 tip-off. But this was because I was worn down. Very worn down.

Hearing from Jonathan through letters and phone calls helped me get through those tough times. One time he called me and I told him my latest story from being on the road during my China season.

"I just had to shower in my hotel with a hose," I said.

"For real?" he asked.

"Yeah. And the water wasn't even warm."

Jonathan couldn't believe it. "The greatest women's basketball player on the planet and she's having to shower with a hose in China? Are you serious?"

I appreciated Jonathan's love and concern for me despite the fact that his conditions were a thousand times worse. We were both living in environments that were not our homes, and both of us were in systems that we couldn't control. Part of my tension was my inability to connect the way I wanted to, as exhibited in the Valentine's Day letters. I was heartbroken during that period to not be there for him. My life wasn't allowing me the space to be there.

I didn't know that I was being emptied to make space for something new. But I was still committed to this massive thing, basketball, so I continued to give it everything I had.

◆ ◆ ◆

Game 5 of the 2016 WNBA Finals. The Minnesota Lynx are playing our rival that year, the Los Angeles Sparks. The Lynx escaped elimination in Game 4 and now are playing at home. In a tough and tight game with twenty-four lead changes, Candace Parker from the Sparks makes a layup with 19.7 seconds left on the clock and puts LA up by 1. After we take our last timeout, I drain a turnaround baseline jump shot to give the Lynx the lead again at 75–76. Only 15.7 seconds remain on the clock, and both teams are without timeouts.

The Sparks inbound the ball, but their fadeaway jump shot hits the rim long. LA's power forward Nneka Ogwumike grabs the rebound, shoots, and then sees the ball blocked back to her. Nneka catches the ball just as she falls backward, launching her second attempt as she falls to the court. The ball drops in and puts LA ahead by 1 point with 3.1 seconds remaining. With no timeouts, we are forced to take a desperation half-court shot, but it's not enough.

Losing the finals in front of eighteen thousand of our fans is awful. It is the hardest loss of my career because we really played well enough to win. When I come back home to Georgia, I am weary and worn out. Not just because of my schedule and the way our season ended. I've experienced another loss as well with Team Jonathan.

◆ ◆ ◆

I remember something Papa once told us. He said that he had once gone to one of the most high-powered lawyers in town and had given him Jonathan's papers explaining his case. The lawyer told him the simple and brutal truth.

"Mr. Flowers. Once you're in the prison system, it's almost impossible to get out."

Over the years, Jonathan kept bumping up into the same argument: He needed a legal reason to get back in court. Time after time, there was new information and evidence that he learned about, but there was all this red tape involved. That's the way our criminal justice system is set up—to keep you in there. Exonerating an innocent person is nearly impossible, even when you have clear evidence like the form that showed another unidentified fingerprint. It's far easier to convict an innocent person than it is to exonerate an innocent person in our system.

People from different nonprofits along with pro-bono lawyers had worked on his case throughout the years, but they had had limited resources and time. Despite having even fewer resources, Jonathan worked and researched any possible avenues to get his case back in court. And he found one. In 2014, Jonathan's team of advocates contacted the prosecuting attorney for St. Charles to inform him of the undisclosed fingerprint records that had been discovered by Reggie and asked that he consider reopening and investigating Jonathan's case. Our team met with the prosecuting attorney in his private chambers shortly after this, and the meeting was short. The prosecutor didn't fight it. They knew there were undisclosed fingerprints, yet they had never disclosed this information to Jonathan and his team. They allowed us to have them, however. Jonathan's team and the prosecuting attorney agreed to proceed with post-conviction "touch DNA" testing, but we would have to pay for it despite it being their job to find the actual perpetrator. The unidentified fingerprints were sent to a lab for analysis.

Touch DNA testing was a forensic method of examining evidence from a crime scene using only a little, itty-bitty piece of physical evidence like a fingerprint. We held on to hope that the testing would discover something, but unfortunately the DNA testing failed. Too much time had passed. It was likely due to the degradation of genetic material after almost twenty years of being in storage. If only someone had tested these fingerprints years ago when they were still viable. If only Jonathan had had a chance to even ask about testing them.

Our latest attempt to get Jonathan home was dead.

I felt like I was living a tale of two lives. One moment, I'd be bruised up in a game over in China; then next I'd be learning about an update on DNA testing from Jonathan. I'd be sitting out on the deck of my room at the Rio Olympics while the man I wanted to marry was just getting out of the hole. I'm grinding my way to the WNBA finals, and meanwhile Jonathan is grinding away trying to get a second chance at being heard. Time after time we had nonprofit groups come in and help, then go missing and seemingly abandon Jonathan's case.

Learning the news about the DNA case felt far worse than losing the finals. It was a roller-coaster ride we were on.

With the Lynx's season over and the effort to bring home the most important person in my life failing, I felt very low. I called my agent and told her how I was feeling.

"I can't go back overseas right now," I told her. "I think I need to stay home the whole off-season this time."

The past six seasons in Minnesota were taking their toll on my body, mind, and soul. I explained a little of this to the *Star Tribune* when discussing my decision not to play in China for another season.

"What we do here is hard," I said about the Lynx. "We make it look easy sometimes, but it takes a toll, playing at the highest level you can year after year."

I knew I needed a break. I needed to pause and reflect on how I was living out my purpose. I was thriving as player, but was I thriving as a human? Not only was my body desperate for healing, I also wanted to be present for my loved ones, close friends, and church family. I needed to be present that way, too.

"You need to be able to find joy in something that requires so much of yourself," I said in an interview with the *Star Tribune*. "I have to have that deeper meaning in my work and in my everyday life. It is important to remind ourselves why we do what we do."

As I shared my heart in the interview, nobody knew that the difficulties I spoke about went far beyond the basketball court.

"It's tough, but you can still find joy in the struggle. Going through a season with a lot of struggles, I got a lot of practice. You have to set yourself up for joy, give yourself the best opportunity to have that going on inside."

◆ ◆ ◆

I've always been a super private person, so my relationship with Jonathan had always been kept close to my heart. Yet when we began to "date" in our own unique way, I knew that I needed to tell people I trusted. A small group that knew my heart and would give wisdom, accountability, and support as we did our best to love each other. "This can't just be a you-and-me thing," I once told Jonathan. "We have to have some people walking alongside us. Not *everyone*, but at least a few to be praying with us and helping us navigate these very different waters." So I created a team of people we could lean on and count on for their prayers. They were affectionately known as our prayer warriors. Jonathan and I felt the safety of having a small group of people besides Cheri, Reggie, and Mom know what was going on.

Jonathan and I had talked more about what it would take to get him home. We knew his case needed more attention. And honestly, I felt like I had been sitting on the bench and watching from the sidelines for far too long. I wanted to be put into the game. I wanted to do more. So, after telling my agent, Lindsay Kagawa Colas, about needing to stay home, I also felt it was time to let her know about Jonathan's story. She was blown away and as outraged as our family was.

Her wheels were spinning with ideas to do something powerful for Jonathan:

"Do you want to start a nonprofit? . . . We can make a documentary! . . . I need to connect you with Mike!"

She jumped into action like the superhero I've known her to be. Jonathan had mentioned making a documentary before, so we were on the same page with moving forward with that method of bringing awareness to his cause. I was also eager to connect with the person she said could really help me learn more about the world of criminal justice reform. I was so relieved and felt like a weight had been lifted off my shoulders because Lindsay was passionate about empowering me to help others.

I have help!

I was not alone in trying to figure out how to advocate from my platform.

"Tell me what you want to name the nonprofit and we'll get started," Lindsay said.

Feeling the wind at my back from that phone call, I discussed this new idea with Jonathan, and we both felt the excitement of this new potential vehicle for change. He had helped me learn so much, and soon I'd be connecting with more people to educate me. Lindsay connected me with Mike de la Rocha, who shared with me many of the broader issues of criminal justice reform. I was feeling so overwhelmed by the brokenness I was discovering, and was feeling even more devastated for Jonathan's struggle. But then Mike gave me the best advice he could have given me.

"Maya, this machine is so massive and it's easy to feel discouraged. I would encourage you to pick a lane and run in it. That way you can stay above water in this long fight toward justice."

Mike taught me a term: prosecutorial misconduct. *Whoa—that's a mouthful!* I thought when I first heard it. I had to slowly practice saying it a few times before it stuck in my mind. He also explained to me about the power of prosecutors and the role they play in our justice system. How they are essentially one of the most powerful actors in our justice system because they bring the charges and basically "set the rules of the game." They have what's called absolute immunity, which makes it illegal for them to be sued for their misconduct in the courtroom.

I learned that prosecutors have a very important job, but there's also the temptation for them to cut corners and abuse their power in order to "get the win" and get the conviction of who they are bringing a case against. This mindset of "winning at all costs" can pervert justice. I thought about the fact that we need to redefine what a win is in our justice system.

A win isn't simply a prosecutor getting a conviction, but a win should be measured by how well the final judgment impacts the flourishing of that community.

This was how my nonprofit Win with Justice was born. Let's win because the outcome is thoughtful and thorough justice, not just the appearance of justice.

Is this an easy way to approach to justice? Not always.

But are the people in our communities worth the effort to change this mindset? Absolutely!

I love this name!

Now I needed to think about what kind of nonprofit this would be.

I was learning about reform and how our systems had been subtly structured to dehumanize a certain class of people. My first reaction was *Let's fix what's wrong with the structure!* But I heard the Lord remind me that, ultimately, we can build the most brilliant structure we want, but without love, it will be in vain. Mankind has always had the ability to take something good and use it for evil purposes. It's a temptation none of us are free from.

We have such a brilliantly structured democratic republic as Americans, but it all depends on the people of our communities running the republic for the good of the people. The heart of the citizens will determine if the system is used for abusing its people or for the flourishing of its people.

I wanted to create something that would help model and inspire the hearts of the people to love our neighbors more. I also wanted it to be a place where people could learn, get educated, and find resources that would empower them to be more intentional about voting for their local district attorney. Finally, I wanted it to be a place that would put Jonathan's fight for freedom on display. Shine light on his plight and ask others to advocate for him, too.

The spirit of Win with Justice was now clear in my mind. I love the term "spirit of the law" because it focuses on the heart of the matter. And as human beings, we flourish when the heart of the matter is love. We can have the most amazing laws, but if we engage in the law with evil motives, we can find loopholes and twist it for our desired outcome. I had seen it up close in Jonathan's plight time and time again. People abusing their power in order to hide the truth, which ends up causing people like Jonathan, his family, and his community so much grief and pain. But when we focus on approaching the law with the right spirit of goodwill toward man, we can watch our communities be more alive than ever.

◆ ◆ ◆

Now that Win with Justice was in the works, we decided to have an awareness event near Jonathan's hometown to have a meeting of the minds and share his story. We set a date of January 2017 and reached out to local media outlets in St. Louis to invite them to learn about this awful and local injustice.

None of them showed up.

This was discouraging, but we didn't let this stop us. Family, friends, and Jonathan's pro-bono lawyers at the time showed up, and we had a very meaningful time. It was the starting point for our next phase in the journey of telling the public about Jonathan. Jonathan had already started getting some of his resources together from some local guys he knew, and my agent found a videographer to come to the awareness event. Our goal of making a documentary to raise awareness was now in play.

If I was going to be an advocate for Jonathan, I needed to be more informed about the system he was in. Jonathan had shown and taught me so many things throughout the years, but I needed to take a step back and learn about the history of how this system came to be.

Jonathan's awareness event

Chapter Twenty

THE SHIFT

(2017–2019)

(M)

I WILL BUILD MY LIFE UPON YOUR LOVE, it is a firm foundation. I will put my trust in You alone and I will not be shaken.

The worship song soared in Atlanta's Georgia Dome as I sang along with over fifty thousand college students at Passion 2017. Young men and women from all over the world had gathered for this popular conference started twenty years ago by Pastor Louie and Shelley Giglio to worship together and hear from great Christian speakers and musicians. The mission of Passion Conferences was to "see a generation leverage their lives for what matters most." I felt a wave of wonder inside me as we praised our Heavenly Father.

This wasn't the first time I had been in the Georgia Dome with feelings of excitement. I could still remember the time in seventh grade when my mom and I drove downtown to watch the open practices of the teams competing at the 2003 NCAA Women's Final Four in Atlanta. Watching those great players on those great teams only confirmed that it was something I wanted to do one day. Yet on this day, basketball was far from my mind. My heart was open, and I felt reinvigorated.

As the new year began, I found myself able to attend the Passion conference for the first time. There is an irony in this as I look back on that season of my life. "Passion" was a key word for 2017. At first, I would be full of it during my much-needed winter break in the off-season. Being able to spend Thanksgiving at my house in Atlanta was a blessing, and so was regularly going to church and connecting with people. As a pro, I had never been able to be present at a church gathering week after week. So, when people began seeing me for a second and third Sunday in a row, they looked at me and asked in amazement: "How are you here again?" I surprised them when I said I planned to be home for a while. A strange thought, right? Seeing Maya Moore several days in a row!

Music was really my first love, and I've discovered it's one of the ways God has gifted me to serve my church family. During this time, I was able to get more into songwriting with a new friend I had met. In fact, that year my mom went behind my back and bought me an early birthday present, an acoustic guitar I named Red Velvet. In the last few years, I've probably written over thirty songs with the assistance of this surprise gift!

It was a blessing to begin to unlock this side of me that I hadn't been able to really develop because of my commitment to the grind. During this off-season, I wanted to stop, rest, and remember the joys deep inside my soul. It was nice to slow down and let the Lord be the Lord without me running at a hundred miles per hour. I was able to show up at church and grow in my spiritual disciplines, since I had created space in my schedule to do that. I had said no to the big overseas money, so I could say yes to being refilled by God in the way He was leading.

Along with this, I was able to visit Jonathan during the awareness event at the start of the year as well as other times. I poured myself into learning what it meant for me to be a citizen. I had been an athlete all my life, but I was also a citizen. I began to have extensive conversations with lawyers and watch documentaries and read books and really pay more attention so I could learn. There was so much I had to understand and discover.

My eyes were opened when I watched the 2016 documentary *13th*. As a part of the Black community, I have a certain level of awareness about our history in this country. But Ava DuVernay's powerful documentary woke me up in an explosive way. *13th* explored the history and evolution of racial inequality and brutality in the United States, focusing on the fact that our nation's prisons are disproportionally filled with Black and Brown bodies. I knew some of the things it covered, but I was given more clarity and context to these issues. It was mind-blowing to see the film break down the reality that slavery, through the Thirteenth Amendment, subtly morphed into mass incarceration through the means of our criminal justice system.

Of course, it was impossible to view *13th* without thinking of Jonathan. Especially with interviewees like Michelle Alexander, the author of *The New Jim Crow: Mass Incarceration in the Age of Colorblindness*, and Bryan Stevenson, who penned *Just Mercy: A Story of Justice and Redemption*. Alexander states in the documentary that "there are thousands of people in jails right this moment that are sitting there for no other reason than because they're too poor to get out." And Stevenson shares that "the Bureau of Justice reported that one in three young black males is expected to go to jail or prison during his lifetime, which is an unbelievably shocking statistic."

The New Jim Crow and *Just Mercy* were two powerful books I read along with others, all in search of knowledge and education about how our justice system worked. I had the chance to meet Bryan Stevenson and the staff at the Equal Justice Initiative, a nonprofit providing legal representation to individuals who had been wrongly imprisoned, unfairly sentenced, or abused while in prison. The group down there in Montgomery, Alabama, did such great work and became a great inspiration and educational resource for me. They had a dedicated and amazing staff who had done so much work that assisted me in knowing what real change looked like in the area of justice reform.

I continued to connect with Mike de la Rocha, who was the leader of Revolve Impact. They were a creative agency that helped influencers become educated on causes that they were passionate about. They had a branch called Athletes for Impact, which was a global network of athletes across sports committed to justice and equity. Mike was essential in helping me connect the history of the struggle with solutions for the present.

I was eager and motivated to study the history of the systems that impacted our country and communities. My passion for this grew as well as my resolve to be a strong advocate for Jonathan. But unexpectedly, I didn't have the same amount of passion for basketball when I began to play again.

◆ ◆ ◆

As I had discovered more of myself, more of my purpose, and what my heart beats for, the more I felt the urge to live in that purpose. So shifting back to an in-season lifestyle was pretty jarring for my soul. As the 2017 WNBA season began, I found out my heart was not in it the way I was used to. I just didn't have it. My passion was at an all-time low, and I wasn't sure how to process it.

Yes, I would call this my passionless season, but I still played hard and (spoiler alert) the Lynx still won the WNBA championship.

It was the weirdest and most unnatural thing to feel this way. Anybody who knows me knows that I'm all in with whatever I do with passion and determination. Yes, I've probably said that before, but I'm mentioning it again because this was so unlike me to feel this way. I'm the conviction person, but it seemed like my convictions were living somewhere other than Basketballville.

Perhaps my struggle with passion impacted my shooting in our first six games. Even though the Lynx went 6–0, I was shooting a career-low of 31.5 percent overall and only 28.6 percent on my three-pointers. My scoring average of 13.3 points and only 2.8 free throw attempts were the lowest they had been since my rookie season. The numbers didn't alarm me. I knew there were lots of other ways I impacted the game besides shooting the ball, and I wasn't going to overthink any of this. I was still going to play like I always had.

Some of those closest to me on the team noticed the change in me. Not just in my scoring but more so in my spirit. When they asked if I was okay, I told them the truth: "No, I'm not okay." But I didn't know what to do. I was Maya Moore . . . one of the faces of the league. I couldn't lose my passion! So I just kept moving.

As the season progressed and the feelings inside me didn't change, I was gifted by a friend with a book. *God Has a Name* by John Mark Comer helps us see and remember that the God of the Bible is a personal being. He wants to be in a real relationship with us, and He wants us to be real with Him . . . good, bad, or ugly. So I prayed.

"Listen, God. Abba. I can't keep doing this."

Abba is an affectionate way to call God "Father" in Hebrew that I had made a habit of using.

"You're gonna have to do something! This isn't safe. I'm gonna get injured if I'm not focused and into this. I feel so fake; I can't live like this anymore. I'm gonna sit here until you tell me something!"

And just like any loving father would do, God heard me and answered me. I felt like He whispered to my heart to *hold on* and trust Him.

It is going to work out for good, Maya. Just move like you believe me. I will restore you.

So I started to move in my belief that there was something glorious coming through this painful and confusing time. Day by day, I came back to life. I actually finished the season really well, feeling and playing way more free. By the time we finished the regular season with a 27–7 record, including a 20–2 start, I had more energy and more bounce in my step.

It was another dramatic series with the Los Angeles Sparks (who else?) in the 2017 WNBA Finals. We split the first two games in Minnesota, then split the next two in LA, bringing Game 5 back to Minneapolis. The Sparks trailed 79–67 with less than two minutes remaining, but they made a crazy 9–0 run to narrow the margin to only 3 points with thirty-four seconds left.

I had been really spoiled to have some of the best of the best who ever played or coached the game by my side through so many championship experiences, and this was no different. Led by the unstoppable play of my teammate Sylvia "Sweet Syl" Fowles, we had gotten to a point in the game where we had a chance to seal the lead. The play did not start off as planned, and we were in all-out scramble mode as LA furiously tried to pressure us into a turnover. One thing led to another, and I ended up getting a handoff from Syl, weaving side to side, then pulling up off of one foot just inside the free-throw line for a quick jumper that slid in to clinch the lead.

As my teammate Plenette Pierson would say after the game to describe that moment:

"EVERYBODY, CALM DOWN."

The crowd went bananas, Syl got finals MVP, and we had won our fourth title in seven years.

◆ ◆ ◆

During my basketball season, Jonathan was never far from my heart or mind. We were still close, trying to have a relationship and stay connected. I encouraged him and he encouraged me. We remained loyal friends and tried to live life in our two very different universes. I missed what I experienced in the spring of just being home and rooted and feeling more alive.

For years, Jonathan had been doing extensive research to determine the best attorneys, hoping and planning that if the day ever came when he had the financial means, he would know who was ready for the job. We had talked about our desire to have an excellent firm represent him. And Jonathan gave me a worst-case-scenario view on how expensive legal work could be. He wanted me to be aware of that, and I appreciated his honesty. By now we had years of relationship under our belt, so I felt comfortable supporting him in every way I could because he knew what he was doing.

"I know nothing about this world," I told him. "So I'm totally depending on your expertise and whoever you decide is best; I'm behind you. I want to cover the costs to get you a lawyer that can do this right."

Our plans went into action in the spring of 2017, when Jonathan became officially represented by attorney Jessica Hathaway. While she learned and mastered the enormous amount of details for his case, Jonathan worked diligently away on crafting his habeas petition. Thankfully he was doing very well in his current housing situation, staying in a unit where they trained men who were on their way home and transitioning back into society. He had been in this program years ago but now they brought him in to lead the men as a mentor.

My success with the Lynx gave me an even bigger platform and opportunity to share about these issues. One great opportunity came with the Players' Tribune when former NBA all-star Jerry Stackhouse interviewed Reggie and me for a video series called *First Step*. This series featured athletes who were fighting today's social issues. The five-minute video allowed me to share how I got involved with prosecutorial reform.

"I lived in a kind of a middle-class home, and I didn't really have a lot of experience with the justice system or prisons or really being aware of that world," I began the video by saying. "My perception has changed from thinking *If someone's in jail they're supposed to be* to *There's a lot of factors—it's not that simple.*"

It felt good to share Jonathan's story and to hear Reggie publicly share about his own personal journey with it. He and Cheri had been fighting to right the wrongs of Jonathan's conviction for the past ten years all while working and raising a family.

"The lead detective said he took him into a room," Reggie shared. "He didn't tape. He didn't bring any cameras in there. He didn't even bring another police officer in there. It was just a comedy of errors to me. . . . And the more I looked at it, the more it just struck a chord in me that, man, we gotta do something for this young man."

We were able to talk to Jonathan over the phone at Jefferson City Correctional Center so he could share from his heart and show appreciation for being able to share his story. Not even being able to interview Jonathan in person just reminded me of his appalling situation, and I expressed how it made me feel.

"I get pretty worked up when I see injustice," I said. "And so I couldn't pretend like I didn't see this happening. Jonathan essentially becoming a part of our family over all these years, it just really motivated me to want to help. If people can see me taking that risk to go on this journey, hopefully it can free them up to want to do the same thing."

Another opportunity to share our message came in a different form of media. Along with Kansas City district attorney Mark Dupree and Fair and Just Prosecution's executive director Miriam Krinsky, I was able to collaborate in writing an op-ed for *USA Today* titled "A 'Win' for Justice."

"As a professional athlete, an elected prosecutor [Mark], and a justice system leader [Miriam], we work in the public eye and are privileged that our communities have bestowed tremendous trust in the work we seek to carry out. To live up to that trust, both on and off our respective 'courts,' we believe that we need to bring a new vision to our justice system that moves beyond simply a result-driven finish line and instead brings a broader lens to promoting safe and healthy communities."

The piece addressed our concerns about the justice system, about lengthy prison sentences for people charged with low-level offenses, about the emphasis on incarceration over treatment, and about the win-at-all-costs mentality from prosecutors. But we also expressed the hope we felt about the changes we saw sweeping over the nation with a new wave of state and local elected criminal justice leaders.

Not long after that, in January 2018, I was able to pen a piece in *ESPN The Magazine* that was written specifically to Black athletes. "Don't ever forget that you are a citizen—a part of a community," I told them. "With being an athlete there comes privilege and responsibility—mainly the responsibility to never stop seeking to understand your fellow citizen and neighbor—more importantly, the ones who aren't exactly like you."

I shared my journey of stepping into the world of mass incarceration in America and witnessing the double standards and unchecked power.

"The American dream of freedom for all of its diverse citizens can only work if we, the people, work it! And as athletes, we know the process to achieving goals better than most."

As an athlete who had been the beneficiary of playing under legendary coaches like Geno Auriemma and Cheryl Reeve, I had watched them cast beautiful visions for our team's culture. This was what I was passionate about now—casting life-giving visions. I wanted my platform to paint visions that said *This is how good we can be.*

◆ ◆ ◆

With another off-season arriving, I decided to not go overseas again and stayed home to enjoy another winter and spring in Georgia. Then, out of the blue, my agent called me three weeks before the new year with an offer to seriously consider.

"Diana is leaving her team in Russia. Do you want to take her spot?"

This was big news. Diana Taurasi was one of the greatest to ever play, and this Russian team had a big budget and professional resources to offer its players. It seemed like a no-brainer, but I wanted to stay home.

I only had a few days to decide, so I considered what I'd be giving up as well as what I'd be gaining.

The club's offering me more money than I've ever made in my career. . . .

I'll miss my restful rhythm at home, but I have gotten some rest this fall. . . .

The players there are super talented, and we'd be so good. . . .

It's only four months. . . .

And I'll be set up to stay home next off-season with what they're paying me. . . .

Yes, I can do this. . . .

Wait . . . how cold is it in Russia?

In January 2018, I made my debut in the Russian league with UMMC Ekaterinburg. My mom came over with me, and we lived in an apartment in Ekaterinburg in Central Russia. We didn't lose a game after my arrival and eventually won the EuroLeague title playing against Sopron in Sopron, Hungary. Thankfully I stayed healthy and God allowed me the grace to play really well.

There was a team of around thirty prayer warriors whom I was starting to update on a regular basis. So that spring from Ekaterinburg I shared in more detail where things were with Jonathan's case. In the update, I explained about a new player we had hired for his legal team.

> Last spring we set a goal of having a petition ready to be filed for Jonathan by the fall of 2017. Things were moving in that direction but a divine delay came in the form of an excellent, well respected, local investigator (Kevin) who we hired around November. Although we are anxious to get the petition filed for Jonathan's freedom, we now see how very impactful Kevin's work will be in making J's case

even more rock solid. Jonathan is very pleased with how Kevin is working and what he is finding. Even more evidence in Jonathan's favor is being found and Jonathan is very encouraged.

I also shared once again how I was able to partner with the Players' Tribune last fall to film a video with Jerry Stackhouse that talked about everything connected to the cause of prosecutorial reform. It had turned out so great with Jonathan being a part of it, so it was wonderful to share the resource once again. I loved being a voice for Jonathan, but nothing beat hearing his *own* voice share the hope he had.

"Just because you're in prison doesn't mean that you let prison overtake you and let it beat you down," Jonathan said. "You have to keep going."

As always, that bright light that I first saw in Jonathan back in 2007 still burned. Maybe brighter than ever. The video continued to share the mission of Win with Justice.

"The people in our society who maybe have the least means are the most vulnerable," I said. "And if we don't protect and fight for the most vulnerable in our community, what kind of community are we? Ultimately systems work or fail because of people."

Jonathan was able to share his future dreams.

"The way I feel about it, it doesn't stop when I go home. It doesn't mean that's the end. I want to reach back and be ready to help all I can and also be an encourager."

◆ ◆ ◆

There was a quick transition from playing over in Russia to starting the new season in Minneapolis, a quick blink of a week before starting to play with the Lynx in May. I was energized to be back with my teammates but also felt weary.

"Oh my goodness," my mom said as we both turned to take in the shocking image.

As we drove to the Target Center for the Minnesota Lynx's home opener, we turned a corner and saw me floating in the sky. There I was, standing in an iconic pose stretched out wide over a massive billboard on the side of a building covering an entire city block.

I knew that the Jordan Brand was planning to do a big promotion for the start of the 2018 WNBA season, but I didn't realize it would be *that* big. There I was posing in the same way that Michael Jordan did in his classic "Wings" poster in the late '80s, with outstretched arms and my right hand palming a WNBA basketball. To replicate this image of Jordan was an incredible honor.

Even though my image appeared larger than life in that moment, I was really feeling a different call from the One who gives life. And that call had finally become clear. Later that year, I would have the realization that for the first time in my whole life, I could stop playing basketball. And I did.

◆ ◆ ◆

"THE SHIFT"

February 6, 2019

The Players' Tribune

I will not be playing professional basketball this year.

There are different ways to measure success.

The success that I've been a part of in basketball truly blows my mind every time I think about it. But the main way I measure success in life is something I don't often get to emphasize explicitly through pro ball.

I measure success by asking, "Am I living out my purpose?"

I learned a long time ago that my purpose is to know Jesus and to make Him known.

Some of you may know about the verse from the Bible that I include in my autographs: Colossians 3:23.

I take the time to leave people with a little insight into who is the foundation of my approach, passion and motivation.

"Whatever you do, work at it with all your heart, as working for the Lord. . . ."

My announcement is about how I'm shifting the focus to the whatever.

My focus in 2019 will not be on professional basketball, but will instead be on the people in my family, as well as on investing my time in some ministry dreams that have been stirring in my heart for many years.

I will certainly miss the day-to-day relationships with my teammates and basketball family this season, but my no for the 2019 pro season allows me to say yes to my family and faith family like I never have before.

I'm sure this year will be hard in ways that I don't even know yet, but it will also be rewarding in ways I've yet to see, too.

I'm thankful to my Lynx family and others close to me who have been walking with me during this shift, and I'm excited to see what the future holds.

Minnesota Lynx media day

Chapter Twenty-One

FIGHTING
IN FAITH

(2018–2020)

(J)

AS MAYA GRINDED it out over in Russia and then proceeded to have another all-star year with the Lynx, I was grinding away as well on another petition. This was going to be the biggest petition for freedom I ever wrote. Every day I sat in my cell researching and note-taking and typing away on my typewriter, crafting a habeas petition that would be the first draft to give over to my legal team. Monday through Friday, I worked all day long, taking a break only on the weekends, then resuming work at 6:00 a.m. on Monday morning.

I had come a long ways from that young kid who entered a library for the first time and could barely read. The advice the prison lawyer named Maxwell gave me so many years ago at The Walls never left me.

The key to your freedom is in those books.

Like so many instrumental people in my life guiding me in the right direction, Maxwell was right. I knew my freedom came from knowing how to argue my case in the most effective way, and I had learned how to do that in a place that didn't want people to learn.

Jonathan Irons, a Missouri prisoner in respondent's custody and petitions this Court, pursuant to Rule 91, for a writ of habeas corpus vacating his convictions for first-degree assault, armed criminal action, and first-degree burglary and his sentence of fifty (50) years.

This wasn't the first habeas petition I had worked on. Filing a habeas corpus is an extraordinary procedure that's based on Missouri Supreme Court Rule 91. There were basically three reasons why you could file: acts of innocence; cause and prejudice, which can be a Brady violation; and jurisdictional issue. We were raising four claims for my relief in this petition. First, we raised the Brady violation about the fingerprints, claiming that the State withheld exculpatory evidence. Second, we made a due-process claim based upon the undeniable fact that my conviction was secured through the perjured testimony of the victim and sole eyewitness to the crime, Stanley Stotler. Our third claim was that since I was a juvenile at the time of the crimes, I had been improperly certified and tried as an adult. And the fourth claim was on the ineffectiveness of my trial counsel for failing to object to the admission of the gun, which was deceptively suggested by the State at trial to be the weapon involved in the crime, and for failing to interview and call a witness on my behalf at trial.

Along with the new evidence we had discovered about the fingerprints on the form, we also found out that the O'Fallon Police Department had substantially enhanced my photo in a lineup of six photos that they gave the victim to look at while he was still in the hospital. They were never supposed to go to the victim and ask him to guess who did it, but they did and actually recorded it in a police report. It was clear that they blew up my picture for the purpose of making it stand out the most among the other photos. That was indicative of tampering with a witness and using improper suggestion techniques. Then there was the previously suppressed evidence of police misconduct by Detective Hanlen, the detective who claimed I had made a confession even though it wasn't recorded or witnessed by anybody else. We had a police blog that impeached his credibility. He was a crooked cop.

The habeas corpus petition didn't simply have to effectively argue the reasons why the judge should review my case once again. The petition needed to have a specific structure and form, much like a book might. There were the parts such as the introduction and factual background and newly discovered evidence; then there were the headings and subheadings, and sub-subheadings under those. The language needed to be official and specific, and every bit of information needed to be cited and referenced. For example, when I wrote that *Lt. Casteel did not receive any significant leads, information, or a clear description of a suspect from the dispatcher immediately after Mr. Stotler reported the incident,* this needed to be followed with the reference citation labeled *(Tr. 90-93).*

After giving the background details of my case and then what happened in court, the habeas needed to argue why I should even be issued a writ of habeas corpus. This was where the real work came in this epic document. So much time and research needed to be spent in identifying other cases and examples that were similar to mine, thus providing legal support for why my case should be seen again. This took scouring volumes and volumes of legal books and former cases and documenting them. An example of this light and easy reading is as follows:

Therefore, this Court can review the merits of petitioner's Brady claim if petitioner "can 'establish that the grounds relied on were not known to him' during his direct appeal or post-conviction case." Id. at 126 (quoting State ex rel. Simmons v. White, 866 S.W.2d 443, 446 (Mo. banc 1993)); see also Duley, 304 S.W.3d at 161-162.

This wasn't something that you finished in a week or even in a month. The habeas petition ended up being over ten thousand words long. And to quote Maya, it was quite brilliant.

◆ ◆ ◆

By the time I finished the first draft of the habeas petition, I had a team of lawyers to send it to. In fact, I had my own "dream team" of lawyers working with me that I had the privilege of handpicking. I was already working with Jessica Hathaway, but I had sensed that this was going to be too much for one lawyer, and she had agreed with me. So I had spoken with Maya about pursuing more lawyers, and her response was short and sweet.

"Go get them," Maya said over the phone. "We got it. I just came back from Russia. We're good."

So that fall I welcomed three more seasoned and high-quality lawyers onto my team. Kent Gipson and Taylor Rickard from Kent Gipson Law out of Kansas City, Missouri, were ones that I had been wanting to connect with for years. And Dan Hunt was a major local lawyer in Jefferson City who would be crucial in seeing my case through since it was so vital to have local representation in a case like this. These were huge and critical additions since each lawyer added an exceptional skill set, experience, and strength to my case. We were so thankful that the Lord had helped us assemble this amazing team.

Another important person we hired was a well-respected and local private investigator named Kevin McClain. He investigated the blog where Detective Hanlen bragged about his illegal and unconstitutional police misconduct, referencing numerous activities like planting evidence at crime scenes, manufacturing false evidence in order to obtain a search warrant, failing to report the misconduct of other police officers, and hindering a prosecution. The detective also had a civil suit filed against him for police misconduct while he was working on my case, a fact that never came to light until years after I was convicted. I was pleased to see what Kevin uncovered in his investigation. It was crucial since we needed to confirm this material on the detective before we put it into the habeas petition.

We officially filed my habeas corpus on December 21, 2018. It was a long, hard, and painful journey, but we had finally finished it! After so many denials, part of me said, *This will be denied, too.* But this time, something different filled the air. I had a feeling I was about to go home.

The state prosecutor's office had other ideas.

◆ ◆ ◆

I knew before anybody else did the decision Maya made to step away from the game. She had told me some of the things she had been dealing with over the years, like feeling exhausted and disconnected and wanting to not go overseas. I knew she was dealing with a lot of anxiety, but just like I didn't tell her all the gritty details of what was happening to me in prison, she did the same thing with sparing me details of her pain. One of the few moments we ever actually fought was near the end of her time with the Lynx when I wanted to help her but had no idea how to. She had told me she had been crying but didn't know why. I didn't realize it, but there was nothing I *could* fix. My job was simply to be there and listen to her.

When Maya told me she wasn't going to play for the Lynx next season, I felt conflicted.

"I don't want to be the reason for that," I told her.

"It's not just that," Maya said.

She explained that she wanted to prioritize some other things that were centered around family and ministry, which to her was one and the same. Her first ministry was her family and church family, and she wanted to be present for us. She wanted and needed rest, and she wanted to have the space to be more engaged in some critical things, both public and private.

After Maya shared "The Shift" with the public, a lot more people started paying attention to my case since she had stepped away from the game and was advocating for me. There were priorities that were more important than the game of basketball that she wanted to give her time and presence to, and of course one of the biggest priorities was my fight for freedom. She needed to have the emotional and mental wellness to be present in my fight, Maya told me, so there was no way she could have done this if she kept playing basketball.

After filing my petition at the end of 2018, the judge gave the State thirty days to come up with a response or they could file for an extension if they needed more time. So on January 21, exactly one month after I filed my petition, the State filed for an extension. A month later, they did the same thing. We weren't extremely discouraged because we were assuming that the State was going to do this. Since the petition was so rock solid and difficult to challenge, we were curious to see what they were going to come up with.

We knew they were just trying to delay and scramble in order to save face. On March 22, 2019, the State finally filed a response. This was huge since we didn't have to deal with any more delays from them. The next step was to have a council status hearing where the judge ultimately was going to decide whether this was a case worthy of going forward or whether my petition should be dismissed and be denied. The hearing was set for May 13.

Our hope was for the judge to truly see my case and say that this needed to go to an evidentiary hearing. If that was the case, the judge would set a date for that hearing. Essentially an evidentiary hearing was where the judge would be able to look at all the evidence fairly with me and my lawyers present in the courtroom. We hoped this hearing would be set for sometime later that summer.

◆ ◆ ◆

Maya's prayer warriors update for April included our recent bit of great news. She had been working hard to compose an op-ed for Black History Month that would raise awareness for my case and for justice reform, but unfortunately at the time the couple of places they tried to get the op-ed into didn't use it. (But it was for the best, because it would later be featured in *Vogue* magazine.)

"I was kind of discouraged," Maya said in her voice memo to the prayer warriors. "I was pretty mad actually about that, but God reminded me about how He is in control and will provide, because about ten days later, my agent emailed me and said that the *New York Times* wants to get involved and cover Jonathan's story, my involvement in Jonathan's story, and they want exclusivity to cover this case. And my mouth dropped. I said, 'I'm sorry . . . What? The *New York* what? Not the *Nebraska Times* but the *New York Times* wants to cover the story right now?' I was just blown away and God reminded me, *I got you.*"

The timing was perfect. Kurt Streeter from the *New York Times* came to Missouri to cover my case along with a photographer, and they not only interviewed Maya and her family, but at the last minute they were able to miraculously get into the prison and interview me in person along with taking pictures of me. We knew it was monumental for the *Times* to come in while the State was crafting their response to the habeas petition and the judge was starting to make decisions.

"It's just the perfect time to have this case go so much bigger than it already is right now," Maya said in her message to the prayer warriors. "So just a huge, huge praise of how the *New York Times* is now involved. And it's going great and it's the right person covering it, and he's hoping to have an article—his first article—done sometime in April, maybe early May, which is perfect timing for Jonathan's case."

The article by Kurt Streeter was titled "Maya Moore Left Basketball. A Prisoner Needed Her Help," and it was a well-written and moving summary of the journeys Maya and I had been on our entire lives. Inside it gave more context to the connection Maya had with me, and it also gave me a chance to share my story. We were, of course, still keeping our relationship private to the public. Yes, it was once true that Maya "began to consider Irons as she would a sibling." But it had been six years since I made Maya stop in the middle of our conversation by saying something a brother wouldn't say to his sister. Hopefully later this year, we could share more with the world when I got out of prison.

After the council status hearing in May, the judge determined there was sufficient reason to move ahead with an evidentiary hearing, but it would be a while before an actual date was set. Our hopes of having it in late summer soon turned to late September, but the State naturally came back and said they weren't available. So it eventually got pushed back to October 9. That had been our worst-case scenario, but the State had taken every opportunity they could to make the process as bad as it could be.

All we could do was continue to work hard and wait and be patient.

◆ ◆ ◆

In September 2019, we launched a Change.org petition where Maya shared my story with both a video and an article.

"Hello, everyone. My name is Maya Moore, and I'm here to ask you to join me in demanding a fair trial for Jonathan Irons, who has been wrongfully incarcerated since 1997. . . ."

I was moved watching the video of Maya talking about my story and walking the same halls I once walked in the now-abandoned Missouri State Penitentiary.

"I've known Jonathan for over a decade, and I'm fighting to make sure his case gets a fair review and calling attention to the prosecutorial misconduct that I believe resulted in Jonathan being wrongfully sent to prison for fifty years as a teenager. Will you stand with me and demand new evidence be considered?"

I still couldn't believe that this beautiful, talented, and amazing woman was out there helping me fight for my freedom and my life. She was speaking out for me.

"I'm dedicating my life to freeing Jonathan the same way I dedicated myself to each game in the WNBA," Maya said. "And it's why I need your help today. I urge you to join me in asking Judge Daniel Green and Missouri Assistant Attorney General Patrick J. Logan, and the Office of the Missouri State Attorney General and the Office of the District Attorney of Saint Charles County to take into account the undeniable facts of Jonathan's case, and provide him justice."

When Maya told me about the *tens of thousands* of people signing up to help my case, my mind was blown. How could all these people actually care about me? I couldn't fathom so many people out there seeing me for the first time in my life. There was a time in The Walls when I had virtually nobody out there. No one. My life and my case and my hopes had all been buried deep into a stone pit. But to now have the eyes of the world seeing the injustice taking place was incredible.

Over 270,000 hearts would eventually sign the petition.

In October, I read Maya's latest update that she sent to our prayer warriors. With the evidentiary hearing almost here, we depended on God as a family now more than ever.

Hello PWs! OCT 2019

We are ONE week out from the big Evidentiary Hearing where Jonathan's legal team will finally get to present all the evidence for Jonathan's freedom in front of Judge Daniel Green in Jefferson City, MO.

Since the last update my media/nonprofit team and I have been on the grind most of September spreading the word about Jonathan's story and the general cause of Criminal Justice Reform. It has been an exhausting yet so rewarding and powerful three weeks as so much light has been brought to his cause and the Evidentiary Hearing will have many eyes on it (so the proceedings won't be done in the dark!).

Thank you for EVERYONE's faithful prayers over this past year and beyond and know that Jonathan is so grateful and has literally felt the prayers of you all and the provision of our Almighty, ever-present Father! We are in the final stretch! The Final Four, if you will!

Some praises:

- Jonathan is doing very well, he is safe, peaceful and his 4-person legal team are ready & prepared for the hearing!

- The Change.org petition that I shared with you all recently has been a huge success in building momentum for Jonathan's cause and gives all of us a lot of encouragement that people care!

- We have successfully captured some great content through the resources I recently obtained through Wasserman Media Group (the agency that represents me)! We are going to be able to get into the prison to interview Jonathan!

- NBC has started to cover our story and produced an excellent piece on the *Nightly News* and *Today Show* last week and it was very well done!

Finally, here are specific ways to pray this week leading into the Hearing:

1. Judge Green will have a heart for justice, wisdom & urgency for Jonathan's freedom. And we won't need another hearing.

2. Favor, protection, wisdom & skill for Jonathan and all of his legal team as they deliver the evidence at the hearing: Kent Gipson & Taylor Rickard (Kansas City legal team), Jessica Hathaway (St. Louis Lawyer) & Dan Hunt (Jeff City Lawyer).

3. Wisdom and favor for me as I continue to tell this story well and encourage us to keep our eyes on Jesus.

4. The Assistant Attorney General Patrick Logan to have the conviction to act justly, God to change his heart and to have the humility to not delay justice. And that all plans for evil would justly turn against them and be used for God's glory.

5. Strength, Peace, and Protection for all of us who will be attending the hearing on OCT 9th to support Jonathan! That we will be emotionally anchored in the Truth that God will have his way and we can remain steady during the hearing.

6. For the Lord to continue to protect, provide & strengthen Jonathan & give him a mighty peace & trust as we go through this next step!

7.   Finally, that all Witnesses and people being called to speak during the hearing would have the grace to tell the truth clearly and for them to be protected and safe all week!

Remember . . .

The Hearing is Wed October 9th at 9am Central Time if you'd like to pray in real time.

As always, thank you eternally for standing and fighting in Faith!

God is Strong & God is Good. Amen.

"Then Job answered the Lord and said: 'I know that you can do all things, and that no purpose of yours can be thwarted.'" —Job 42:1–2 ESV

◆ ◆ ◆

I knew it was time to tell Maya. She was visiting me at JCCC, and as she went to the vending machine, I made up my mind to let her know my intentions. Over the years, the intimacy we had shared was likened to a married couple, yet at the same time we were trying to navigate the uniqueness of our situation. Always trying to honor the Lord and His design for marriage as a sacred covenant, but also realizing this was a very unusual and broken situation. So Maya and I did our best to love each other well, growing our emotional intimacy, always hoping to be together one day but knowing it wasn't time just yet.

As she walked back to our table carrying a couple of waters and sat down in the low chair, I studied her eyes. They had always been so full of compassion, so open to listening and learning. So authentic.

"Let me ask you a question," I said to Maya.

"What's up?"

"Will you marry me?"

Maya began to say something, but I held up my hand. "Don't answer yet. I don't want you to answer just yet. I want to wait till I'm home. You know—if and when I go home."

"*When* you come home," Maya said.

"Okay. *When* I come home. I want to do it that way. I don't want to marry you while I'm in prison. I don't want you to be tied to this. I don't want you to be anchored to me while I'm in here."

"You're coming home."

Maya advocating for Jonathan to Michael Jordan and the Jordan Brand Family in Monaco, 2019

Chapter Twenty-Two

THE TRUTH IS OUT

(2019)

(M)

I LOVE STORIES of faith, and I believe we are on the brink of seeing ours fulfilled.

As I walk into the Cole County Courthouse in Jefferson City with my family on October 9, 2019, I know that all of us are doing what we've been doing for years: moving in faith. After delay after delay with the State pushing back the date as far as they could, we've finally arrived to the evidentiary hearing. I'm hopeful and have been planning for this for quite a few months. I've not only been praying for this day, but I've also been preparing for another big day.

Very few people have any idea that Jonathan and I are a couple. So who would believe that I've been working with a wedding planner and finding a venue and doing all sorts of things for our wedding? All in faith.

Preparation can be the difference between success and failure. As I was making plans in anticipation for our long-awaited wedding, I prepared the same way I've approached the game, like I've said so many times before.

"It's going to come down to your work ethic, your preparation, your chemistry, your attitude as a team. At this level, there are so many details that have to come together."

We are as ready as any team I've been on entering a championship. This past year has been an abundance of blessings, adding amazing free agents to Jonathan's team and signing veteran players. Our lawyers are ready. Our witnesses and experts are lined up. I'm no longer on the sidelines; I'm busy working with Jonathan, Reggie, Cheri, and the rest of our team.

We know that today is the chance to lay out all of our evidence and to show that our claims are not procedurally barred, that the judge can overturn Jonathan's conviction. We believe the judge will most likely see that it's not procedurally barred, but chances are he will set a date for another hearing. In that hearing, he'll be able to overturn Big J's conviction. I'm hoping it's today, but Jonathan has reminded me that in cases like this, the judge often breaks it up just to give each side a fair chance to present whatever they have and to give the State time to put anything else together before he overturns that conviction. It's frustrating because we've already responded to the State on paper saying why this isn't procedurally barred, but this has to happen in a hearing in front of a judge. Hopefully the judge will agree with us and then choose a date very soon to meet again or maybe even overturn the conviction today.

We have a room full of people supporting Jonathan—Reggie and Cheri; Papa and Hamaw Flowers; me and my mom; my former grade-school teacher Joni Henderson; and several other friends and family. ESPN, the *Jefferson City News Tribune*, and other local reporters are there as well in the courtroom. They don't allow video or photography for this hearing, but we are still all able to be there in person. And so is Jonathan. This will be the first time he has been able to set foot in a courtroom since his trial in 1998.

I can't wait to see Jonathan in person in this place. We bought him a suit so that he could show up at his own evidentiary hearing in respectable clothes. We did so much research to get him properly fitted for his suit. Then we got word that the State objected to this request, so the judge shut down our attempt to get him the nice clothes.

As we sit in the wooden pews in the seating area, we watch as Jonathan steps into the courtroom in an orange jumpsuit and handcuffs. Our hearts sink within us as we also see they've put shackles on his feet, clanking every time he walks.

Jonathan looks at all of us.

"Clothes don't make the man," he tells us.

I can't believe the State didn't allow him to wear his suit or any regular clothes, but that's just the reality of his injustice and what's going on. Jonathan takes a seat at the table next to his legal team and gives us a confident look.

"God is a chain breaker, you hear me? God is a chain breaker."

It doesn't take long for Jonathan to shine his light in the courtroom. When he sees Reggie and Cheri's twenty-five-year-old son all dressed up in a suit, he has to comment.

"Ooh. You lookin' sharp."

We laugh and feel a bit more at ease. It's amazing that the man in shackles is trying to make all of us feel less burdened. But that's just one reason why I love him.

(J)

"All rise," the bailiff says.

For years I've been waiting to hear those words and wanting to finally stand in a court of law to speak out about my case. I never had a chance to during my trial. Today is the day I am free to rise. Today I get to have a voice.

Just like everything else the State has done, they refused to let me wear the suit Maya got for me. I don't care about that except for the fact that it's so cold in here and I'm freezing. This orange jumpsuit isn't doing me justice. That's okay—it's not gonna bring us down. I'm sitting next to my squad—Kent Gipson, Taylor Rickard, Jessica Hathaway, and Daniel Hunt, while on the other side Assistant Attorney General Patrick Logan is executing the interests of the newly elected Attorney General Eric Schmitt. The Honorable Daniel R. Green is presiding over this hearing. Even before we are able to call our first person to the stand, the prosecutor says that this hearing is to argue about whether or not there should be an evidentiary hearing.

"Is that what you still thought we were doing today?" the judge asks him.

"Yes," Logan says.

The judge asks Gipson if that's what he thinks we're doing.

"Our understanding is we're going to have a hearing on the entire case, because procedural bar issues are intertwined with the merits of the Brady claim," Kent Gipson says.

They're still trying to play games with me. After all this time and all the credible evidence.

Judge Green lets us proceed. It's only fitting that Reggie is the first one to be called to the stand. Daniel Hunt from our team begins asking him questions. Reggie explains how he and Cheri got to know about me and my case, and how things didn't make sense the more he learned about it. After giving our backstory, Reggie reaches the point where he describes finding something he hasn't seen before on the latent fingerprint report.

"So let me hand you Exhibit No. 3, if you can tell me what this is," Hunt says to Reggie.

Reggie holds and looks down at the document. "This is the latent report that was in that folder we got when we went to the O'Fallon Police Department."

"Okay," Hunt replies. "So let me hand you Exhibit No. 9, and if you can identify that for me."

"This is a latent report that was actually entered into evidence during the trial, and that was in the public defender's box that I had."

"So with respect to Exhibit No. 3, prior to that day and going down to O'Fallon Police Department, had you ever seen that document before?"

Reggie shakes his head. "No, I had not."

"And was that in any of the files that you got or at any time?"

"No. I went through everything in those files, and I had never seen this before."

Reggie is as cool and calm as he might be talking to me in the visitation room at JCCC. Hunt continues with his questions.

"So Exhibit No. 9 there that you have there in front of you, is that the only report that was in the trial file?"

"That was the only part in the trial file, and it actually had a stamp that it was admitted into evidence during the trial. So that's the one that was admitted into evidence during the trial."

As Hunt gets more into the details of the fingerprints, he asks Reggie if he ever met with an expert or anyone regarding the prints, but before Reggie can answer Logan interrupts.

"Objection, relevance and beyond the scope of the pleadings."

It's not been the first of Logan's objections.

"I think old habits die hard, but you realize you get a do-over at the court of appeals," Judge Green says. "They may or may not look at the record, and I've already read all this stuff about the fingerprints. But develop your case as you see fit. Overruled."

This is good. The judge has read over everything and knows where we're going. Reggie is articulate in explaining what the State testified to for the original fingerprints they found on the scene of the crime in 1997, how they ran the prints through AFIS (Automated Fingerprint Identification System, which collects and holds fingerprint evidence), and how the prints *did not match* Jonathan and that they all matched the victim.

"They said all of those prints that were found then were—belonged to the victim. And yet this report says otherwise."

Hunt nods at Reggie's answer. This is proving that the police had fingerprint evidence that was never disclosed to Jonathan's public defender.

After discussion of the prints, the topic goes to Detective Hanlen and the blog that Reggie discovered along with the lawsuit against Hanlen during the time of my arrest. This is all setting the stage for what's to come. Reggie is giving context on how we found out about these details. As Hunt finishes his questions, Patrick Logan begins asking his barrage of questions, all trying to find inconsistencies and discrepancies with the details related to Detective Hanlen and my initial interviews with the detectives and the fingerprints.

"There were more than three prints that were lifted. Correct?" Patrick Logan asks.

"No. There were three prints on the glass leading outside of the door and that's the only—where they collected them. Three prints. Out of the three, two were identifiable. That's even right here on the document, identifiable by two. So there were only two that were identifiable. So basically if you're saying that there is a print, those two would have to have belonged to Stotler. Now you have a document that says only one of them was identified, so who does the other one belong to? That was my question."

It's awesome to see Reggie up there, carefully explaining my case in an effective and articulate way as if he's the lead attorney on our team. When Reggie finishes, we call Kevin McClain next, the private investigator we hired to work on my case. The State has another objection.

"Judge, I should have done this earlier, but I'd invoke the rule on witnesses at this point," Logan says.

"I think you're a little late on that one," Judge Green tells him.

Taylor Rickard from our team asks McClain questions related to his investigation on Detective Hanlen and the blog he discovered. The investigator gives specific examples of police misconduct that Hanlen shared on his "war stories" website. McClain's testimony is backing up our assertions that question the character of the detective who led to my conviction.

Christine Sullivan follows McClain on the stand to testify. It's been so long since seeing the public attorney I had back in 1998 that I didn't even recognize her today. Jessica Hathaway starts to ask her questions about her background as a lawyer and how much experience she has. It turns out that Christine started working at the public defender's office in 1998 as an experienced attorney. She worked on countless cases until 2006, when she retired.

"All right," Jessica Hathaway says. "Could you talk a little bit about this case and what generally your defense was by the time of trial?"

Christine's answer is short and concise. "It wasn't him. Somebody else."

"Okay. So is it fair to say this is an eyewitness identification primarily?"

"Eyewitness identification, yeah."

My former public defender confirms that her defense involved eyewitness testimony from a witness claiming I was the guy who did this.

"So the case also involved some evidence about fingerprints?" Jessica asks.

"Yes."

What's she gonna say? I wonder. *What's gonna be her response to the form Reggie found?*

Jessica continues her questioning. "All right. I'm going to hand you what is already in evidence as Exhibit 9."

"Okay."

"Do you recognize that?"

Christine examines the report. "It looks like the latent print report that would have been in my case file from St. Charles County Sheriff's Department."

"All right. And so that's something you've seen before?"

"I'm sorry?"

Jessica repeats her question. "So that's something you have seen before?"

"Yes."

"And that's something you used at trial?"

"Yes."

I feel something jar at me deep inside.

"All right," my lawyer says. "Explain the significance of that in the context of the facts in the case."

"Well, there were no prints attributed to Jonathan Irons."

"Okay. All right. I'm going to hand you what is in evidence as Exhibit 3. So before recently, is that a document that you had seen before?"

Jessica hands my former public defender the form, which she studies.

"No, not to my knowledge. The document that I saw would have been contained in the case file, which would have been turned over by my office to the appellate office. And if Exhibit 3 was not in that case file, it's just not something I would have seen. It's obviously different than Exhibit 9, so . . ."

Obviously different . . .

"Talk about for a minute how that's different," Jessica asks.

"Well, it shows that only one identifiable print was attributed to the homeowner."

"All right."

Christine continues. "And the other print, identifiable print, is who knows, but it is also not attributable to Jonathan Irons."

Not attributable . . .

"So, in other words, it's a print that is not attributable to Jonathan Irons, which the jury heard?" Jessica asks.

"Right."

"And not attributable to Mr. Stotler, the victim?"

"Correct."

I can't believe we're even talking about this here and now, finally, after all this time.

"Now, at the time of trial, was it your understanding that both prints matched Mr. Stotler, the homeowner?" Jessica asks.

"Yes."

"That was your understanding?"

"Yes."

The same question asked twice. Just to make sure it is crystal clear what Christine is saying. Jessica steps across the room with confidence and authority.

"So if you had this document at the time, you would not have that understanding. Correct?"

Christine nods. "Correct."

"Because that particular document shows that there is one print attributable to Mr. Stotler?"

"Correct."

My very foundation begins to rumble as I hold my breath and listen.

"So, when you have cases, you receive discovery—you had been a lawyer for a very long time at the time of this case. Do you review every single document you receive from the State?"

"Yes," Christine answers.

"And the fingerprint evidence was significant to your defense. Correct? The idea that Jonathan is not matching up with these fingerprints?"

Logan fires back right away at this question. "Objection, leading."

Christine is undeterred. "That there was somebody else that did it, yes."

Something inside me—some part long secured and sheltered and silenced—suddenly begins to break.

"So, explain the significance of the fingerprint evidence to your defense," Jessica Hathaway says.

"That someone else was in or out of that house that left the print on an outer door. Not Jonathan, not the homeowner, someone else."

Did I just hear that? Not Jonathan, not the homeowner, someone else?

I try to hold in the tsunami of emotions coming to surface in this courtroom as my attorney continues, but I can't help breaking down.

"Right. And you've already testified that your defense is somebody else did this?"

"Yes."

After all this time, it's finally been spoken and stated and acknowledged in a court of law. The truth. My truth.

I begin to weep with a wailing that echoes off the walls.

"So, if I hear your testimony—" Jessica begins before pausing and saying, "Mr. Irons needs a moment."

Pain pours out of me like a broken dam. It's unexpected and uncontrollable and unspent. Judge Green can clearly see this.

"Let's take a recess," he says.

My emotions move with me into the hallway, but with every step I take, I can feel the change. I feel like I no longer have the shackles on. Despite how cold I feel and how ridiculous I look in this bright orange jumpsuit, I feel this sensation that's never come over me.

I feel free.

The truth has finally been uttered and stated and declared in the most important place it can be heard. I feel free because I know this is not something that can be ignored. Not anymore.

(M)

"I told you!" Jonathan declares down the hallway in an avalanche of emotion. "Finally, the truth is out!"

When Judge Green calls the recess for Jonathan, we follow him out to the hallway. All I want to do in that moment is rush over to him and hold him and tell him it's okay and be close to him. But I know I can't.

"Simmer down, now," the bailiff says. "I understand. I know you're emotional and can see that. But simmer down. Pull it together. You have to go back in there, okay? Can't have everybody out here crying, all right? So just calm down, young man."

Jonathan says, "Okay," as he continues to cry. I'm so close to him, yet I still can't care for him. I can't hold him and tell him how proud I am of him. Even in a place like this, he's looking at us from behind invisible bars in an isolated cell.

When the hearing commences, Jonathan's former public defender continues to be questioned by Jessica as the subject turns to examining if there was even enough probable cause to charge Jonathan in the first place. Logan continues his objections, but Judge Green tells our team to proceed.

Evidence used to charge Jonathan came from an unrecorded and uncorroborated statement that Detective Hanlen said Jonathan made. Now that the court has seen the facts of Hanlen's questionable character, Jessica questions the reliability of his testimony.

"If you had known there was a pending case making allegations of police misconduct, is that something that would have also been material to you in impeachment?"

"Absolutely," Christine says.

Christine confirms that if she'd had this information, it would have been used in Jonathan's defense.

Jessica then moves on and asks Christine to read a voluntary statement by Amber Boeckman. Logan objects for the umpteenth time, but the judge lets it pass. Amber states that Jonathan came over three different times on the evening of the crime, including once at 6:40 p.m., when she had just woken up. This testimony would have proven it impossible for Jonathan to have committed the crime, yet Amber Boeckman was never called in Jonathan's defense.

Our lawyer politely tells Christine that they examined her files on this case and have some questions for her.

"So, you weren't able to judge her [Amber's] credibility as a witness or anything like that?"

"Only what my investigator would have talked to me and written up in her statement, which would have been part of the case file."

Jessica asks one of the most obvious questions.

"So, as you sit here today, can you recall any reason you would not have called her as a witness?"

"I don't recall anything about Amber Boeckman at all. I'm sorry."

"So, you don't recall any strategic or other reason that existed at the time?"

"No," Christine says.

After Jessica finishes her questions for Christine, Logan cross-examines her. After a dozen or so questions, Logan asks the judge permission to approach the witness.

"I've given opposing counsel a copy of what I've marked as Respondent's Exhibit U, and I'm handing it to the witness," Logan says. "Could you just take a look at that for a moment, Ms. Sullivan? And go ahead and look up when you're done."

Christine Sullivan studies the document for a while.

"Now, this piece of paper, does it look like Petitioner's Exhibit 9—I mean, I'm sorry. Exhibit 3?" Logan asks.

"Well, I mean there are differences," Christine says. "Sergeant Luetkenhaus didn't sign Exhibit U. The list of latents box, that's the last box that appears on Exhibit U. Whereas Exhibit 3 has another box below it identifying Mr. Stotler's print as one of the prints, Mr. Irons's prints as none, and Mr. Luetkenhaus's signature."

As she's speaking, I can see Jonathan animatedly talking to his team of lawyers as they examine the same document Logan is discussing. We're not following exactly what's happening. This "Exhibit U" is something we've never seen.

"If I told you that Respondent's Exhibit U was found in your trial file after that was disclosed by Mr. Irons's attorneys to us in discovery, would you have any reason to dispute that?" Logan asks.

"No," Christine says.

(J)

The moment I see the form, I know it's a fake. I can tell that somebody altered it while making a photocopy. I instantly tell my team, whispering, "That's been photocopied!" It's unbelievably obvious. It's the same thing that's just been photocopied with the bottom cut off and a different signature.

When Jessica goes back to follow up Logan's questions, she's calm and cool as she begins to talk about this "Exhibit U."

"So, I'm going to place Exhibit 3 and Exhibit U in front of you," Jessica tells Christine. "Now, I'll hand you a highlighter, if that's okay. Okay. So, I want to just do some comparison of these two exhibits. . . . Do you see a line or a blemish in the middle of the photocopy?"

"Yes."

With the precision of a surgeon, Jessica carefully examines this new document introduced by the State compared to the form we had found about the fingerprints. She asks Christine to circle similar things on each document, including blemishes and lines, and she finds several of the exact same thing on the two documents. Minuscule details are highlighted and compared, leading to the obvious question from Jessica.

"So, in other words, if someone made a copy to create this, it would make sense that these same original blemishes would appear on both?"

"Yes," Christine says.

(M)

At first, we don't know what's happening with this newly introduced "Exhibit U," but after Jessica begins to dissect the form, I can't believe it. I cannot believe what's happening right in front of our eyes. *What are you guys thinking?* All of us sitting here are furious and can't believe this. It's obvious that this new form has been fabricated.

Jessica's questioning tears this doctored version of the fingerprint report to shreds. While we're angry to even see this report, we keep seeing lie after lie being exposed, and we're silently making "dropping the mic" hand gestures with each other, loving seeing our talented lawyer at work.

"So, if a person was to lay a piece of paper on the bottom of Petitioner's Exhibit 3 and make a photocopy of Defendant's Exhibit 3, would it look exactly like Respondent's Exhibit U?" Jessica asks.

"Yes," Christine confirms.

"So, you're a defense attorney, you have been doing this forever, does that seem odd to you?"

Christine agrees that this is indeed odd. Jessica brings up how even though the information at the bottom of Exhibit 3 is different, everything else is exactly the same as Exhibit 3, including the handwriting, the spacing, every idiosyncrasy you can imagine.

"So, if you're a defense attorney and you're seeing this in your own discovery, so as you sit here today, you find that a little odd?" Jessica asks.

"Yes."

"And, you know, respondent just represented to you it sounded like that this was something, Respondent's Exhibit U, found in your actual trial file?"

"I believe that is what he said, yes."

After more discussion from both sides about Exhibit U, we break for lunch and then come back to hear from Dr. James Lampinen, an eyewitness identification expert we hired in 2017 to evaluate the photo lineup and review the eyewitness identification factors in Jonathan's case. He is a distinguished professor of psychology at the University of Arkansas and a cognitive psychologist, the branch of psychology that deals with memory, reasoning, thinking, and language. His specialization has to do with memory as applied to the legal context. We paid him to look at Jonathan's case and examine it since the only reason Jonathan is in prison is because of the testimony of the victim.

Dr. Lampinen has said for years that Jonathan's case could be a case study of all the things *not* to do in eyewitness procedure. While he's on the stand, he breaks down everything with intelligence and truth and reason. Boom, boom, boom. Once again, it's a series of dropping more mics as he details all the things that were screwed up about the eyewitness process in Jonathan's situation. The first and most obvious is Jonathan's picture being bigger than the rest.

"When I initially looked at this lineup back three years or so ago, the thing that popped out at me immediately was that Mr. Irons had looked big, looked big compared to the other photographs," Dr. Lampinen states. "And that was kind of an immediate perceptual thing. It just kind of jumped out at me that his head was a lot bigger than in the other photographs. I then went through and did a simple kind of pixel count measuring from the bottom of each person's chin to the top of their head and kind of quantified. So Mr. Irons's photograph from the bottom of the chin to the top of the head was about twenty-five percent larger than the average of all the other photographs."

Lampinen's testimony is powerful. He speaks clearly, and Logan can barely manage to come up with reasons for objections, though he still does have some. Our eyewitness expert explains the problem with the instruction given to Mr. Stotler when using the lineup. The witness shouldn't feel like they have to choose someone if they don't recognize any of the people shown. But Dr. Lampinen says this isn't what happened.

"According to what I reviewed, what the witness was told was something along the lines of, look at the lineup carefully and pick the person who did it, or pick the person who shot you, or something to that effect. Now, that's suggestive because it implies to the witness that they need to pick somebody. That was compounded by the fact that according to the police report, the victim initially said that he was uncertain about who did it, and then he was encouraged to guess. And that also has the same problem because it implies to the witness you really need to pick somebody even if you're not certain."

A few moments later, Kent Gipson asks, "In all of your career in examining this, have you ever seen anything like that in your life?"

"I've never heard of a case where the police officer tells a witness to guess," Dr. Lampinen says. "In fact, you know, many of the guidelines that law enforcement are taught with are specifically designed to discourage guessing. I mean, the whole point of a proper admonishment is to let the witness know that it's okay not to take to—not to pick anybody."

Lampinen addresses another obvious concern.

"So, another problem with the lineup procedure is that the—in addition to encouraging the witness to guess, the witness made multiple identifications from the same lineups. After the witness was encouraged to guess, the witness said it could be three or it could be six. And, of course, that's problematic, because if a witness gets two choices out of a lineup, it increases the odds that they are going to pick the suspect just by chance. So, imagine I'm the witness and I choose the lineup photos just by rolling a die twice and picking those two numbers. If I were to do that, I would have one chance in three of picking Mr. Irons's photo out of the lineup."

The State continues to object to no avail. At one point, Logan objects only to have Gipson state that he hasn't even finished his question yet.

"He's an expert witness," Judge Green says. "Overruled."

Lampinen uses examples of past cases while also carefully giving examples of what the State did wrong in Jonathan's case. He also brings up the truth of the case to make logical statements that are, as he says, "based on a simple chain of logic."

"The victim could not make a positive identification in the lineup about three weeks after the crime. But the witness did make in-court identifications two and a half months after the crime and nearly two years after the crime. And we know that memory doesn't get better over time. Memory gets worse over time."

Dr. Lampinen effectively goes through how the eyewitness-identification procedures used on Mr. Stotler were unduly suggestive and how there was a high probability of misidentification given the totality of everything. When Logan goes to cross-examine Dr. Lampinen, he only has a handful of questions. There's nothing for the State to really ask him.

We take another break. After that, it's time for Jonathan to get on the stand.

(J)

"Mr. Irons, you do understand that if you are successful on your writ of habeas corpus, that the State could retry you for this crime? Are you aware of that?"

"Yes, sir," I say to Judge Green moments after sitting on the stand.

I'm terrified sitting here. I don't want to be here, but I know I have to go through with this.

"And are you aware that anything that you say here under oath can and would be used against you in that new trial?"

"Yes, sir."

I look him dead in the eyes and don't look away, don't even waver. Judge Green is searching me, and I'm searching him. And I realize something.

Man, he's good. He's good. He cares.

The judge continues. "And I'm sure you've gotten good advice from Mr. Gipson and Mr. Hunt. And so it's more of a formality than I think I'm telling you anything that you don't know. But all that being said, do you want to move forward and testify in this case today?"

"Yes, I do."

As my lawyer Kent Gipson begins his direct examination of me, I feel anxious and tight in this wooden chair. But this is my chance to tell them what happened in my own words. I need to speak for myself. After being asked to tell the court where I was born and about my early upbringing, I begin to calm down as I go back into my memories. As I talk about Granny and being poor and needing to use a five-gallon bucket as a toilet and not knowing my father and my mom having postpartum depression, I feel as if I'm reliving my childhood. I openly admit to my regrets and failures, how dropping out of school was a stupid decision and how I'm ashamed to admit I was selling marijuana.

Then I recount everything that happens when I'm arrested. Once again, I'm sixteen—only sixteen years old, just a kid—hanging out with friends I know in the neighborhood where the crime takes place, then a week later arrested with no idea why. I refuse to write anything and don't make any incriminating statements when Detective Hanlen interrogates me. Kent Gipson then asks me to recount what actually happened during that interrogation.

"Objection," Logan calls out. "This is beyond the scope of the pleadings and beyond the scope of the hearing."

"It's his chance to tell me his side of the story," Judge Green says. "Overruled."

So I tell them everything about those conversations, about the different detectives questioning me, playing good cop/bad cop, about being interviewed without anybody else and without being recorded, about being sarcastic with the guy fingerprinting me, about not knowing the gravity of the situation while being terrified at the same time. I'm able to explain about the gun I had, the .380 I took in self-defense from the hippie who tried to jump me behind the gas station.

After talking about how we tested the fingerprints for DNA but didn't find anything, Gipson ends his examination with the basic questions of why I'm here.

"Now, did you break in a basement window of Mr. Stotler's home on January 14, 1997?"

"No, sir, I did not."

"Did you hide in his closet?"

"No, sir."

"Did you shoot him?"

"No, sir."

"You're completely innocent?"

"Yes."

"And you're saying here today that there was police misconduct in your case, at least two police officers told blatant lies at your trial; isn't that right?"

"Yes," I state boldly. "Yes, absolutely. I don't blame Stotler. In fact, I forgive him. We are both victims. He still hasn't got closure. He may think in his mind that I was the guy, but I was not the guy. And I've spent twenty-three-plus years trying to fight, and prove and holler and scream. You know, I don't have no money. When people saw the truth, they came and they fought for me, and that's why I'm here in this courtroom today. But I did not shoot him or break in his house. I wanted to tell it back then, but Christine said 'You're just a baby. I don't want to put you on the stand because they will try to lie and twist your words up. I don't want to do that.'"

When it's time for Patrick Logan's cross-examination, he tries to twist my words up and down and right and left. But I know exactly how to answer every question. "No. I testified and I said . . ." "No, I did tell her . . ." "No. I testified and I said . . ." At first it feels like he really wants to go at me, but then something seems to just shut him up. For one question, I use some "legalese" in my answer, and I can see Logan's face turning tomato red. He's not expecting any of this, for me to be this well versed in the law, so he stops. He questions me far less than he does anybody else.

He wants me off this podium. He wants me off ASAP.

As both Gipson and Logan state, "Nothing further, Your Honor," and I'm finished with my examination, Judge Green looks over at me.

"Mr. Irons?"

"Yes."

"Be careful going back down there and sitting in your seat."

"Yes, sir. Yes, sir."

He cares. This judge really does care.

As I go back to my seat, the judge's words echo in my mind.

I'm going home. Oh man.

I sit down feeling courageous and happy and relieved.

It's been 8,296 days since I was arrested. Twenty-two years, eight months, and eighteen days.

January 21, 1997, to October 9, 2019.

Over eight thousand days to finally officially declare my innocence and state what happened.

The evidentiary hearing isn't finished; there is more discussion about the fingerprint forms and Exhibit U and Reggie is even called back to the stand. But in my heart, I feel heard and seen, not just by those watching in the crowd or by the lawyers at the tables but by Judge Green. He's the man who will be making the decision on saving another man's life.

(M)

At the end of the evidentiary hearing after all the witnesses have been called and the arguments made, Judge Green says he thinks he has a pretty good handle on everything except for the fingerprint exhibits, so our lawyer Kent Gipson addresses this.

"What I'm going to propose is two things," Gipson says. "One, I think we're going to file a motion to have you compel the running of this print through the Missouri Highway Patrol database, which was never done. And also I think we need to amend our petition to conform to the evidence."

As they discuss running the prints and other things, I become confused, but then I hear the judge ask Gipson and Logan if they think they can have everything ready to go by 12/9. *December 9.* Now I'm alarmed and infuriated.

Watching the spectacle in front of me unfold with the State making it obvious that all they want to do is maintain the win instead of trying to see the truth of evidence, I have one thought raging through my mind.

You're literally fighting against the flourishing of a family.

I dream of walking down the aisle in our December wedding and picture Jonathan in a navy-blue tuxedo, his eyes looking at me with the same light that he carried the first day I met him at JCCC. I hear the wedding vows we speak to each other and the pronouncement the pastor states to make us husband and wife. I imagine watching Jonathan come home to our community in Atlanta and pour out onto the next generation the wisdom he has gained from his life experiences. To see how his laughter and his childlike spirit blesses the kids in our neighborhood. To watch him spend time with Reggie and Cheri and my godbrothers. To witness him bless families with his ability to train up their family dogs. And to behold him becoming a father and beaming as he watches me carry our first child.

The world needs a man like Jonathan Houston Irons living and thriving in it. It needs someone to speak and teach about justice reform. It needs someone to show what loving your neighbor truly means. But the world is missing out because he is handcuffed and his feet are chained together for something he didn't do.

This is how we're treating one of the most amazing humans who's alive right now. We just spent the whole day showing why Jonathan's innocent, but we're going home and he has to go back to a box.

Maya and family entering the courthouse in Jefferson City, MO

Jonathan, Cheri, and Reggie on a visit

Chapter Twenty-Three

BELOVED

(2019–2020)

(M)

WHERE DO WE GO FROM HERE?

In the hours after the evidentiary hearing, my heart was full, worn down and confused. I still didn't have a clear understanding of what was happening.

When I finally spoke to Jonathan later in the night, around 9:00 p.m., he sounded upbeat and explained to me the fullness of what actually happened, how good it was and how encouraged we should be because everything got put out there. He explained how we were going to file a motion to get that one fingerprint run to find out who it belonged to because we could potentially solve the case. It wasn't even our job to do that—the State and the police should have run that print twenty-three years ago—but in good faith we were trying to help bring answers, not cover them up.

I was still frustrated that we had to wait until December 9 for the next hearing.

"Yeah, I didn't see that coming," Jonathan said. "But that was smart. That was Kent's idea. He suggested to the judge to grant that motion to get that fingerprint run so it would prevent them from having any argument to discredit what we're doing in order to damage or attack our evidence."

Regardless of the timing, Jonathan explained to me that the judge had enough to overturn the conviction. And Judge Green seemed to be wanting to do the right thing quickly, so he could rule on it at any point after we got our updated petition and request.

After speaking to Jonathan, I had a renewed sense of hope, so I decided to continue to make wedding plans even while I waited to see what would happen.

◆ ◆ ◆

The days of October and November ticked away, and all I could do was wait and pray. It was the hardest thing I had ever done, knowing so much was on the line for our future and dreams for a family.

Shortly after the evidentiary hearing, I was interviewed by Michel Martin from *Amanpour & Co.* to share Jonathan's story and his latest injustice of still being imprisoned even after the evidence we showed. Michel asked me a very pertinent and powerful question about Jonathan's potential release.

"If he doesn't achieve clemency or perhaps better than that, exoneration, will your faith be tested? Do you feel this will have been worth it?"

"Absolutely," I answered. "I have no regrets. We ultimately don't know what's going to happen, but one of the things that anchors our whole family in this process is knowing that God is sovereign and we're anchored in faith and we know that it's ultimately not in our hands, but any role that we can play in pushing toward justice, we'll put our heads down and pursue that, just like I would pursue a championship. It's definitely been a wild ride, but we just try to focus on the best outcome right now."

My faith was being tested more than ever before. The closer we got to December 9, I felt it best to not do anything else publicly to campaign but instead simply prayed and fasted and asked my other prayer warriors to do the same. But I struggled to hold it together during this time. The waiting was hard, but through my bouts of crying and sadness I clung to God.

I knew the ultimate reason behind this delay. It was because of the State. Every single step of the way, if the State had done the right thing, Jonathan would have been set free and we could have started our family. The State was ignoring the people—the human beings—involved here. They were looking at this as a cold exercise of saving face. Families were being punished—families they had sworn to protect—all for the petty reason of saving face.

As I brought these frustrations to my Heavenly Father, I was reminded of a fun game I sometimes played when I was reading the Bible. I liked to search for the number twenty-three in scripture, whether that was a twenty-third verse or chapter. I would look it up and see what it was saying. This time I landed in a part of the Bible called Exodus, which tells the story of God's people being delivered from Egyptian slavery thousands of years ago. I flipped to the twenty-third chapter of that book, read the first three verses, and was floored at the truth of what God was telling His people.

"You shall not spread a false report. You shall not join hands with a wicked man to be a malicious witness. You shall not fall in with the many to do evil, nor shall you bear witness in a lawsuit, siding with the many, so as to pervert justice, nor shall you be partial to a poor man in his lawsuit." —Exodus 23:1–3

This is literally *our story. Thank you, Abba, for reminding me of Your heart, and that You are for us.*

As December began, I was battling anxiety and wrestling with anger, but God was continuing to teach me things. He was telling me to wait. To remember. And to trust.

So that was what I did, and as I did, I kept my prayer warriors updated. Sending voice memos to them and sharing prayer requests helped me stay grounded. Reflecting on those updates now, they are reminders of God's goodness and faithfulness.

After the December 9 hearing was over, I updated everyone the following month:

PW Update January 2020

Hey, everyone. Happy New Year, it's Maya. I wanted to send you an update for this month. Since the December 9th hearing, we have been waiting for the unidentified fingerprint evidence to be mailed from Body Labs in Virginia to the highway patrol in Missouri. There is a four- to six-week window of time that it can take for the print to get from Virginia to Missouri. And since the order got sent to the labs in Virginia, it's been, I don't know, probably about four or five weeks. So, we're hopeful that in the next week or so, the print will get to the highway patrol and then they can run it through AFIS and we can hopefully find out who the print belongs to if it's somebody in the system. Or if it's not someone in the system, then it will remain unidentified. But we will have done our due diligence and there's literally nothing else to do. But unfortunately, there will be another thirty days or so to wait after that because the state has asked for thirty days to respond to the results of the fingerprint evidence and the judge granted them those thirty days. . . .

PW Update February 2020

We finally got news back about the fingerprints. So, we have literally been waiting since last December to get the prints from Virginia and Bodie Labs. That took six weeks to get to the highway patrol. And then it took three weeks for the highway patrol to respond back, which is kind of anticlimactic because we don't have any new information. . . . And so now there's no excuse, there's nothing left to do but to make a ruling. And so, at the last hearing on January 29, the AAG Patrick Logan tried to request that the next hearing would happen in May. I'm like, *what?* Judge Green's response was absolutely not. And then Judge Green tried to get a February date actually set, but then they ended up settling on March 9. . . . We're pretty confident that the state's going to take their full thirty days and then we'll show up to the hearing and the judge will overturn the conviction. So, it's super exciting. I'm almost in shock because we've just been waiting, waiting, waiting.

And now it seems like we can be pretty confident to know what to expect at this hopefully last hearing. . . .

PW Update—What to Expect March 9

We're so, so close. We're really, really hopeful that March 9 will be the last hearing in that Judge Green will overturn the conviction. . . . Nothing is really sure; it's just the nature of this process. But if and when Lord willing Judge Green overturns the conviction, Jonathan could be home within a day, within two days or ten days, and so it's just really hard to say. . . . The State has the option to appeal the judge's decision, even though we don't think the appellate court would accept the state's appeal. And then the prosecutors in O'Fallon also have to say that they're not going to retry him. So, after all that's said and done, then Jonathan's like free and clear to leave the state. . . .

◆ ◆ ◆

"If the outcome were to go the other way, would all the time you've put into it this fight, the suspension of your athletic career, still have been worth it?"

The question was posed to me during an interview by Sean Gregory of *Time* magazine right before the March 9, 2020, hearing that would determine Jonathan's fate.

"Well, that's a very important question," I said. "I'm more human now than I was ten years ago. I think we are more of who we were created to be when we do things like this.

"We can live shallow, superficial, materialistic lives very easily in our country, in our day and age. I don't think anybody that really invests into someone's life will say that it wasn't worth it.

"You just see so much beauty in things that you just wouldn't have ever thought that you'd see, despite the ugliness of the situation. There are so many people that have been inspired and blessed and felt loved and seen by what I've done, by what my family's done. One of Jonathan's good friends, that he's officially grown up with in there with, was just talking to us around Jonathan's birthday last month; he was just telling us about how the love that he's been able to receive from our family spread into the prison and just other guys.

"It's just so much bigger than just me. You don't want to think about, you know, injustice continuing after March ninth. But it is definitely worth it. And I definitely feel like a different person than I was as an eighteen-year-old before I started getting involved in Jonathan's story. He's blessed so many of us. For all the things that we've given to him, he's given much more to us. So, it's quite amazing. I had no idea a decade ago that I'd be sitting here right now in the middle of this amazing story. So, we're hopeful and we're going to stay hopeful."

We carried that hope to the courthouse in Jefferson City on March 9. Around fifteen to twenty friends and family of Jonathan's came together in the courtroom to hear what Judge Green would finally decide. As unbelievable as this sounds, Jonathan was denied the opportunity to be at this life-changing hearing. So he would have to wait inside JCCC and figure out a way to get phone time that morning so he could call us to find out what even happened.

After the judge came in, he asked if either side had any more arguments to present. Jonathan's team of lawyers said no and Missouri Attorney General Eric Schmitt's team of lawyers said no as well.

"I have had a chance to review all the evidence taken in the case," Judge Green said. "It will be the judgment of the court that the petitioner has established he is entitled to habeas relief on his Brady claim under claim one of his first amendment habeas petition. This court will issue a judgment granting petitioner a conditional writ of habeas corpus in order that his convictions be vacated and petitioner be discharged from custody. Judgment will be up online available later on today."

After the judge said we were going to take a short recess, pretty much everybody in the room applauded and stood to hug one another and rejoice at the news. I just sat there in disbelief for a moment with my hands on my head. *Is this really over?* I felt a rush of relief at hearing the conviction was overturned, but I also had this unexpected fire in my chest. I was angry.

Why did this have to take so long?

The attorney general could have ended this mess months *ago!*

How's Eric Schmitt getting away with this?

We finally had the justice to free Jonathan, but justice still felt incomplete. I had seen too much during these hearings and my heart was still raw from justice delayed. I was jolted back into that courtroom moment when I felt my mom put her arms around me like she had so many times before. I dried my tears and let out a sigh I had been storing for years.

"Free."

It felt good to utter that word.

(J)

I waited for Maya to pick up the phone as I called to hear the news. The first sound I heard was a room full of cheers and screams, and I nearly dropped the receiver in my hand. I felt overcome with a strong cyclone of relief blowing through me.

"Oh my gosh," my choked voice said. "What happened? What? Say it again?"

"Overturned," Maya declared. "Overturned!"

I broke down and barely could stand. "Oh, God, I love you. Oh, thank you, Jesus."

As I wept with joy, I called out to the guys around me. "They overturned it, y'all! Overturned my case, man!"

Just like the tears spilling out of me, I immediately began to sing a song we had sung at the prison chapel.

"I am free. Praise the Lord. I'm no longer bound. And it's a blessing. Praise the Lord. Hallelujah. I'm free!"

This was the news we had been hoping and praying for, but the fight still wasn't over. Now there was the process of getting me released. We planned to push for the prosecutors in St. Charles County to decide not to retry me and for the State not to appeal the judge's decision. But prosecutors have so much power and are charged with so much responsibility in making sure justice can be done. In this case, the State could not care less about justice. All they wanted to do was keep me behind bars for as long as they could.

◆◆◆

What follows is an example of why we need prosecutorial reform in the United States. Most prosecutors are elected by the people, and they also have absolute immunity, meaning they can't be sued for misconduct in the courtroom, even in cases where they've presented falsified evidence or coerced a witness. So it's easy to see how dangerous it is to have prosecutors who are overly concerned about maintaining a high conviction rate or saving face when a conviction is overturned. And even though my case was overturned, we had to wait for the State to do the right thing. There was no bond, of course. The State had fifteen days to decide if they wanted to appeal.

AG Schmitt waited until the fifteenth day at 4:30 p.m. to say he wanted to appeal Judge Green's decision. We also had time to respond, but we only took two days. Then they had fifteen more days to respond to our response. It goes on and on and on. The Court of Appeals has it for a little over thirty days, and my lawyers filed a motion to expedite it. That's what sped it up. When it came back from the Court of Appeals, the court issued a scathing twenty-seven-page order condemning the AG's behavior by saying "the State's reliance on untruthful trial testimony . . . borders on the incredulous."

Despite this clear rebuke, the State still had the option to file one last appeal to the highest court in Missouri. So back and forth we went. Another round of fifteen days. Then another. Back and forth to the Supreme Court of Missouri, where it sat for thirty days. We filed a motion to expedite for the Supreme Court because there's certain dates that the Supreme Court of Missouri rules on cases like this. And they're only twice a month. Since there was a two-month break they took around this time, we filed a motion to expedite so that I wouldn't have to stay in prison until the fall. When the ruling date came, the Supreme Court essentially said, "Stop it and release him immediately."

It was done.

This finally happened at the end of June. All of this, of course, is briefly summing up months of stalling by the State. Months of time and money. Months of awful anxiety for my family knowing that each of the prisons in Missouri were being overtaken with COVID-19 cases. It was just a matter of time before it reached JCCC. Prisons are a breeding ground for viruses like this one as we had no access to health and safety protocols. We asked the attorney general Eric Schmitt to consider all this and stop fighting my release, but he resisted. All for what reason? Why?

Freedom for the innocent should not be this difficult to find.

◆ ◆ ◆

Stepping out of Jefferson City Correctional Center into broad daylight under an open blue sky, I took my first steps in the world as a free adult. The person they locked up twenty-three years ago was just a child who barely knew how to read or write, a kid scared out of his mind, a boy forced to fight grown men to protect his own manhood. Then that kid met Hugh Flowers, who inspired him to believe in himself, who gave him the confidence to know he was intelligent, who showed him he had value. That kid started going to the library and reading everything he could, and he learned to read and write, and then he learned how to type and how to argue the law. He grew into a man who helped other men go home before he was able to, but now he was finally free.

As I walked toward Maya and my family and friends, I lifted my hands and arms in praise to God. Maya fell to her knees as she wept. Reggie waited for me, and we embraced. Then Maya and Papa Flowers joined us and we all held one another in love and in tears and in hope. It was the first time I ever hugged Maya longer than two seconds. I didn't have to follow the prison rule of letting go after "one Mississippi, two Mississippi." Cheri came over and began to howl as I hugged her and lifted her off her feet.

So many years. So much work and waiting. I finally felt like I could breathe, like the weight of the world was no longer suffocating me. With cameras around us, Maya asked me to describe how I felt in one sentence.

"Oh God ... Life. I feel like I can live life now. I'm free. I'm blessed. I just want to live a life worthy."

♦ ♦ ♦

Kneeling beside the gravestone planted on a grassy knoll, I finally could say goodbye to Granny. I touched the marble and broke down in tears.

"I'm home, Grandma," I said, patting the gravestone.

I kissed my fingers and put them against this memorial.

Florence Bell Spears

July 30, 1914

February 3, 2004

Beloved Mother and Grandmother

Maya and Reggie had accompanied me to my grandma's gravesite in Wentzville so I could fulfill a promise I had made to her sixteen years ago while I was inside The Walls.

"When she died, I didn't find out for, like, three weeks," I told Maya. "The prison didn't tell me. She was in the ground for three weeks before I found out. I had to call. She was my mother, my grandmother, my father, and my grandfather. And my friend. She used to play with me and scold me when I was out of control. I'm home, Grandma. I'm home."

Coming back to Wentzville was a reminder of where I came from and who I used to be. I was just a country boy who came home from school and played with his dogs. I went out into the woods and fished and hunted and climbed trees and played with my friends. Playing things like pickup football. I was a normal kid loving being outdoors and enjoying life.

Enjoying life.

Granny was there for me even when I wasn't there for her. She never left me even after I had nobody. She would have still continued to love me and pray for me and be there for me, but it had been her time to go. She walked with me as long as she could.

I thought about all the people that had walked alongside me in life, who were still walking with me. There's a misconception out there that once you give your life to Christ, it's all good. No. You need people to walk with you. And even when I got put into prison, men like Papa Flowers found me and walked with me and showed me how to live. They corrected me when I was wrong. They were like, "Hey, man, don't do that. If you do that, this is what's going to happen." And when I did a good job, they'd be like, "Good job, man! Keep doing that!" They would talk with me. Help me process my day, what I was feeling. If a CO was harassing me, they'd pull me aside and ask, "How you doin'?" They would encourage me. "You can't focus on that. You're not here to focus on them. You gotta keep your eyes up. Just read that Bible." They'd have Bible studies with me.

Every day, just walking with me.

Maya and Reggie and Cheri and their family had been walking with me for so long. There had been times that I was ready to give up and push everybody away, but their love for me kept me going. I knew I was going to need it as I adjusted to life. I wanted to rest, to take things slow, and I was surrounded by people who loved me and had my best interests in mind, so they were going to take care of me. Just like how Granny used to take care of me. I planned to listen to them, to study and learn all I could so that when I had the time, opportunity, resources, and provision, I would reach back and help other people.

I hoped this story would one day bless people and give them hope in dark times.

♦ ♦ ♦

All I ever wanted for Maya was to know and experience what it felt like to be loved. To be someone's beloved. So, if it didn't work out for us, she could at least know what it was like and choose a guy who would love her just as much. We couldn't see our relationship with our eyes, so we had to see our relationship with our hearts. I wanted to treat her good, to spoil her, so that if we couldn't be together and someone else came long, she could say, "If you won't treat me at least as good as a man in prison treats me, then you ain't got a shot." She deserved the best.

After being released from prison and the excitement of the day started to wind down, I couldn't wait any longer. We had gathered to celebrate my release at a hotel Maya and family were staying at that evening. I couldn't believe I was finally free and my future with Maya was right in front of me. I took Maya aside to a more private part of the hotel suite; then I dropped to my knee and looked up at her with a smile.

"Will you marry m—"

"Yes!" she said before I could get all the words out. "Of course I will!"

Back in JCCC when I asked her to marry me but didn't let her answer my proposal, I knew deep inside that I might not go home. I wanted her to know how deeply I felt about her, about us, but at the same time, I wanted her to be free to go continue living her life if I remained inside prison. If she did find someone else, I was going to cheer her on and tell her to go. Thank God I didn't have to let her go. Now we were going to be teammates for life.

"All right, let's get home," Maya told me. "We have a wedding to get to."

*Jonathan walking out of prison
after being exonerated on
July 1, 2020*

Maya

Jonathan and teacher Joni Henderson

Papa Flowers

EPILOGUE

(2022)

(M)

OUR HOME REMINDS me of where we came from. Jonathan grew up in the woods and Papa Flowers lived on a farm when I was born, so it seems natural for our house to be surrounded by trees and fields and rolling hills. It makes me think of the times Mom and I drove out to the farm every weekend for family get-togethers and meals. There is nothing more cherished than family. Jonathan was taken and locked away from the only family he had, but for many years, I remained far from my own family as well. Both of us are back home now, building a life and a family together.

When I think of our story, I think of the seeds that were sown so many years ago in Jonathan. A seed has to be buried and remain in the dark so it can have strong roots. It takes time for those roots to grow, to sprout up its stem and to show new life. Papa Hugh Flowers sowed seeds inside Jonathan; he saw somebody and felt moved to act. When you do that long-term, you can see a life transformed. When you are faithful and you just keep going and remain anchored in love, you can see life come out of death.

In July 2021, I was able to share my thoughts on this when Jonathan and I spoke with Robin Roberts on *Good Morning America*.

"The way we can have impact is not just about being the biggest and farthest and the widest and the loudest, but it's really about everyone in their sphere of influence figuring out a way to go narrow and deep in trying to model and show people the richness—the life. I feel like a lot of us are searching for purpose and for meaning and for reasons to get up, and sometimes they're not as far away as you think. Sometimes they're right around you and it's just about continuing day by day being faithful to pouring out what you can to those people around you and you'll realize you'll find your life in those narrow and deep ways."

◆ ◆ ◆

In the midst of writing and researching this book, I come across a letter I don't recognize.

"Hey, what is this letter?" I ask Jonathan.

He glances at it and knows right away. "That's my new year's prayer that I wrote before I met Reggie and Cheri, the one where I was at my wit's end. I call it my prayer petition because I'm petitioning God."

With all the letters we've found and gone through, I hadn't read this letter yet, so I ask Jonathan to read it out loud.

"'Heavenly Father, I humbly come to You in the name of Jesus Christ, and I ask for your forgiveness for my sins and transgressions against You and Your will. Thank you for creating me, for my excellent mental health and physical health. Being a father and mother to me, for protecting me, for giving me a stable place in a godly family after your own heart—'"

Jonathan stops and looks up at me.

"So this is me praying this in faith," he says. "I didn't have that godly family yet."

He continues on with reading his thanks to God.

"'For sending me the help that I need to fight for my exoneration and liberation, and for blessing me on a daily basis even during those times where I have been the furthest away from your perfect will and plan for my life. My Lord, my Father, my one and only God, please hear my prayer and grant my requests that I have petitioned you for if it is in accordance with Your will. Because Your will always comes first and will be done. Like King David, I trust you. Please do not ever let be me ashamed. You are my strength and I commit my life and my spirit to You as it should be.'"

The help that I need to fight for my exoneration and liberation . . .

Jonathan prayed this before that help ever came.

"So the following are my petitions," Jonathan says. "I list them out. 'Number one. I pray that You allow me to overwhelmingly feel Your love and Your mercy; that You give me abundant favor and blessings; that You keep me safe; that You help me and those that are with me defeat my enemies that come against me, and seek to oppress me; and that our relationship grows stronger. I need to always feel Your love and know that I am Your son, my dear Heavenly Father.

"'Number two, I pray that You deliver me, exonerate me, and liberate me early before the summer in this year 2006, as I understand time, and very quickly from the wrongful conviction and from being locked away in this man-made prison and the prison system. Redeem my name and restore me with my godly family in the free world society so that I can live for You, be a blessing to people, bring the message of hope that You have given me, prosper and thrive abundantly, and give glory to Your name by testifying that You are good and merciful, and that You heard my cry and rescued me. Upon hearing the testimony that You have given me, my Lord, who would not look to You and give glory to You, who would not trust You? And my Heavenly Father, I desire to be set free from this place, You know that I do not belong here. Please do not delay my deliverance any longer. This is the desire of my heart and You said that You would give me the desires of my heart. And You are not a liar and You are not cruel and evil. I trust You and I have faith in You that You will come quickly to deliver me.'"

As I think back to how many years ago Jonathan prayed this, I am reminded about a valuable lesson I learned when Jonathan didn't come home in December 2019. I feel like we need to have an open hand when hoping for God to move and having faith for something to happen. We have to leave space and allow God to be God in His fullness of how He wants to unfold something.

"'Number three. I pray that You keep me safe, bless, and prosper my family that was given to me by You my Heavenly Father.' Again, praying that in faith. 'Let us grow closer and strengthen our ties with each other. I know that I rightfully belong with them as part of the family and that You have placed great love in our hearts for each other. This I know is Your will.'"

I shake my head. "You're literally describing *us* before we were us. Reggie and Cheri weren't even in your life then."

Jonathan continues reading. "'Number four. I pray that You allow me to greatly succeed and prosper in all that I do and help me to think on those things that are pleasing to You and give me clarity of thought at all times. Number five. I pray that You help me strengthen my mind, body, and spirit greatly as well as improve my character. Number six. I pray that You allow me to hear your voice clearly and know when it is You sending me messages. Number seven. I pray that You abundantly bless, keep, safe, and prosper Rick, Anthony, and those that are helping me with my case that I have not mentioned or do not know about that seek to ensure that I am exonerated and set free. Give them all an overwhelming and unending desire to help me; give them the time, energy, assistance, resource, finances, and whatever else that they may need, and let their efforts be successful and the ending result of their efforts be that I become exonerated, redeemed, and set free into society once again to stay as a successful member of the free society. Please do not let their labor be in vain, nor let their prayers to free me be unanswered or denied.'"

"So those were guys in your life helping you at that time?" I ask.

"Yeah. But I'm also speaking into the future without even knowing," Jonathan says. "I'm praying for people like Kent and Taylor and Jessica and Daniel. So here's the final paragraph. 'My dear Heavenly Father, I trust You and I depend on You and I love You more and more every day. Know that I am not a saint and that I am not without sin. I humbly pray that You grant all seven of my requests. I want to be able to say with total confidence and have proof that my Heavenly Father is my deliverer and my fortress, that You are truly merciful, and that You are a God of love. What message would it send to Your people if I, a youth in Your heavenly family, cried out to You and You ignored my pain and chose not to deliver me out of my bondage? Our thoughts are not Your thoughts, but we know that You do not take pleasure in seeing us suffer, otherwise You would not have sent Jesus Christ. So having faith in You means trusting You by relying on evidence of things not seen and the substance of things hoped for. I thank You for hearing my prayer and granting in advance all seven of these prayer requests. Respectfully submitted to you, Jonathan.'"

By the end of reading the prayer, there are tears running down both of our cheeks.

"Like . . . what?" I say in disbelief. "Unbelievable."

"I felt like the Holy Spirit was helping me write that," Jonathan tells me.

"So this was 2006. You were how old?"

"It was right before my birthday, so I was twenty-five going on twenty-six when I wrote that prayer. I typed it on my typewriter and made two copies. Like I told you, I burnt the first copy and eventually gave Reggie and Cheri the other copy. I told them, 'You're an answer to my prayer,' and then gave it to them."

"This is such a treasure," I say to Jonathan. "This New Year's prayer is something our children's children will treasure. This is like family foundational, chain-breaking stuff. And you had no idea what that was going to turn into."

Jonathan grins, and then he leans over to me and places his hand on my expecting belly. "He answered all seven of those prayers. In His time."

Seven months into my pregnancy, I know God has answered those prayers and so many more.

◆ ◆ ◆

It only seems fitting to end this book with a new life. A new beginning and a new promise. Jonathan Jr. was born on February 7, 2022, weighing nine pounds and measuring twenty-two inches.

I've known I wanted to name him after Jonathan for a long time. When I tell Jonathan this, his heart beams.

"Why do you want to name him after me?"

"Well, darling . . . I just really feel that all of who you are needs to be continued. Your essence—your legacy—your character—all of that needs to continue. I'm just so proud of you and honored to have your name. I think our son will be, too."

So we know that we are going to name him after Jonathan, and he will be Jonathan Houston Irons Jr. One night shortly after we are married, we are lying in bed and it hits me. The first part of Jonathan's middle name sounds like Papa's first name: Houston and Hugh.

"What if we just spell 'Houston' 'Hughston'?" I ask Jonathan.

He looks at me with a glorious joy in his eyes. "I love it."

We both get chills. Papa Flowers is the reason Jonathan and I have a story, so we love honoring his legacy. Papa showed us how a legacy was made. Legacies are made and held by being deeply committed and invested in people over time. Sometimes when you see injustice, you have to act. And sometimes taking action means telling yourself, "I don't know the solution, but I'm going to keep moving to try to love this person who is worthy of love because they're a person."

That's what our family has done—keep moving. And what I've always done. Who could have guessed that this would lead to Jonathan and me falling in love? But as Jonathan says, we didn't fall in love. We rose in love. He told me that we weren't falling, that we were rising. We are rising in love.

It's hard to remember that eighteen-year-old girl who first met Jonathan and began a journey with him. He's blessed so many of us. For everything that we've given to him, Jonathan's given much more back to us. I could never have believed that in the midst of a career where I wore the number 23, I would also be in the middle of this profound twenty-three-year-long story of love and justice.

But the story isn't finished. In fact, in so many ways, it's just begun.

MAYA MOORE IRONS and JONATHAN IRONS

*Cheri and Jonathan on his
wedding day, July 10, 2020*

One-year anniversary celebration

Daddy Jonathan and Baby JJ at three weeks

Irons family at Family Camp, June 2022

Jonathan Freedom Air Jordan 1 created by Maya

NOTE TO THE READER

THANK YOU FOR letting us share our story with you. Not only is it a victory story, but it's also the story of miraculous perseverance. The kind only God can give. We know the reality that people in Jonathan's situation rarely get to come home, but we're trying to make that reality more attainable. It's only a victory story if people look, care, and act.

Our story of transformation proved that there are no quick fixes. Twenty-three isn't just a number on a basketball jersey but it is also the number of years it took to free a blameless juvenile. Transformation takes time. It takes being a better neighbor and becoming someone who learns about a person who is different than you. It takes not frantically guarding your own comfort and privilege, but rather using the power and privilege you have to empower others.

This doesn't have to happen again!

We can be a better community. We can be better if we care about dignifying and valuing people. We also do that by caring about justice. The following are some resources that have played a big part in preparing us for our journey:

BOOKS
How We Love Matters by Albert Tate (I purchased the audiobook and loved hearing it in the author's own voice)
Just Mercy by Bryan Stevenson
The New Jim Crow by Michelle Alexander

FILMS
13th, a documentary by filmmaker Ava DuVernay (please note this film has moments of mature content)

PODCASTS
Race & Redemption
BEMA Discipleship (there are many episodes but the more you listen, the more you learn about the heart of justice)

PLACES TO VISIT
Visiting the Legacy Museum and memorial was one of the most moving experiences of my life. It's a must see! Plan your visit here:
MuseumAndMemorial.eji.org

WIN WITH JUSTICE
Our goal with Win with Justice is also to help you be a more informed voter as you elect your next local prosecutor, district attorney, or attorney general.
WinWithJustice.org (be sure to click on the Toolkit and Media tabs)

ORGANIZATIONS WE PARTNER WITH
For the People
Today, there are thousands of people in our prisons who can be safely released. Their continued confinement is unjust. Prosecutors now have the power to make it right. They can remedy excessive sentences. They can restore families. They can make changes. They can do this for the people.
ForThePpl.org

The Exoneration Project
By investigating and petitioning courts to reverse wrongful convictions, the Exoneration Project is dedicated to restoring justice. The Project works with community-minded organizations to advocate for exonerees so they are able to reenter society with the support they need to succeed. Anyone seeking help with their case should contact:

The Exoneration Project
c/o Intake Department
311 North Aberdeen St.
Third Floor Suite E
Chicago, IL 60607

Here is their website: ExonerationProject.org

Before making contact, we would suggest that you write up a clear, concise case summary that outlines the facts of your case, including details of the crime as well as the specific charges you were given and the sentence(s). It is very important to do research on your own first to determine what legal avenues or laws apply that can serve as a gateway into court to be heard. It is a good idea to have someone (an English teacher, law student, or journalist, for example) read through your summary first to help you edit it, and also to give you feedback on whether it is clear and understandable.

The Lentium Group

Excellent training for your community or organization on navigating the complexities of racial diversity while also discovering the beauty of diversity. I attended a workshop and it was some of the most impactful training I (Maya) ever received.
Lentium.org

IF YOU NEED A LIFT

These are encouraging resources to add to your rhythm of growth. . . .

The Chosen (the episodes of this TV series have been a staple for Movie Night in our home)
Angel.com/watch/the-chosen

Transformational study:
See Jesus
SeeJesus.net

Get trained:
SeeJesus.net/training/see-jesus-workshop

Sample study:
SeeJesus.net/sites/default/files/content/POJ%20Sample%20Lesson.pdf

Book: *Garden City* by John Mark Comer (all of his books are fantastic)

Book: *The Very Good Gospel: How Everything Wrong Can Be Made Right* by Lisa Sharon Harper

Book: *What If Jesus Was Serious?* and *What If Jesus Was Serious About the Church?* by Skye Jethani

LEARN MORE

Learn more about your local Conviction Integrity Units (CIUs); they are a way to safeguard against wrongful convictions.

MIND-BLOWING STAT FROM MAYA

I was able to hit *The Shot* (chapter 17) for my team in the 2015 WNBA Finals on October 9, 2015. Little could I have known that I would sit shocked in my room on the day I realized that Jonathan's evidentiary hearing (chapter 22) actually happened on October 9, 2019. Exactly four years to the day!

FINAL THOUGHT

We are complex, multilayered human beings created to know each other and to be known in real relationship. Taking time to be in real relationship is the start of real change. We weren't designed to grow alone.

Our hope is that the following prayer becomes your own, asking God this question: "How can I become more of who I was created to be?"

SELECTED SOURCES

Abrams, Jonathan. "Connecticut Women Win National Title." *New York Times.* 7 April 2009. https://www.nytimes.com/2009/04/08/sports/ncaabasketball/08women.html

Adamec, Carl. "UConn women enjoy life at the top." *Journal Inquirer.* 30 January 2008. https://www.journalinquirer.com/archives/uconn-women-enjoy-life-at-the-top/article_c32b7e7a-803c-56a9-9c13-6b696b4a481f.html

Associated Press. "Moore helps Huskies get 18th straight win vs. Orange." ESPN. com. 24 February 2010. https://www.espn.com/womens-college-basketball/recap?gameId=300550183

Blount, Rachel. "Maya in the middle." *Star Tribune.* 1 June 2011. https://www.startribune.com/maya-in-the-middle/122756434/

Fuller, Brian. "Moore, Huskies Ready for Syracuse." *Register Citizen.* 24 February 2010. https://www.registercitizen.com/news/article/Moore-Huskies-ready-for-Syracuse-12089077.php

Gay, Jason. "The Team That Forgot How To Lose." *Wall Street Journal.* 18 November 2010. https://www.wsj.com/articles/SB10001424052748704648604575621090523076212

Hays, Graham. "Times change, but Auriemma hasn't." ESPN.com. 27 November 2009. https://www.espn.com/womens-college-basketball/columns/story?columnist=hays_graham&id=4694904

Helin, Kurt. "Maya Moore becomes first woman signed by Nike's Jordan brand." NBCSports.com. 20 May 2011. https://nba.nbcsports.com/2011/05/20/maya-moore-becomes-first-woman-signed-by-nike's-jordan-brand/

Hiro, Brian. "UConn expedition: Elite Huskies arrive to face resurgent Aztecs." *San Diego Union-Tribune.* 20 December 2007. https://www.sandiegouniontribune.com/sdut-uconn-expedition-elite-huskies-arrive-to-face-2007dec20-story.html

Longman, Jeré. "After Injury, Greene Gets New Game for UConn." *New York Times*. 1 April 2010. https://www.nytimes.com/2010/04/02/sports/ncaabasketball/02uconn.html

Longman, Jeré. "UConn Women Own the Longest Streak." *New York Times*. 21 December 2010. https://www.nytimes.com/2010/12/22/sports/ncaabasketball/22uconn.html

"MSP Riot of 1954 Had Far-Reaching Impact." *News Tribune*. 16 September 2014. https://www.newstribune.com/news/2014/sep/16/msp-riot-1954-had-far-reaching-impact/

Streeter, Kurt. "Maya Moore Left Basketball. A Prisoner Needed Her Help." *New York Times*. 30 June 2019. https://www.nytimes.com/2019/06/30/sports/maya-moore-wnba-quit.html?action=click&module=RelatedLinks&pgtype=Article

Streeter, Kurt. "Jonathan Irons, Helped by W.N.B.A. Star Maya Moore, Freed From Prison." *New York Times*. 1 July 2020. https://www.nytimes.com/2020/07/01/sports/basketball/maya-moore-jonathan-irons-freed.html

"UConn's Moore a freshman phenom." *News-Times*. 19 March 2008. https://www.newstimes.com/news/article/UConn-s-Moore-a-freshman-phenom-46368.php

Voepel, Mechelle. "Moore shines even in the shadows." ESPN.com. 7 April 2009. https://www.espn.com/womens-college-basketball/ncaatourney09/columns/story?columnist=voepel_mechelle&id=4051030

Voepel, Mechelle. "Ever-relentless Huskies win again." ESPN.com. 14 February 2010. https://www.espn.com/womens-college-basketball/columns/story?columnist=voepel_mechelle&id=4917562

Voepel, Mechelle. "Imperfect game caps perfect season." ESPN.com. 6 April 2010. https://www.espn.com/womens-college-basketball/tournament/2010/columns/story?columnist=voepel_mechelle&id=5062743

Voepel, Mechelle. "UConn's Moore leaves incredible legacy." ESPN.com. 3 April 2011. https://www.espn.com/womens-college-basketball/tournament/2011/columns/story?columnist=voepel_mechelle&id=6288546

Youngblood, Kent. "Maya Moore renewed her spirit, then upped her game for the Lynx." *Star Tribune*. 14 May 2017. https://www.startribune.com/maya-moore-renewed-her-spirit-then-upped-her-game-for-the-lynx/422179453/